The World Turned Inside Out

AMERICAN THOUGHT AND CULTURE
Lewis Perry and Howard Brick, Series Editors

The World Turned Inside Out

American Thought and Culture at the
End of the 20th Century

James Livingston

ROWMAN & LITTLEFIELD PUBLISHERS, INC.
Lanham • Boulder • New York • Toronto • Plymouth, UK

Published by Rowman & Littlefield Publishers, Inc.
A wholly owned subsidiary of The Rowman & Littlefield Publishing Group, Inc.
4501 Forbes Boulevard, Suite 200, Lanham, Maryland 20706
http://www.rowmanlittlefield.com

Estover Road, Plymouth PL6 7PY, United Kingdom

Copyright © 2010 by Rowman & Littlefield Publishers, Inc.

British Library Cataloguing in Publication Information Available

Library of Congress Cataloging-in-Publication Data

Livingston, James, 1949–
   The world turned inside out : American thought and culture at the end of the
20th century / James Livingston.
      p. cm. — (American thought and culture)
   Includes bibliographical references and index.
   ISBN 978-0-7425-3541-1 (cloth : alk. paper) — ISBN 978-1-4422-0117-0 (electronic)
   1. United States—Intellectual life—20th century. 2. Popular culture—United States—
History—20th century. 3. Political culture—United States—History—20th century.
4. Social change—United States—History—20th century. 5. United States—Politics
and government—1981–1989. 6. United States—Politics and government—1989– 7.
United States—Social conditions—1980– I. Title.
   E169.12.L558 2010
   973.91—dc22   2009025274

⊗ ™ The paper used in this publication meets the minimum requirements of
American National Standard for Information Sciences—Permanence of Paper
for Printed Library Materials, ANSI/NISO Z39.48-1992.

Printed in the United States of America

This book is for my favorite teachers,
Mike Fennell and Marvin Rosen

The Lord maketh the earth . . . waste, and turneth it upside down. . . . And it shall be, as with the people, so with the priest, as with the servant, so with his master, as with the maid, so with her mistress. . . . The earth shall reel to and fro like a drunkard.

—Isaiah 24:1–2

Certain dualisms have been persistent in Western traditions; they have all been systemic to the logics and practices of domination of women, people of color, nature, workers, animals—in short, domination of all constituted as others, whose task is to mirror the self. Chief among these troubling dualisms are self/other, mind/body, culture/nature, male/female, civilized/primitive, reality/appearance, whole/part, agent/resource, maker/made, active/passive, right/wrong, truth/illusion, total/partial, God/man. . . . High-tech culture challenges these dualisms in intriguing ways. It is not clear who makes and who is made in the relation between human and machine.

—Donna Haraway, "A Manifesto for Cyborgs"

Social revolution in America has so far proved a dream; cultural revolution has been an important reality.

—Henry F. May, *The End of American Innocence*

Contents

~

Foreword

Howard Brick and Lewis Percy, Series Editors

Over twenty years ago, this series on American Thought and Culture began with the aim of offering concise, provocative volumes that, taken together, would survey the long span of American intellectual and cultural life from the sixteenth century to the present. Since then, the output of richly documented monographs in the field has continued to grow, sustaining the demand for inventive historical syntheses. The goal of the series has always been to bring together readable, well-informed books that stand on their own as introductions to significant periods in American thought and culture. There is no attempt to establish a single interpretation of all of America's past, for the range of American experiences and their change over time would frustrate any such attempt. All the authors in the series, innovative practitioners in the field in their own right, bring their own independent research to bear as they strive for a broad reach in interpretation. They aim to explore issues that are of critical importance to the particular period under discussion and, on that basis, to cast new light on the whole of American experience as it both shaped and was transformed by that time.

The series now nears completion with the publication of this and two other forthcoming volumes treating discrete periods of the twentieth century. The culture and intellectual life of the United States remain subjects of heated debate. Scholars of the mid-twentieth century often assumed that the country bore a common culture that could be summed up in a few basic themes or characteristic dilemmas. By the 1980s, historians were more likely to recognize a plurality of thoughts and traditions in the American past. Variation and contention among the multiple strands of American consciousness made it difficult to achieve a synthetic view of the culture in times past. Nonetheless, the relation between the many and the one continues to preoccupy historical observers. Few historians today are likely to challenge a strong emphasis on diversity among subcultures in American life. At the same time, the international primacy this country has attained—for example, as a purveyor of mass culture or the vanguard of a "war on terror"— again poses the question of what collective identity or cultural wholeness Americans share. As the United States looks out on the world at large, and the world looks back, who are "we"?

James Livingston's book provides the capstone of the series, the volume that treats "American thought and culture at the end of the twentieth century." In the roughly twenty-five years surveyed here, the multiplicity, tension, and conflict at play throughout American history seemed to reach a high pitch in a transformation of experience and consciousness that Livingston describes as turning the world "inside out." Historians have become accustomed to seeing the end of the twentieth century as the site of one or more profound "turns"—the "right turn" in U.S. politics signaled by the rise of Ronald Reagan and the sudden reversal Reaganism seemed to initiate in putting "free markets" in place of "the welfare state," as well as the "postmodern turn" that tended to undermine a trust in science, reason, progress, and moral order that was assumed to characterize U.S. culture in large part since its beginnings.

Livingston weds these "turns" together in ways that profoundly recast what we think they meant. The political, economic, social, and cultural phenomena of the years stretching from the Reagan to the George W. Bush presidencies indicate far less than a conservative ascendancy in American life. Indeed, the apparently vehement disputes between the Left and Right over social policy as well as culture and morals more often than not mistook or masked the drift of things. In economic affairs, public authority and responsibility, as well as the social foundations of market exchange, continued to grow rather than diminish, and in the broad reach of culture, the "postmodern Left" not only secured leadership of what Livingston calls the "pilot disciplines" of academic liberal arts but also proved more in tune with popular sensibility than conservatives did—despite the common charge of "elitism" laid against cultural innovators.

In penetrating analyses of some of the most popular art forms at the end of the twentieth century—horror movies, comics and cartoons, TV shows depicting vampires and their slayers, and hip-hop music—Livingston shows how common it has become for Americans to confront, and in some ways to accommodate, the erosion of customary barriers and boundaries that long defined the private family and the public world, masculinity and femininity, sexual norms and "deviance," the human body and alien creatures, the nation and global affairs. All those things customarily kept apart as "inside" or "outside" the comfort zones of American experience have been shuffled together, and remarkably, American culture has gamely striven for new kinds of balance amid uncertainty. That does not mean that new and unsettling problems are easily resolved, as Livingston explains in his sober reflections on the course and coming future of U.S. relations with the wider world. But it does show that American thought and culture remains malleable and ever changing in the realm of flux it inhabits.

~

Preface

The World Elsewhere Is Not

The title of this book is a variation on a theme found in the Old Testament—in Isaiah, it's in the epigraphs—and developed in Christopher Hill's great book of 1972, *The World Turned Upside Down*. The prophet Isaiah predicted what servants and slaves everywhere called "jubilee," the redistribution of property that would change everything. The historian Hill wrote about a "revolt within the [English] Revolution" of the 1640s, which, if successful, would have enfranchised more people and more rights than resulted from that extraordinary upheaval. This movement of radicals, of Levellers and Diggers, of beggars, vagabonds, poets, and thieves—this movement, he wrote, "might have established communal property, a far wider democracy in political and legal institutions, [and it] might have disestablished the state church and rejected the protestant ethic."

There are no "might have beens" in this book. I write about the cultural and intellectual revolution that changed North America and the world after 1975. It was so successful—it was so formative, causative, and measurable—that we can take it for granted, and then look past it, to the point where some of us even argue that conservatism took over American thought and culture after 1980.

But this cultural and intellectual revolution did turn the world inside out, in three related senses. First, it complicated the ways we could perceive the relation between our insides and all of what we normally designate as outside. The difference between private and public, for example, became a problem rather than an assumption at the end of the twentieth century. So, too, did

xiii

the distinction between foreign and domestic policy get blurred when the post-Vietnam all-volunteer army rebuilt itself as a social program dedicated to affirmative action and when terrorists without state sponsors became a central feature of globalization. Meanwhile, excremental visions became the norm of performance art and the mainstream of cartoon politics as anal probes from outer space and the Santa (Satan?) from the sewer challenged Disney's constituency—what had been expelled from our bodies somehow became the raw materials of our revised interiors, that is, the stuff of our thinking.

To put it another way, the personal became political, and vice versa, but not just because feminists said it should—although we must attribute the original slogan and its radical connotations to feminism. We were all confused by the shifting boundaries between the so-called private sector and the so-called public sectors whether we were speaking of economic growth or the relation between our inner selves and our outward appearances. We still are. For example, we still ask, can public spending stand in for private investment? Should the government supplement or replace private enterprise? Does the specter of socialism still haunt the American imagination? We still ask, what is the outer limit of the family, a presumably private domicile? And what is a family, anyway? Where's Dad, the family guy? We still ask, can the government invade this familial space and tell the females that they don't have control over their own bodies?

Second, the cultural and intellectual revolution of the late twentieth century brought the world that was once elsewhere into the room and onto the screen where we were watching TV or sending e-mail and later Googling ourselves. Either we turned the machine off or we became citizens of the whole world, no borders allowed. There we were, face to virtual face, with every imaginable kind of person—also every imaginable kind of cyborg, vampire, angel, or demon—and what did we do? We let them into our lives and turned the world inside out. Even the difference between animals and human beings or between machines and men seemed to dissolve at the end of the twentieth century.

Third, and this may be the same thing, all those strangers, all those Others out there—cyborgs, simians, animals, Asians, immigrants, women, homosexuals, people with disabilities, whatever—suddenly acquired substantive identities that required our very close attention and our scrupulously ethical attitude toward their prospects. The world once elsewhere had moved into the cultural space where white, male heterosexuality had long been the norm. All these believably sentient beings were close by, and they were demanding their rights, even the animals and the immigrants and the homosexuals.

This book explores American thought and culture in the aftermath of the fabled 1960s. The argument is that the tendencies and sensibilities we associate with that moment decisively shaped intellectual agendas and cultural practices—from the Congressional Budget Office to the cartoon politics of Disney movies—in the 1980s and 1990s. By this accounting, the so-called Reagan Revolution was not only, or even mainly, a conservative event. By the same accounting, the Left, having seized the commanding heights of higher education, was never in danger of losing the so-called culture wars. At the end of the twentieth century, in short, the United States was much less conservative than it had been in 1975.

This book takes supply-side economics and *South Park* equally seriously. It treats Freddy Krueger, Buffy the Vampire Slayer, Ronald Reagan, and Judith Butler as comparable cultural icons. In doing so, it formally recapitulates the aesthetic movement specific to the late-twentieth-century moment of "postmodernism"—when artists, writers, and intellectuals working in every imaginable medium, from movies and TV to novels and newspapers, adjourned any remaining distinction between high and low culture. In doing so, that is, by depicting this moment on its own terms, the book recaptures the complexity, the pathos, the idiocy, and the achievements of a past that is not even past.

Everything from skeletons to sexuality came out of the closet toward the end of the twentieth century, and we're still wondering what to do about it. This book could help us decide.

Acknowledgments

My principal debt in writing this book is to Howard Brick, who urged me to write it and then helped shape it with incisive comments. Thanks also to his coeditor, Lewis Perry, whose later reading reshaped it. I hasten to add that neither would endorse all my arguments.

I wrote this book with four audiences in mind, and I would like to acknowledge them here as components of my ideal reader. The first is the students who never got "to the present" in the courses they took in high school and college because their teachers never made it that far. The second is the baby boomers who experienced this late-twentieth-century moment as I did, but probably never got around to analyzing it. The third audience is the literate reading public that craves serious discussion of movies, music, and politics, probably in that order. The fourth is the divided fraction of the reading public that wonders why antirealist art forms like cartoons and comics have such a hold on the American imagination.

Friends, colleagues, former students, and even relatives spent a lot of their valuable time reading and discussing the book while it was in progress. They have helped me to strike the right tone in writing for a broad, nonacademic audience, I believe, and they have meanwhile contested my conclusions, corrected my errors, and laughed at my jokes. I am very grateful, then, to Mike Fennell, Christopher Fisher, Keith Haynes, Bruce Robbins, Marc Chandler, Joan Wallach Scott, Brian Connelly, Jonathan Arac, Patricia Rossi, Jackson Lears, Shannen Dee Williams, Kristoffer Shields, Matthew Roth, Andrew Livingston, Leland Livingston, Julia Rossi Livingston, Matthew Friedman,

Gregory J. Renoff, Ross Posnock, Louis Ferleger, Elise Salem, Colin Koopman, the Department of American Studies at Rutgers University, and readers of my blog, www.politicsandletters.com, where I tried out ideas and parts of chapters. My bandmate Matt Friedman also helped with the illustrations and saved me from stupid mistakes in writing about music and singing about architecture.

I inflicted several chapters on three undergraduate classes at Rutgers University, where I teach, because college students are part of the book's intended audience. Among the undergraduates who were quite critical, but also quite helpful, with their comments and who supplied references from their own research, are Al-Zamar McKinney, Jonathan Lackey, Tracy Dimond, Chris Mindich, Robert Knowles, Sabrina Taylor, Brian Katinas, Dan Devine, Jason Yellen, Elizabeth Jacobs, Mike Vuono, Susanna Policros, and Dylan Errickson. I am also grateful to the students in my spring 2006 course on twentieth-century American culture, who endured the spectacularly awful movie *I Spit on Your Grave*, or *Day of the Woman*, then discussed it with wit and intelligence.

At Rowman & Littlefield, Niels Aaboe, Michelle Cassidy, and Elaine McGarraugh shepherded the manuscript through production with expert care, pointed questions, and good humor. It was a pleasure working with them.

~

Chronology

Books are italicized, movies, plays, and TV shows are shown in quotation marks; an asterisk indicates best picture.

1970   "Little Big Man."

1971   "Sweet Sweetback's Badasssss Song"; "Shaft."

1972   "The Godfather," the original; "Superfly."

1973   Supreme Court decides *Roe v. Wade* on grounds of right of privacy; Organization of Petroleum Exporting Countries doubles prices of crude oil, inflating consumer price index and contributing to "stagflation"; Congress passes the War Powers Act, limiting presidential discretion in declaring and fighting wars; Latin America's 9/11, the overthrow of Salvador Allende, the democratically elected president of Chile, with U.S. connivance; Daniel Bell, *The Coming of Post-Industrial Society*; Martin Scorsese's first feature, "Mean Streets"; "High Plains Drifter"; George Gilder, *Sexual Suicide*.

1974   President Nixon resigns in August; "The Texas Chain Saw Massacre," the original; "Chinatown"; "The Godfather, Part II."

1975   Frank Church's Senate committee condemns U.S. illegal intervention in Chile and elsewhere; James Q. Wilson, *Thinking About Crime*; Seymour Martin Lipset & Everett S. Ladd, *The Divided Academy*; Gayle Rubin, "Notes on the Traffic in Women," in Rayna Reiter, ed., *The Anthropology of Women*; Samuel P. Huntington, et al., for the Trilateral Commission, *The*

Crisis of Democracy; Daniel Bell, *The Cultural Contradictions of Capitalism*; New York City, on verge of bankruptcy, pleads for federal aid.

1976   Jimmy Carter elected president; "Rocky"*, the original; "Taxi Driver."

1977   Charles Lindblom, *Politics and Markets*.

1978   Congress passes FISA, the Foreign Intelligence and Surveillance Act, limiting surveillance of U.S. citizens by government agencies; "I Spit on Your Grave," aka "Day of the Woman"; "The Deer Hunter"*; "Halloween," the original; Irving Kristol, *Two Cheers for Capitalism*; Will Eisner, *A Contract with God*.

1979   Iraninan Revolution, capture of American hostages; Sandinistas come to power in Nicaragua; Soviet invasion of Afghanistan; "Apocalypse Now"; Jimmy Carter cedes Panama Canal.

1980   Ronald Reagan elected president; Lester Thurow, *The Zero-Sum Society*; "Friday the 13th," the original; Solidarity Movement in Poland.

1981   George Gilder, *Wealth and Poverty*; "Ms. 45"; Solidarity crushed.

1982   Michael Novak, *The Spirit of Democratic Capitalism*; Michael Jackson's "Thriller"; "Blade Runner"; "Poltergeist"; "First Blood."

1983   MTV debuts; "Scarface"; Barbara Ehrenreich, *The Hearts of Men*.

1984   "Nightmare on Elm Street," the original; "Terminator," the original; Ronald Reagan re-elected; Paul Craig Roberts, *The Supply-Side Revolution*; Charles Murray, *Losing Ground*; William Gibson, *Neuromancer*.

1985   Perestroika and Glasnost in USSR: economic reform and press freedom inaugurated by Communist Party General Secretary Mikhail Gorbachev; Solidarity resurfaces in Poland; Don DeLillo, *White Noise*; "Rambo: First Blood, Part II."

1986   "Platoon"; Art Spiegelman, *Maus*; David Stockman, *The Triumph of Politics*; Joan W. Scott, "Gender: A Useful Category of Historical Analysis."

1987   "Robocop," the original; "Lethal Weapon," the original; Robert Bork nominated to Supreme Court by Reagan; Toni Morrison, *Beloved*; Alan Bloom, *The Closing of the American Mind*; Judith Butler, *Subjects of Desire*.

1988   George H. W. Bush elected president.

1989 Berlin Wall breached; Velvet Revolution begins in Czechoslovakia; "The Simpsons" debuts on FOX; "The Little Mermaid."

1990 "Dances with Wolves"*; Roger Kimball, *Tenured Radicals*; Judith Butler, *Gender Trouble*; Noel Carroll, *The Philosophy of Horror*.

1991 The "First Gulf War" against Iraq; "The Silence of the Lambs"*; "JFK"; "Beauty and the Beast"; "Terminator 2"; Clark Kerr, *The Great Transformation in Higher Education*; Donna Haraway, *Simians, Cyborgs, and Women*.

1992 "Defense Policy Guidance" memorandum authorized by Dick Cheney and Paul Wolfowitz leaked from Defense Department; Bill Clinton elected president; "Reservoir Dogs"; Arthur Schlesinger, Jr., *The Disuniting of America*; William Bennett, *The De-Valuing of America*; Carol Clover, *Men, Women, and Chain Saws*; Kaja Silverman, *Male Subjectivity at the Margins*.

1993 Terrorist bombing of World Trade Center by al Qaeda associates; federal siege at Waco compound of Branch Davidian sect led by David; Scott McCloud, *Understanding Comics*; Tony Kushner's "Angels in America" opens on Broadway.

1994 "Pulp Fiction"; Tricia Rose, *Black Noise*; S. H. Fernandez, Jr., *The New Beats*.

1995 Lynne Cheney, *Telling the Truth*; Tim LaHaye & Jerry B. Jenkins, *Left Behind*, Volume I; "Braveheart"*; "Toy Story"; Terrorist bombing of Oklahoma City federal office building by Timothy McVeigh.

1996 Bill Clinton re-elected president; Robert Bork, *Slouching Toward Gomorrah*; Samuel P. Huntington, *The Clash of Civilizations*; "From Dusk Til Dawn."

1997 "Buffy the Vampire Slayer" debuts on the WB channel; Project for a New American Century launched by William Kristol, Donald Rumsfeld, Dick Cheney, et al.

1998 Richard Rorty, *Achieving Our Country*; "Saving Private Ryan."

1999 "The Matrix," the original; "Fight Club"; Susan Faludi, *Stiffed*.

2000 Al Gore wins popular vote, George W. Bush elected president by Supreme Court decision in *Bush v. Gore*; Michael Hardt & Antonio Negri, *Empire*; PNAC, "Rebuilding America's Defenses."

2001 Coordinated terrorist attacks on Pentagon and World Trade Center, 9/11.

2002   National Security Strategy statement issued by White House; Andrew Bacevich, *American Empire*; Joseph Stiglitz, *Globalization and its Discontents*.

2003   American-led invasion of Iraq; Robert Kagan, *Of Paradise and Power*.

2004   George W. Bush re-elected president.

2005   Anti-American insurgency peaks in Iraq.

2006   Insurgency continues in Iraq; housing prices flatten after fifteen years of steady increase.

2007   George W. Bush announces a "surge" of additional troops in Baghdad; global financial crisis begins in August, then intensifies with outright failure, federal bailout, or private buyout of several large investment banks in New York City.

2008   Barack Obama elected president.

CHAPTER ONE

~

"From Dusk to Dawn"
Origins and Effects of the Reagan Revolution

In the very late twentieth century, capitalism seemed triumphant throughout the world—that is why everyone was debating the meaning of "globalization" (on which see chapter 6 below). But in the 1970s, capitalism did not look like the wave of the future. Then, as now, it seemed to be on its last legs. Remember, the Soviet Union—the "evil empire," as Ronald Reagan would call it—was still intact and was about to invade its neighbor Afghanistan (yes, the very same Afghanistan the United States invaded in 2001). Communist China's drive to industrialize was in full stride. And socialist movements in Latin America were flourishing; the Nicaraguan Sandinistas, who came to power in 1979, were merely the most visible and effective of these movements.

At the cutting edge of capitalism, however, back in the United States, the economy was a mess and the future of private enterprise was in doubt. The "oil shock" of 1973 to 1975, which tripled the price of imported crude oil—and thus the price of gasoline—still crippled automobile manufacturing, the signature American industry; indeed, the Chrysler Corporation had filed for bankruptcy and begged the U.S. Congress to come to its rescue with outright grants and guaranteed loans. The housing market and consumer spending were severely cramped by double-digit interest rates and unprecedented inflation (to the tune of 20 percent per year). Moreover, occupational safety and environmental protection, the new watchwords of government regulation and public opinion, had apparently trumped the requirements of economic growth. Back then even the Federal Reserve was clueless. And everybody knew it.

Meanwhile, New York City, the financial headquarters of the capitalist world (then still known in Cold War parlance as the "free world") was close to bankruptcy. Huge swaths of Brooklyn and the South Bronx were smoldering ruins. Garbage rotted in the streets of Manhattan. The subways were visibly decaying, most dangerously after dark—not because graffiti artists were sculpting a new underground alphabet, but because the physical plant was expiring and the middle-class commuters were fleeing. And the intersection of Broadway and Forty-second Street—Times Square, where the ball drops on New Year's Eve—was not a tourist destination unless your purpose in coming was pornographic. It was a sexual bazaar, an open-air brothel even in winter, where hustlers, performers, and pimps often outnumbered pedestrians.

Many interested observers—from filmmakers like Martin Scorsese to social scientists like James Q. Wilson—saw these mean streets as thoroughfares to the future of the nation; for they seemed to have channeled the social, political, and cultural extremes inherited from the 1960s and then closed the off-ramps. The plight of New York City was, in this sense, a symptom of systemic failure, of disease in the larger body politic. It was a miniature version of a general crisis in capitalism. And everybody said it.

At any rate the cultural and intellectual history of the late twentieth century was framed by the perception of this bifocal crisis. For example, the ambivalent yet rigorous defense of capitalism which goes by the name of neoconservatism was a direct result of both the general crisis in capitalism and the specific spectacle of New York City. So too was "deregulation," the movement to lighten the visible hand of the state which was originally sponsored by liberals like Ted Kennedy and Jimmy Carter. And so was the Reagan Revolution, the touchstone of contemporary conservatism.

The Supply Side

Let us look more closely, then, at the fears and the hopes—and the ideas—this crisis created. Whether liberal or conservative, those who examined the economic problem typically interpreted it as a political issue animated by deeper cultural change that started in the 1960s. Whether liberal or conservative, their short-run solution was ideological exhortation and their long-run solution was victory in a protracted war of cultures that would necessarily engage the hearts and minds of every American. To solve the economic problem was to convince the American people that unleashing market forces would reinvigorate freedom, progress, and morality—or that state-centered planning for growth would underwrite liberty, equality, and democracy. As we shall see, it was a hard sell either way.

The economic experience of the Great Depression and the Second World War had established a Keynesian consensus in Washington which guided both Democratic and Republican administrations during the Cold War (ca. 1947–1989). In fact, the Republican presidents before Reagan were big-government liberals—Richard Nixon imposed mandatory wage and price controls to subdue inflation, and Gerald Ford followed suit. The Keynesian consensus, from Left to Right, was based on two assumptions. First, government policies, especially decisions on spending (the federal budget) and interest rates (the Federal Reserve), were the keys to economic growth. Second, the scale of consumer spending was more important than the scope of private investment in determining the rate of economic growth.

This consensus expired in the late 1970s as a result of an economic reality—the new combination of price inflation and lower productivity that went by the name of stagflation—and an intellectual movement that came of age at the same moment. The maturing movement was crucial because it explained the new reality and offered an alternative. In its absence, a larger dose of Keynesian policies would have seemed natural and necessary. This intellectual movement was the supply-side revolution that gave Ronald Reagan the broadband credentials he needed to win the presidential primaries and then the presidency itself. In the name of renewed growth, its proponents—Jack Kemp, Jude Wanniski, Paul Craig Roberts, Arthur Laffer, David Stockman, Irving Kristol—wanted to repeal the welfare state and liberate the private sector from every impediment, including taxes. As Stockman, a Michigan congressman who would eventually run Reagan's Office of Management and Budget, put it, the supply-side program "required the radical dismantling of state-erected barriers to economic activity."

It also required tax cuts because increased investment would not happen unless entrepreneurs could keep most of the wealth they generated. This was a matter of incentives, according to the supply-siders, who drew on a large body of research (much of it done by Martin Feldstein of the National Bureau of Economic Research) showing that higher tax rates on personal and corporate income caused lower investment. The loss of tax revenue after the cuts they proposed would be more than offset, they argued, by the gain in tax revenue generated by the faster growth determined by greater investment, which would, in turn, be elicited by the incentive of higher retained earnings. Their argument never made any empirical sense—the numbers just don't add up, as George H. W. Bush pointed out in 1980, when he ran against

Reagan in the primaries—but the arithmetic was beside the point. The supply-siders were arguing that individual saving and private investment, not consumer spending and government policies, were the keys to economic growth. They were arguing against history.

For the history of the twentieth century is the record of economic growth accompanied, perhaps even caused, by declining saving and investment, on the one hand, and rising consumption, on the other. It is also the record of massive market failure: No one except the most devoted disciples of Milton Friedman can still believe that the Great Depression was the result of the Federal Reserve's mistakes (see the appendix on the 2008–2009 economic crisis). Once you acknowledge these simple facts, the supply-side argument sounds more or less absurd. But it was never offered as merely a recipe for economic growth—it was the blueprint for a moral renewal through which the American people would relearn the virtues of hard money, balanced budgets, and real work. Wealth creation would replace redistribution, as Stockman and many others put it. By this they meant two things. First, the limits to growth animated by markets were artificial bureaucratic conventions, not natural environmental constraints. Faster growth through deregulation would underwrite social justice by generating the jobs necessary to get the poor off the welfare rolls.

Second, a transparent relation between effort and reward, between work done and income received, had to be reestablished by the wider application of market forces. Otherwise the American people would continue to shrug off the welfare state's transfer payments, which permitted wages without work. They would continue to be morally corrupted by the state's largesse. As Stockman summarized it: "As an intellectual and moral matter, this comprehensive supply-side doctrine had a powerful appeal. It offered a rigorous standard of justice and fairness, and provided a recipe for economic growth and prosperity—the only viable way to truly eliminate poverty and social deprivation."

The supply-siders called themselves conservatives, of course, but their doctrine was radical, even utopian—it was a "conservatism of yearning," a "rootless nostalgia for roots," as Peter Viereck, an avowed conservative, once put it. The doctrine was radical in the sense that its inventors repudiated that big part of the past that we call the twentieth century. It was utopian in the sense that its proponents constantly cited "classical truths" as if these were impervious to counterarguments grounded in historical consciousness and experience. George Gilder's influential body of work in the 1970s is a perfect example. This quirky Harvard grad made his bones by writing a book called *Sexual Suicide* (1973), in which he argued that feminism threatened

Western civilization, and then by writing a flurry of magazine articles that would become the core of another book, *Wealth and Poverty* (1981), the most energetic and engaging manifesto of the supply-side revolution.

Historians will someday think of Gilder as the George Fitzhugh of his time—as a man of principle who didn't and wouldn't notice the irreversible tendencies of his century. For now, however, we must treat him as a profoundly important intellectual whose ideas shaped policy and public discourse for at least a decade. *Sexual Suicide* brought him wide notice as well as notoriety. Here he argued that the key to the "intractable problem" of the "hardcore American poor" (a.k.a. black folk) was the lack of married men. Bachelors don't work as hard as husbands, Gilder claimed. So the lack of a marriage contract in the nether realms of American society, where the "underclass" congregated, consigned the poor to a future of poverty. More generally, the breakdown of the family caused by feminist revolt against patriarchal norms had produced a huge crop of men, white as well as black, without attachments to wives and children, men who were meandering through adulthood without the kind of commitments and ambitions marriage and family normally produce. Observers on the Left, among them Barbara Ehrenreich, also noted that a new surplus of bachelors was abstaining from the affective attachments that could become long-term commitments under the emotional tutelage of the family. Their solution to the problem— it echoed the attitude of the nineteenth-century "women's movement"—was to search for ways women and children could survive without men, which meant rethinking the nature of the family and calling for public policies that recognized women's social positions and political concerns.

Gilder's solution to the problem, so conceived, was to restore the "male role" of breadwinner in the traditional family. His solution, in other words, was to turn back the clock, to sink roots in sand dunes long since washed away by the tides of historical change. For by the 1970s, the traditional family was already becoming an anachronism, and no amount of rhetoric would restore it. The rate of divorce tripled between 1960 and 1982; by the mid-1980s, 50 percent of marriages ended in divorce, and at least 25 percent of all children were growing up with no more than one parent. In 1967, half of all women in their thirties were married mothers who remained at home full time; by 1982, only a quarter were so occupied. More than half of all women, married or not, were in the workforce by the 1980s, and the American family had diversified accordingly. According to the 1990 census, most families did not fit into the "traditional" category because they were headed by single women, or were based on homosexual partnerships, or were otherwise anomalous from the "anthropological" standpoint Gilder adopted. And so on. Gilder may have been urging a worthy cause—although, come to think of it, *The Simpsons* does question the function of our fathers—but he might as well have been denouncing the law of gravity.

Or was he on firmer ground? What if the decline of the traditional family was not the inevitable result of social, economic, and cultural changes since 1960? What if this decline was instead the artificial result of misguided public policy? Gilder didn't bother to ask—for him, the family was one of those "classical truths"—but Charles Murray, yet another quirky Harvard grad with backing from the American Enterprise Institute (AEI), did ask. His startling answers were contained in a book, *Losing Ground*, which was published in 1982 to the delight of the supply-siders. They had already read his AEI research papers of the late 1970s, where he argued that welfare—that is, Aid to Dependent Children (ADC) as sponsored by the federal government—had destroyed the traditional family by giving poor women the financial incentive to bear children but stay single (the recipients of ADC could be neither married nor employed). In the absence of this transfer payment, Murray insisted, the family would not be at risk, and neither would the larger culture, because the benefits of marriage and work would no longer be obscured, even canceled, by government policy. Dependence on the dole would disappear, and with it the "urban crisis" exemplified by New York City.

Meanwhile, Murray claimed, a criminal "underclass" that was simply unable to take advantage of job training, food stamps, educational subsidies, or welfare would have to be taken off the street. In this scenario—which could have been borrowed from almost any Western movie from 1939 to 1962, from *Stagecoach* to *Liberty Valence*—a vigilant law and order cleared the way for self-reliance and stable families, and thus for civilization as such. Angry pimps with too many prostitutes and "welfare queens" with too many bastards would soon give way to husbands with jobs and wives with children just as renegades and outlaws had given way, once upon a time in the West, to the superior force of armed settlers and hired guns. In effect, then, Murray was writing a political screenplay that spoke to the social disorder and ethical ambiguity on display in most films from the 1960s and 1970s. Moral exhortation had already replaced social science. In other words, the imperative mode of argument, where personal conviction ("authenticity") and narrative form count for more than mutually agreeable exhibits of empirical evidence—where a new, opinionated relativism reigns—had already become the norm by 1980. But notice that it was not the handiwork of the academic Left.

This imperative mode of argument dominates Gilder's *Wealth and Poverty*, the anthem of the Reagan Revolution. Almost every paragraph contains a sentence that begins or ends with the kind of certainty we associate with evangelical faith; phrases like "there can be no doubt," "no one denies," "there is no question" etc., sprout in this ideological hothouse so profusely that the reader has to wonder why the book had to be written. In the absence of controversy, after all, writers are unnecessary. But then Gilder was enlisting in the culture war of his moment, when the *sources* of poverty were becoming a new issue. He argued that poverty was, in fact, a structural problem, just like liberals claimed. But the problem in question was, again, cultural, not economic. It was again a result of the shortage of fathers, which in turn meant a surplus of feckless, useless males without attachments, commitments, and responsibilities—that is, without the moral anchor of familial obligation.

Gilder wanted to make the case for the supply-side revolution, however, so he also launched a theoretical assault on the Keynesian consensus. In this airless room of relentless abstraction, the eternal truth of Say's Law—"there cannot be a glut of goods caused by inadequate total demand" because "the sum of the wages, profits, and rents paid in manufacturing a good is sufficient to buy it"—is repeatedly asserted, to the point where it becomes an explanation, or at least a label, for almost everything in human history. Indeed, Gilder invokes it to describe the gift economies of aboriginal cultures as well as the investment strategies of modern capitalists; by this historical accounting, everyone in every time and place has acted in accordance with its dictates. So he can earnestly announce that "Say's Law, in general terms, is a rule of all organized human behavior," and then say, equally earnestly, that "Say's Law in all its variations is the essential enactment of supply-side theory."

The Disregard for Capital

But so what, you might ask, if Gilder insisted that Say's Law is a transhistorical dimension of human nature? What's the bottom line here? What was the "cash value" of these theoretical incantations? Good questions. The assault on the Keynesian consensus was designed to demote consumer demand and to promote private investment as the key to growth; it was designed, that is, to increase the incomes of the wealthy, on the assumption that such a shift in the distribution of income shares would enhance investment. This was not a hidden agenda; it was clearly stated by everyone involved. If supply creates its own demand, as Say's Law stipulates, we should not worry about the scale of consumer demand, and we should not, by the same token, penalize private investment by taxing it heavily. Here is how Gilder explained the program: "But the essential point is fruitless to deny. Producers play a leading and initiatory role in eliciting, shaping, and creating demand. Investment decisions will be crucial in determining both the quantity and the essential [sic] pattern of consumer purchases." Or again: "The crucial question in a capitalist country is the quality and quantity of investment by the rich."

Now, if "investment by the rich" rather than consumer demand is the engine of economic growth, the policy-relevant question becomes, how do we redistribute national income away from consumption toward saving and investment? In short, how do we reward capitalists for doing their job? The indispensable first step, according to Gilder and his fellow supply-siders, was to cut taxes on investment income, for that move would persuade rich folks to stop buying larger mansions, faster cars, and bigger yachts—to stop consuming so conspicuously—and start investing their money in goods production. Again, this redistribution of national income was not a hidden agenda. It was articulated as early as 1974 by Alan Greenspan, later of Federal Reserve fame, and it was the centerpiece of Reagan's presidential campaign in 1980.

The supply-siders were fighting a rear-guard action against what Henry B. Kaufman, the Salomon Brothers partner who was the most influential stock market analyst of the 1970s, called "The Disregard for Capital." In a speech delivered at the New York Economic Club in May 1980, then widely circulated as a photocopy, Kaufman declared that the American people were no longer satisfied with the merely formal equalities afforded by the modern liberal dispensation—most of them, he claimed, were now clearly committed to something that resembled socialism. "Fundamental change has been taking place in our society over the last five decades," he noted, and insisted that such change had finally produced a "democracy oriented toward an unaffordable egalitarian sharing of production rather than equal opportunity."

Kaufman's counterpart on Wall Street, Felix Rohatyn—he was the investment banker who steered New York City away from bankruptcy—similarly lamented the advent of a "padded society" that had smothered market forces in the name of income security for all. They both agreed with the diagnosis offered a few years earlier by the Trilateral Commission, a high-profile group of accomplished intellectuals and business leaders from Japan, Western Europe, and the United States, which blamed a "welfare shift" in federal spending priorities—a shift away from defense and toward domestic social spending—for empowering new voting blocs and thus endangering both the future of economic growth and the "governability" of American democracy: "The political basis of the Welfare Shift was the expansion in political participation and the intensified commitment to democratic and egalitarian norms which existed in the 1960s."

Notice that the dissatisfaction with business as usual, and the fear of impending alternatives to private enterprise, together created a consensus that included figures from every part of the political spectrum. The liberal Trilateral crowd upstaged Jimmy Carter by dominating his cabinet; then the "conservative" supply-side crowd chewed the scenery of Reagan's presidency by slashing taxes and burning the budget. But they all agreed that capitalism was broken and needed some kind of fix. More specifically, they all agreed that "a new balance between social and economic objectives," as Kaufman put it, had to be written into government policies. Otherwise the perceived requirements of social justice would continue to block the known requirements of economic growth, that is, personal saving and private investment. So the supply-siders were not a voice in the wilderness; they were just the loudest in a growing chorus of critics which doubted that capitalism would survive the 1970s unless it received the equivalent of shock treatment. In this sense, the intellectual origins of the Reagan Revolution were not exclusively conservative.

Even the die-hard Keynesians, and there were lots of them, understood that the stagflation of the 1970s represented a new challenge to their theoretical assumptions and policy prescriptions. Lester Thurow of the Massachusetts Institute of Technology, for example, wrote a book called *The Zero-Sum Society* (1980), which fed into Rohatyn's almost apocalyptic writings of the early 1980s by arguing that the enfranchisement of new interest groups had created political deadlock in Washington. Economic policy had accordingly become an illogical, even idiotic patchwork of pork-barreled compromise. Like Rohatyn and Lloyd Cutler of the Trilateral Commission (he would become Carter's White House counsel), Thurow proposed to solve this problem by streamlining and centralizing policy making in the executive branch. Robert Reich and Ira Magaziner, both later employed by the Clinton administration, meanwhile wrote books like *Minding America's Business* (1979), which recommended Japanese-style "indicative planning"—low-cost government loans to rising industries, higher interest rates, and worker retraining for declining industries—as the cure for what ailed us. The Keynesian diagnosis of stagflation led, therefore, toward state capitalism.

So maybe David Stockman was right to suggest that he was a soldier in "the war between the statists and the anti-statists, between those who wanted government to dominate every aspect of American life and those who didn't." Surely Ronald Reagan's campaign rhetoric tapped into the powerful antistatist tradition of American politics. He knew as well as anyone that the revolution which created the United States of America was animated by commitment to the sovereignty of the people, not the state or its agencies. The founders understood the appeal of classical republicanism, especially its reading of virtue as the product of political action; they nonetheless believed that the sphere of liberty was society, in market transactions among equals under law, and that the sphere of power was the state, where domination and corruption rather than mutuality ruled. Reagan restated and amplified this opposition between liberty and power by insisting that "government is the problem, not the solution." His supply-side principles, however belated, were an integral part of his attachment to the antistatism of "original intent."

By 1980, American voters were willing to try an alternative to the Keynesian consensus—the big-government liberalism—that had characterized the programs of every president since Calvin Coolidge left office in 1929, in part because they knew that public policy wasn't solving their economic problems, in part because they hoped that increased private investment would. They were always skeptical of Reagan's programs (every poll of the 1980s showed they liked the man better than the policies), but they rolled the dice and hoped for the best.

Conservatism Old and New

Meanwhile conservative opinion was becoming more visible, more respectable. William F. Buckley Jr., the founder of *National Review* who had opposed the civil rights movement and who had once proposed to limit the vote to property-holders, still appeared weekly on public television (the fourth channel in most households) as the "moderator" of a wonkish talk show. Then conservative icon Milton Friedman, the famed economist from the University of Chicago who won the Nobel Prize in 1978, was featured as the talking head of a PBS series that let him expound on his ideas about the causative relationship between markets and freedom. This was a breakthrough for conservative opinion, even though his monetarism—the rate of growth in the money supply determines everything, he argued—was inconsistent with the implied activism of supply-side doctrine. For the guileless Friedman indirectly introduced millions of viewers to Friedrich von Hayek, the Darth Vader of modern economics, as if he were just another theorist from the mainstream.

Hayek was the Austrian who insisted that socialism was preposterous as well as evil because it supposed that the market could be subordinated to reason. For Hayek, as for Friedman, market forces were the source of freedom precisely because they could not be known from any standpoint—precisely because they could not be manipulated by individuals or companies or governments. As long as the rights of private property were inviolable, they assumed, and as long as everyone was subject to the same anonymous laws of supply and demand, liberty and equality were possible. From this premise, they argued that only capitalist societies could be free societies. They also argued that the citizens of a free society could not even try to create a just society; for to do so would be to modify the arbitrary results of market forces in the name of justice and thus to staunch the economic source of freedom.

As Irving Kristol, by all accounts the founding father of neoconservatism, noted at the time, this argument's rigorous indifference to justice would be simply intolerable to most Americans. But he didn't reject it because it wouldn't play in Peoria. He rejected it because it denied modernity itself, the moment when consent—not force and not chance—became the principle of social order and political innovation. "But can men live in a free society," Kristol asked, "if they have no reason to believe that it is a just society?" In a word, no. The "historical accidents of the marketplace," as Hayek and Friedman portrayed them, could not be "the basis for an enduring and legitimate entitlement to power, privilege, and property," not any more than the historical accidents of birth could make the claims of a hereditary aristocracy seem reasonable.

Kristol was trying to detach conservatism from its schizophrenic devotion to free markets on the one hand and tradition on the other. He knew that you can't revere tradition if you admire the "creative destruction" that capitalism brings to life. He knew that you can't insulate the nuclear family from the heartless logic of the market if you accept the dictates of free enterprise. He knew that conservatism had to become more liberal if it were to sound like something more than hidebound devotion to a phantom past. A "combination of the reforming spirit with the conservative ideal," he declared, "is most desperately wanted," and cited Herbert Croly, the original big-government liberal from the Progressive Era, as his source of inspiration.

Kristol also knew that the competitive, entrepreneurial economy Friedman and Hayek posited as the source of freedom was a mere fantasy. Capitalism had long since become a system in which large corporations, not small producers, dominated the market—those anonymous and unknowable laws of supply and demand which once made all producers equally subject to the discipline of market forces had been supplanted by the visible hand of modern management: "There is little doubt that the idea of a 'free market,' in the era of large corporations, is not quite the original capitalist idea." Some producers had more market power than others: some persons (and this is how corporations are legally designated) were more equal than others. So everyone was not "free to choose," as Friedman would have it, simply because he or she inhabited a market society. Corporate capitalism remained a moral problem. For in "its concentration of assets and power—power to make economic decisions affecting the lives of tens of thousands of citizens—it seem[s] to create a dangerous disharmony between the economic system and the political."

We might then say that neoconservatism was born when that problem was acknowledged and addressed by ex-liberals like Kristol. We might also say that Friedman's PBS series was an "elegant tombstone" marking the death of an older conservatism in which the state was a passive spectator and in which the moral problem of market logic—if everything is for sale, how do we preserve public goods (like democracy) that have no cash value?—was happily ignored. Certainly George Gilder was trying to make an ethical case for capitalism by claiming that investing in the hope of private profit was the equivalent of gift-giving in the name of social solidarity. Kristol was trying, too, but he was more subtle and more skeptical than his colleagues on the supply side.

God, Family, Markets

One of his many protégés, Michael Novak, was writing a book at the same historical moment which exemplifies both this ambition to dress capitalism in new moral clothing and the institutional environment that enabled the ambition. Like Kristol and many other neoconservatives, Novak was a former radical disillusioned by the oppressive idiocies of actually existing socialism and disheartened by the political postures of the largely literary Left. As a genuine theologian and moral philosopher—before he joined the American Enterprise Institute as a senior fellow, he was the Watson-Ledden chair of Religious Studies at Syracuse University—he knew that the defense of capitalism required something more than jolly slogans and militant assertions. That knowledge propelled Novak onto the contested terrain of classical social theory, where Karl Marx and Max Weber were still the landlords, and into the fractious space of contemporary religious debate, where "liberation theology"—a distant echo of the early Christian concern with its original constituency among the poor and the outcast—was now the real alternative to received doctrine in the Catholic Church itself.

Novak had two aims in writing *The Spirit of Democratic Capitalism* (1981), whose title was a conscious parody of Weber's classic statement, *The Protestant Ethic and the Spirit of Capitalism* (1904, 1930 in English translation). On the one hand, he wanted, like Gilder, to demonstrate that capitalism as such neither impaired the moral capacity of any individual nor contradicted the moral standards of modern society: "There is a strong consonance between the virtues required for successful commercial and industrial practice and the natural moral virtues." In this sense he was rebutting the long-standing claims of socialists—keep in mind that these were also the deeply felt suspicions of most Americans—and addressing the questions Kristol had recently raised. On the other hand, he wanted to directly confront liberation theology and in doing so provide a positive theoretical alternative to Marxism. In pursuing both aims, his itinerary consciously and closely followed the map drawn by Reinhold Niebuhr, the Christian socialist of the 1930s who turned cold warrior in the 1950s.

Novak was using Niebuhr's example to argue with Daniel Bell and Charles Lindblom, two giants of American intellectual life in the 1970s. Bell was the Harvard sociologist who had drawn deeply on Marx in writing *The Coming of Post-Industrial Society* (1973)—he was, not incidentally, a close friend of Irving Kristol, with whom he had founded *The Public Interest*, a hugely influential journal—and Lindblom was the Yale political scientist who had similarly drawn on Marx (as well as Adam Smith) in writing *Politics and Markets* (1977), a quietly incendiary book that explained why capitalism and democracy were at odds. Each of them posited a pluralist order in which there were three separate but interlocking systems (economic, political, cultural). But Bell had discovered a disturbing disjuncture between the economic and the cultural systems—the new capitalist hedonism had trampled the older bourgeois values (what Novak had called "the virtues required for successful commercial and industrial practice")—while Lindblom had (re)discovered a dangerous discrepancy between the economic power of corporations and the political power of individuals (note that this same concern was expressed at the same moment by Kristol himself).

Novak insisted that the moral/cultural system was not out of phase with the economic system because "the most profound of economic motives is almost always—and must necessarily be—family-oriented." Indeed, the "fundamental motive of all economic activity" turned out to be "family-regarding." Deferring gratification, saving for a rainy day, promising to meet one's obligations, all the bourgeois virtues that were visibly decaying in Bell's account of postindustrial society remained intact in Novak's account of democratic capitalism: "self-interest" was just an ugly label for devotion to family. This is a compelling argument, of course, but only insofar as the traditional nuclear family functions as the moral anchor of modern economic man. In its absence, all bets on the future of capitalism are off. Perhaps that is why we still try to read that uncertain future in the fractured state of the family.

Novak also insisted that Lindblom was peddling social science hokum. Corporations were not "disproportionately powerful" actors on the pluralist political scene, as Lindblom had argued; they were leading men, to be sure, but they were directed, for the most part, by governments. Here Novak forgot his own homage to the corporation, "a novel social instrument," as the key structural element of democratic capitalism. But then, his description of the corporation sounded very much like his defense of the family as the device by which self-interest was converted to social purpose: "The assumption behind this invention is social, not individualistic. It holds that economic activity is fundamentally corporate, exceeding the capacity of one individual alone. It requires a social life form which goes beyond the power and the lifetime of one individual."

So Novak settled the ongoing debate about markets in organizing social life and individual opportunities by reference to institutions that either stood apart from markets (families) or actively administered them (corporations). It was an honorable attempt to demonstrate the continuity of capitalism and character, then, but it ultimately failed because it wouldn't address the moral problem of market logic. In fact, Novak defended capitalism by celebrating the "social life forms" that limit the reach of markets in the name of purposes that have no prices—for example, he declared that "the family is a form of socialism that corrects the exaggerated individualism" created by modern market economies. He might as well have claimed that capitalism is tolerable as long as socialism contains its excesses.

Novak's concluding critique of liberation theology was rather less than compelling; for his doubts about the moral contents of free markets were already on display. It also ran counter to the U.S. Bishops' 1982 statement on the economy, which promoted state intervention in markets on behalf of equality. But it did clarify the deepening fissures in American religious thought of the 1970s and 1980s. Liberation theology was not officially launched until 1968 at the conference of Latin American bishops in Medellin, Columbia, when revolutionary hopes in the Western Hemisphere were highest; it had, however, been percolating within the Catholic Church, north and south, since the 1950s. In many ways, it was a theological version of dependency theory, which held that the former European colonies of Asia, Africa, and Latin America remained poor because they were still locked in exploitative economic relations with advanced industrial nations (especially but not only the United States). To abstain from these disadvantageous relations was to act on a "preferential option for the poor," to treat the people who had been left behind by capitalism as if they were the future of the church.

The seminal statement of this radical vision came from the Second Vatican Council of 1965, in Gaudium et Spes ("The Church in the Modern World"). Here the gathered clerics announced that "equity and justice" demanded the immediate removal of the "immense economic inequalities" still separating rich and poor nations: "For excessive economic and social differences between the members of the one human family or population groups cause scandal, and militate against social justice, equity, the dignity of the human person, as well as social and international peace." They also insisted that the real purpose of "economic production" was neither growth nor profit; it was instead "to be at the service of humanity in its totality." So they concluded that the ancient criterion of need, the criterion on which their church had been founded, had a modern application: "Therefore everyone has the right to possess a sufficient amount of the earth's goods for themselves and their family. This has been the opinion of the Fathers and Doctors of the church, who taught that people are bound to come to the aid of the poor and to do so not merely out of their superfluous goods." Indeed, the poor were now deputized to redistribute the wealth on hand when required, as in the biblical injunctions of the Old Testament prophets: "Persons in extreme necessity are entitled to take what they need from the riches of others."

The sequel to *Gaudium et Spes*, which was published in 1971 by the Synod of Bishops as "Justice in the World," was in some ways even more stridently anticapitalist. It recognized, for example, the new issues residing in discussions of the "biosphere," and proposed, accordingly, to limit economic growth in the name of environmental integrity. And it posited a universal human "right to development," which makes participation in political decisions the equivalent of access to economic resources. But "liberation through development" required the eradication of existing inequalities between nations and peoples so that "a new form of colonialism" would not again victimize the poor, wherever they lived.

There was no Bible-banging in Novak's response to this revolutionary theological challenge; his text was Niebuhr, not Isaiah. Instead of a scripturally based treatise on the sources of inequality or the solutions to poverty, in other words, he wrote a social-scientific meditation on the origins of a pluralistic, democratic capitalism. He assumed that dependency theory and its theological adjuncts were nonsense and asked, what kept the Other Americas poor? His answers recalled and recast the arguments of Barrington Moore Jr. (which were, not coincidentally, reminiscent of arguments made by both Marx and Weber). In a seminal book called *Social Origins of Dictatorship and Democracy* (1966), Moore had shown that the original response of the landed nobility to the appearance of world markets in the sixteenth and seventeenth centuries determined the subsequent political history of their countries. Where they responded by imposing a second serfdom on the peasantry—as in eastern Europe—democracy was doomed; where they responded by selling or renting their land to commoners, who in turn hired peasants newly freed from feudal obligations—as in western Europe—democracy became imaginable.

Novak used a similarly Weberian typology to suggest that the presence or absence of markets as such explained nothing; the key to the future was how the political and the moral/cultural systems had shaped the economic system. The roots of Latin American backwardness were then a matter of political and cultural failures that had distorted markets and disabled democracy since colonial times; liberation theology was merely the latest of these failures. Capitalism of the North American kind would redeem, not ruin, the South, for it would bring its adjuncts, political pluralism and moral/cultural integrity, to bear on the hapless products of the Spanish empire. Again, however, Novak had demonstrated that the spirit of democratic capitalism and the promise of American life did not reside in the economic system—in free markets, private enterprise, profit motives, and the like. They were instead to be found in a world elsewhere, in a world removed from economic imperatives: it was to be found in the same place liberation theology had located as its preferred destination. So the neoconservative argument once more intersected with that of the radical opposition to capitalism.

The Spirit of Democratic Capitalism was published by Simon & Schuster with a subvention—a subsidy—from the AEI, where Novak became a senior fellow in 1977. AEI was one of several Washington think tanks established or reinvigorated in the 1970s with big money from self-consciously conservative foundations (Olin, Scaife, Coors), which, unlike older and avowedly liberal foundations (Ford, Rockefeller, Carnegie), had no measurable purchase on American intellectual life. Its inventors understood that they needed to create a new political culture, a new intellectual climate, that would completely bypass the universities—the bastion of the Left—and speak directly to both journalists and politicians. Like their counterparts at the new Heritage Foundation (founded in 1973), they raised lots of money ($10 million a year by 1980), identified issues of concern to conservatives, recruited bona fide intellectuals like Novak, armed them with eager young interns, and said, "Let there be books!" Also academic conferences, press releases, talking points, budget studies, sound bites, and photo-ops. The point was to change the world, and that process, they knew, would have to begin in the marketplace of ideas, where liberals, Keynesians, and socialists were still the most reputable and influential peddlers. This institutional environment was the enabling condition of the "Reagan Revolution" as both an intellectual background and a social network—between them, AEI and Heritage sponsored most of the ideas and many of the individuals (including Stockman, Kemp, Roberts, and Gilder) that mattered in the first Reagan administration.

Why Is There Still Socialism in the United States?

Our question now becomes, how much did they matter? We know already that the intellectual origins of the Reagan Revolution were not merely, or even mainly, conservative. Were its consequences just as ambiguous? Let us look at the effects of the supply-side revolution and the larger neoconservative movement on what Novak called the economic and the moral/cultural systems. Marginal tax rates on corporate and individual incomes were cut substantially (by half) in 1981, in keeping with the idea that higher retained earnings would mean greater investment in goods production. But the fifty corporations with the largest tax benefits from the legislation of 1981 reduced their investments over the next two years. Meanwhile, the share of national income from wages and salaries declined 5 percent between 1978 and 1986, while the share from investment (profits, dividends, rent) rose 27 percent, as per the demands of supply-side theory—but net investment kept falling through the 1980s. In 1987, Peter G. Peterson, the chairman of the Council on Foreign Relations and former secretary of commerce under Richard Nixon, called this performance "by far the weakest net investment effort in our postwar history." And yet the gross national product grew rapidly and the stock market surged after the short recession of 1982–1983.

The Reagan administration did reverse the welfare shift decried by liberals and conservatives alike. Between 1980 and 1987, for example, the human resources component of federal outlay fell from 28 percent of the total to 22 percent, while the defense component rose from 23 percent of the total to 28 percent. Meanwhile, federal funding for state and local spending on public welfare and education declined in real terms (after accounting for inflation) in the 1980s. Journalists and historians subsequently identified this reversal of budget priorities as the means by which the wily Reagan bankrupted the Soviet Union—the Kremlin had to match the American defense buildup or lose credibility—and "won" the Cold War. But it always had primarily domestic purposes rather than foreign policy implications: perestroika over there was an unintended consequence of the supply-side revolution over here.

Moreover, Reagan's reversal of the welfare shift almost broke the bank back home. Federal budget deficits tripled in the 1980s, reaching levels unmatched except in wartime; by 1986, annual interest payments on the national debt exceeded corporate profits as a percentage of gross national product. For the Reagan administration did favor "free markets," but couldn't complete the agenda of "deregulation" started under Jimmy Carter; in fact, federal regulatory expenditures increased more than 21 percent in real terms between 1981 and 1990. And Reagan did make the "restoration" of national defense a principal priority, but he couldn't stop the growth of government spending on entitlements or transfer payments such as Medicare, Social Security, family assistance ("welfare"), educational assistance (grants or loans), and veterans' benefits. The Congress wouldn't stand for it, and so the budget deficit just kept growing. This was not a result of liberal Democratic majorities; avowedly conservative Republican congressmen were equally determined to keep federal funding for local and state transportation projects, equally unwilling to dismantle Medicare or reduce Social Security benefits, and equally eager to regulate the economy on behalf of their constituents.

As David Stockman explained in 1987, "[p]olitical reality blew a large hole in the side of the [budget] cuts he had proposed in his capacity as director of Office of Management and Budget:" the free market and anti-welfare state premises of the Reagan revolution were not going to take root." The ultraconservative economist Robert Higgs agreed: this so-called revolution "fizzled," he claimed, because "politics as usual" reasserted itself as early as the spring of 1981. So we might say that the economic system installed and maintained by the Keynesian consensus miraculously survived the supply-side assault. But we should then ask how, and also wonder why anyone still believes that Reagan made an economic difference. What political reality was so powerful that it thwarted the electoral mandates this conservative president could honestly cite? Let us ask the question more pointedly: Was Henry Kaufman right about that majority of Americans committed to an "unaffordable egalitarian sharing of production"? Put it as plainly as possible: Did an unspoken socialism become a bipartisan purpose—politics as usual—in the late twentieth century?

One way to answer the question is to notice the dizzying range of regulatory agencies, federal statutes, and executive orders which, then as now, limit the reach of markets in the name of purposes that have no prices. A laundry list of such agencies, statutes, and orders would merely begin with the Federal Reserve System, the Food and Drug Administration, the Federal Trade Commission, the Securities and Exchange Commission, the Federal Deposit Insurance Corporation, the Federal Communications Commission, the Federal Aviation Agency, the Occupational Safety and Health Administration, the Environmental Protection Agency, the Equal Employment and Opportunity Commission, the National Weather Service, the Federal Emergency Management Agency, the National Institutes of Health, the Centers for Disease Control, the National Science Foundation, the National Endowment for the Arts, and the National Endowment for the Humanities. And so on, unto acronymical infinity.

To this incomplete laundry list, we should add the post-Vietnam armed services—the "volunteer army" that now serves as a job-training program and a portal to higher education for working-class kids, of every color, who enter adulthood with great expectations but without good grades, real diplomas, or athletic scholarships. Our new model army is, of course, one dimension of Reagan's efforts to reverse the welfare shift. But if this massive part of the federal budget is not domestic spending to promote equal opportunity and social mobility—guns *and* butter, we might say—what is it? And to our apparently endless list we should also add the thousands of nongovernmental organizations and nonprofit institutions that stand athwart the free market, modulating and containing its arbitrary forces. As we shall see in chapter 2, the most important of these hybrids are institutions of higher education, where the public and private sectors now meet to plan the future, and where about a third of Americans now congregate, almost every day, whether as students, teachers, or staff.

Another, more prosaic way to answer the question about an unspoken socialism passing for politics as usual in the late twentieth century is to measure the growth of transfer payments in this period. Transfer payments represent income received by households and individuals for which no contribution to current output of goods or services has been required. By supply-side standards, they are immoral at best and criminal at worst because they represent reward without effort, income without work—because they conform to the ancient Christian and the modern socialist criterion of need ("From each according to his abilities, to each according to his needs"). But they were the fastest-growing component of income in the late twentieth century, amounting, by 1999, to 20 percent of all labor income. From 1959 to 1999, transfer payments grew by 10 percent annually, more than any other source of labor income, including wages and salaries; by the end of the twentieth century, one in every eight dollars earned by those who were contributing to the production of goods or services was transferred to others who were not making any such contribution.

But did the American electorate ever rise up against this unspoken socialism? Not really. Neither did their representatives in Congress. There were, of course, local rebellions against property taxes in the late 1970s, the most successful of which happened in California under the rubric of Proposition 13. But it took a notoriously neoliberal president, Bill Clinton, to "end welfare" as we knew it, and he couldn't slow the growth of federal transfer payments anymore than his predecessors could. Indeed, the "crisis" of Social Security which consumed so much newsprint, airtime, and blog space in the early twenty-first century was largely a matter of chart–mongering and hand-wringing about this seemingly irresistible urge to detach income received from work done.

The detachment of income from work, the essence of socialism, abides, then, just as unobtrusively, but just as steadfastly, as The Dude, who unwittingly foiled the venal designs of that outspoken neoconservative, the Big Lebowski. The specter of communism may have retired to the dustbin of history, but its first cousin still haunts the economic system of modern capitalism, even in the United States, even in the aftermath of the "Reagan Revolution."

And the moral/cultural system? Did neoconservatism triumph where the supply-side revolution failed? According to its most ardent supporters, absolutely not. Here, too, they say, the liberals and the leftists and the lesbians won. They have a point. American culture was much more liberal, open, and electric in 1990 than in 1980, and then again in 2000, no matter how you frame the issues of gender, sexuality, and race, no matter how you characterize music, movies, and other performance arts. And that culture was increasingly popular, visible, and even politically significant *outside* the United States, as the sound tracks and dress codes of the Eastern European revolutions of the early 1990s will attest: from Poland to Czechoslovakia, rock and roll, blue jeans, and T-shirts identified the personnel of a post-Soviet order.

Whatever the issue—whether sexuality, gay rights, reproduction, education, women's rights, racial equity, equal opportunity, affirmative action, or freedom of expression—the domestic debate was joined in the 1970s and 1980s, was intensified in the 1990s, and was always lost by the so-called cultural conservatives who kept citing "family values." For the New Left of the 1960s grew up and got jobs in all the right places, especially, but not only, in higher education. Here is how Robert Bork, whom Reagan nominated to the Supreme Court in 1987, explained this process ten years after the Senate voted decisively against his confirmation: "It [the 1960s] was a malignant decade that, after a fifteen year remission, returned in the 1980s to metastasize more devastatingly throughout our culture than it had in the Sixties, not with tumult, but quietly, in the moral and political assumptions of those who now control and guide our major cultural institutions. The Sixties radicals are still with us, but now they do not paralyze the universities; they run the universities."

Again, the United States was a much more liberal place after Ronald Reagan. We will explore the evidence in more detail in chapter 4. In the next two chapters, meanwhile, we turn to the academic sources of this evident yet unknown result of the culture wars.

CHAPTER TWO

~

"Tenured Radicals" in the Ivory Tower:

The Great Transformation of Higher Education

The so-called culture wars of the late twentieth century were fought, for the most part, at the shifting borders of the American university, the new center of "knowledge production" in the postwar era. The goal of the combatants, from Left to Right, was to clarify and (re)define the proper uses of higher education in the United States. But in a broader sense, the culture wars were debates about the promise of American life; for, by the 1970s, the principal residence of that promise was widely assumed to be the new "meritocracy" enabled by universal access to higher education.

These conflicts often turned on the meaning and significance of obscure academic doctrines such as deconstruction, which apparently invalidated any possibility of a stable truth claim about written texts; they often degenerated into pointless arguments on the role of Western civilization—both the European past and the required course—in sponsoring the concepts of reason, justice, and representative government; they often got stuck at the rhetorical stage of "political correctness," where both Left and Right could accuse the other side of harboring inane ideas about the realities of research, teaching, and public service. These conflicts nonetheless illuminated different versions of the usable past and the impending future of America which reached well beyond the sacred groves of academe. For as Arthur Schlesinger Jr. put it in 1991, "the debate about the curriculum is a debate about what it means to be an American."

We might even say that the "culture wars"were a symptom of the fourth great watershed in the history of higher education. By the same token, we might say that they were judgments on the historical moment—the 1960s—in which this educational watershed was both cause and effect.

The university as we know it, a secular city unified only by commitment to intellectual inquiry, is little more than a hundred years old. The university as such is about eight hundred years old; it was invented in the thirteenth century by the so-called scholastics, the learned priests who, with the help of ancient philosophy, tried to square Catholic doctrine on usury with modern uses of money at interest. Thereafter, higher education was mostly a matter of learning to reconcile God and Mammon, of keeping faith with purposes larger than your own, whether you learned the lesson in a seminary, a college, or a university. Certainly the curriculum of the private colleges founded in England and North America before 1800—Oxford, Cambridge, Harvard, and Yale are the blueprints—would suggest that both the religious archive and the effective conscience of modernity found their homes on campus.

The modern *secular* university emerged in nineteenth-century Germany as a nation-building device. Its inventors thought of it as a way of articulating a culture—not a religion—that would forge the citizens of a unitary, sovereign state from the raw materials of different classes, regions, and peoples. In such a setting, the humanities did not make up the "core curriculum" of the university; they constituted the university. The research program here was scholarship that demonstrated the cultural continuity of ancient Greece and modern Europe. Reputable scholars showed that each modern, civilized nation stood at a different remove, or at a different angle, from the Athenian origin, but that each had developed a unique identity in the form of a national literature by appropriating that origin. And so the idea of the canon was born.

By the end of the nineteenth century, American educators and legislators were building a new, hybrid system that borrowed from the German model—many of the young PhDs who invented and staffed the new American universities had been trained in Berlin—but that didn't merely reproduce it. We can date the formal beginning of this system, the third great watershed in higher education, from 1884, when the Johns Hopkins University established the first graduate programs in philosophy and history. But its roots lie in the land grant college acts of 1862 and 1887, which used federal resources to lay the foundations of the state universities that came of age in the 1890s, from Michigan to California; and its effects are evident in the transformation of private institutions—among them, Stanford, Chicago, Cornell, Northwestern, and Columbia—which was meanwhile accomplished by imitation of the public universities. And so "the politics of liberal education," as we now say, were present at the creation of the modern American university because the university itself was the product of political purposes.

The new model of higher education in the United States was, however, neither public nor private. And its immediate inclusion of science and business courses in the college curriculum meant that the humanities would have no monopoly on the future of the university or the larger culture—the canon was always in question, and it always included renegade texts from disreputable sources. As usual, the American university did not measure up, or down, to the more romantic and elitist standards of European education. Its curriculum and clientele never abstained from the commercial culture that surrounded and permeated it, and by the 1940s its managers, public and private, had begun to imagine the consequences of universal access.

And yet as late as 1960, only a third of high school graduates in the United States went on to college, and of these privileged students, only 38 percent were women, and only 7 percent came from ethnic minorities. In 1960, there were about 3.5 million students in all American colleges and universities. By 1970, however, their numbers had more than doubled to 7.5 million because, for the first time in the history of higher education, more than half of all high school graduates went on to college of some kind. The number of faculty members increased proportionately, by almost 70 percent, as the system sorted into the three tiers we now take for granted (universities, four-year colleges, community and county colleges). Most of this increase came in the five years after 1965, when the number of new positions created and filled by institutions of higher education exceeded the entire number of faculty positions filled in 1940. Many of these new hires were understandably moved by the "new social movements" of the 1960s, particularly civil rights, Black Power, environmentalism, and feminism, but, as we shall see, they didn't always get tenure.

By 1980, enrollment in colleges and universities had grown by another 60 percent to twelve million students, a fourfold increase since 1960. Meanwhile, the social composition of the student body changed dramatically. Women were less than 40 percent of undergraduates in 1960; by 1980 they were a solid majority of a much larger cohort. Minorities were less than 7 percent of undergraduates in 1960 (about 210,000 students); by 1980, their numbers had grown sevenfold to 13 percent of all undergraduates (about 1.6 million students). The social composition of faculty and professional staff changed accordingly, but less dramatically, as the net number of new positions dwindled after 1970 and almost disappeared after 1980. For better or worse, the politics of liberal education had nevertheless changed irrevocably.

This almost incredible expansion of higher education—the fourth great watershed—was not an accident, and as with other such massive quantitative changes, it had qualitative effects both inside and outside academe. One way to explain it as the product of careful deliberation rather than a random development is to claim that the Soviet scientific achievement of 1956—the successful rocket launch of Sputnik, an automatically orbiting satellite—galvanized public opinion and government resources in the United States, pointing both toward greater investment in education as a vital dimension of national defense. There is much to be said for such an explanation, in part because it dissolves the distinction between domestic programs and foreign policy. Even so, it tends to reduce the great transformation of higher education in the 1960s and 1970s to a late episode in the Cold War. That explanatory tendency is a problem because this transformation began long before the Soviet Union and the United States squared off in the 1950s as contestants for the loyalties of the "Third World," and it remains, in our own time, as evidence of a fundamental historical transition that has nothing to do with the Cold War.

The great transformation of higher education began, in this sense, as an intellectual upheaval that reached a verge in the 1940s and became a kind of common sense in the 1950s. The Keynesian Consensus discussed in chapter 1 was the policy-relevant economic theory that authorized this upheaval. The GI Bill, which gave veterans of World War II significant incentives to abstain from the labor market and go to college—you could reduce unemployment and get a free education, all at once—was one of the new public policies that expressed the same upheaval. So was the Master Plan for the University of California, which, as implemented in the 1950s and early 1960s, made education the basic industry of the most populous state. And so, too, were the federal policies of the 1960s, which sought to increase equality of opportunity, to reduce regional educational disparities—the South was still a backwater at best—and to create universal access to higher education through tuition grants and admission mandates.

Postindustrial Intellect

The intellectual upheaval that figures as the backstory of these policies and the great transformation they enforced—the most consequential "reform of institutions of higher education in the Western world in eight hundred years," according to Clark Kerr, who wrote California's Master Plan—was the discovery of a "postindustrial society." Daniel Bell, whom we met in chapter 1, is the scholar most consistently associated with that discovery, but he has always insisted that he did no more than integrate the findings of many other scholars, from Raymond Aron to Amitai Etzioni, whose mid-century work was shaped by some sense of an ending. "The sense was present—and still is—that in Western society we are in the midst of a vast historical change," Bell noted, "in which old social relations (which were property-bound), existing power structures (centered on narrow elites), and bourgeois culture (based on notions of restraint and delayed gratification) are being rapidly eroded."

The eclipse of modern-industrial society and the concurrent emergence of a postindustrial society meant, according to Bell and his antecedents, that goods production and manufacturing would give way to a "service economy" in which occupational opportunity and standing would derive from open-ended access to knowledge (in effect, from universal access to education); that power derived from ownership of property would decline accordingly as social status would come increasingly determined by theoretical knowledge and technical skill; and finally that culture, having "achieved autonomy," would replace technology as the fundamental source of change in Western society. So conceived—and nobody, from Left to Right, bothered to quibble with this new periodization of Western civilization—a postindustrial society required rather more nerds than had previously been thought usable or tolerable.

Intellectuals—"persons who are not performing essential services," as Everett Ladd and S. M. Lipset, two influential academics, characterized their own kind—became crucial in such a society, where the production of strange new ideas is more important, perhaps even more profitable, than the production of tangible goods. And the university quickly became the place these nomads—these intellectuals, these ideas—could call home. So, from Left to Right, everyone agreed by the 1970s that professors, the intellectuals certified by their well-educated peers in the universities, held the key to the political future of postindustrial society. "Colleges and universities are the wellspring of the ideas around which we organize ourselves," as Lynne V. Cheney put it in bitter retrospect, in 1995. Here is how Kerr himself saw the future twenty years earlier: "Once economic growth depended upon new land, more labor, more capital. Increasingly it now depends upon more skill and new knowledge. . . . [Thus] intellectuals have become a real force in society. In some ways they are taking the part once played by the peasants or the farmers, and later by the trade union movement in social change."

Once upon a time in the 1930s, as this story goes, capital and labor had engaged in a great class struggle for control of the point of production. Now the great divide was between the intellectuals who congregated in academia, where an "adversary culture" flourished, and the rest of Americans, who frequented a conformist, consumer culture. At the historical moment when new knowledge, technical skill, and theoretical acumen became the rudiments of economic growth and national security, what the New Left of the 1960s called the "new class"—the white-collared "professional-managerial class," or PMC—had apparently inherited the earth. At any rate it had taken over the universities, and by all accounts the better universities housed its most adversarial elements. The revenge of the nerds was complete by the time Ronald Reagan took office.

Well, almost. There was a remarkable shift in the politics of professors after 1969, but that shift reflected a larger public disavowal of the war in Vietnam, and even after the epochal election of 1972, the social sciences—the most outspoken and critical of academic fields—had not been seized by an intemperate radicalism that would become a wholesale "anti-Americanism." Ladd and Lipset were emphatic on this point in their massive and authoritative study of professorial politics in the 1960s and 1970s: "Most academic social scientists are not radicals, and do not seek or support radical change in the polity of the academy. While far from being apologists for all or most policy initiatives of the ruling elites of the country, the vast majority of social scientists are also far from being advocates of a fundamentally new constitutional order. They are critics *within* the system."

So the university had become the site of significant struggle by the late twentieth century as an incident in the emergence of a postindustrial society. Again, by the 1970s, everyone, from Left to Right, agreed that it was the social and intellectual terrain on which the promise of American life would be decided, for better or worse. But if the rambunctious social scientists harbored by the university were still part of the loyal opposition as late as 1975, if they were still "critics *within* the system" long after the spirit of the 1960s had expired, what was all the fuss about "tenured radicals" in the 1980s and 1990s? What were they doing that was so outrageous? What, in other words, was the real difference between the combatants in the culture wars, aside from the obvious fact that one side (the Left) controlled the commanding heights of the higher learning, and the other (the Right) wanted a foothold there, at the level of intellectual authority now determined by the university, the cultural pivot of postindustrial society?

From Left to Right, What Is to Be Done?

The New Left that flourished in the 1960s later told its own story as an unfolding tragedy that began in 1968, when "years of hope" gave way to "days of rage," when left-wing activists, having given up on the American electorate, either tried terrorism—the Weather Underground of Students for a Democratic Society, the Progressive Labor Party, the Symbionese Liberation Army, and so on—or retreated to the ivory tower of academe. The New Right that meanwhile emerged in the 1960s and 1970s similarly told its own story as an unfolding tragedy that began in 1968, when left-wing activists, having been defeated by the American electorate, either tried terrorism or took over the ivory tower of academe. Both tellers of the tale were correct, of course, because they told pretty much the same story. But what was the moral of the story they told?

The Left's complaints about America as newly framed by academic locutions were familiar to anyone who had merely watched the network news in the 1960s and 1970s. The United States was built on a foundation of racism. Slavery was the origin, of course, but racial oppression did not end when the "peculiar institution" did, in 1865. In fact, the enforcement of white supremacy got more ugly, more violent, and more effective in the early twentieth century. The civil rights movement and its successor, Black Power, had tried to redeem the promise of the Declaration ("all men are created equal"), but inequality was still the rule. The United States was also built on a foundation of sexism. Females had been systematically excluded from the public sphere since the seventeenth century, and no amount of voting would change the assumption that women were better off at home with the kids than at work. Women's Liberation in the late 1960s had questioned this common sense, of course, but here, too, inequality was still the rule as late as 1980.

What then was to be done? The question was not yet political. As rephrased by the academic Left, it went something like this: Why does inequality persist in a society committed, at least on paper, to its eradication? Why can't we live up to our own beliefs, our own promises? Or is our notion of equality flawed? Is it too formal, too contractual? Why does it seem to allow for, perhaps even require, racial difference, sexual difference? In view of this accommodation of racial and sexual difference, why can't it acknowledge the role of ethnicity in shaping American politics? What powers hold us in their thrall, and what is power, anyway? If the state is not its only source, where does it come from, how is it expressed, who are its agents? Speaking of power, did old-fashioned imperialism drive America's bloody "intervention" in Vietnam? Or was this grisly war an accident, a deviation from the principles of U.S. foreign policy?

The form of the answers was in many ways more important than their content. That form was urgent, angry, categorical, above all cultural—a hardline, Marxist emphasis on "structural" (read: economic) causes of American idiocy was already quaint in the 1970s. And before long, this form became the content of critique as such, in keeping with the collapse of distinctions between appearance and reality, or surface and depth, or known and knower: the medium and then the messenger became the message. And so cultural politics was born. Its key words were race, gender, and class (read: identities), and, as methodological matters, pragmatism, feminism, multiculturalism, postmodernism, deconstruction, relativism, and revisionism.

The Right's complaints about America were less familiar to those who had merely watched the network news in the 1960s and 1970s, for two reasons. First, the mass media had depicted movements for racial equality as consistent with the best hopes and oldest promises of the nation. It was not until the early 1970s that Black Power began to look dangerous, or at least divisive, and even here most journalists were residually sympathetic to the cause because they knew that the FBI was funding a flamboyantly violent counteroffensive against the Black Panthers. Second, as more and more females entered the workforce out of necessity as well as choice, the palpable obstacles to equal pay, the sexual politics of the workplace, and the epic inertia of the family—when was the housework going to get done?—became pressing issues for most women, even those uninterested in a feminist critique of patriarchy. This rapidly increasing labor force participation may well account for the easy passage of the Equal Rights Amendment (it outlawed discrimination by employers on the basis of sex) by both houses of Congress in 1972 and its ratification by thirty states within a year. But no matter how conservative you were in 1973, it was hard to argue with the claims of both black folk and working women on the promise of the Declaration.

What then was to be done? The question was already quite political, in part because the Supreme Court's decision in *Roe v. Wade* also came in 1973, at the moment of the liberal legal ascendancy—the low point, by all accounts, of American conservatism. As rephrased by the intellectual cadres of the New Right, which were consigned to the outer darkness of extra-academic think tanks and journals, that question went something like this: How can anyone talk about persistent racial or sexual inequality after the Civil Rights Act of 1965 and Title IX of the Educational Amendments Act of 1972? Who says we haven't lived up to our founding beliefs? Haven't we provided genuine equality of opportunity (not outcomes), in keeping with our commitment to the free markets afforded by capitalism? And shouldn't we affirm sexual difference—aren't men and women fundamentally different? But why should we acknowledge ethnic identities in political deliberations? Isn't that a way of renouncing the "color-blindness" of the Constitution? What powers hold us in their thrall, and why are they concentrated in the universities and in the mass media—movies, radio, music, TV—that congregate on our coasts? And how can anyone say that imperialism was America's motive or purpose in Vietnam or in the world? Aren't we the country that rebuilt Japan and Germany after routing them in World War II? We have massive military power, to be sure, but has it not always been deployed for the common global good?

Here again the form of the answers was in many ways more important than their content. Here again that form was urgent, angry, categorical, and above all cultural. Here again the messenger became the message, and so seemingly private, personal attributes became public, political issues; in short, the personal got political. The key words of this intellectual program were the same as those of the Left, but, as we shall see, the Right did tend to treat certain cultural categories—particularly family, Western civilization, nation, modernity, canon, and reason—as given facts, and thus as self-evident premises of its countercritique.

Race, Class, and Gender

Let us have a look at the contested meanings of these key words, then, but as we do so, let us bear in mind that the populations and purposes of the Left and the Right were changing quickly in the 1970s, 1980s, and thereafter, to the point where conventional political geographies were becoming moot. Many late-twentieth-century conservatives, for example, were "old liberals" who understood themselves as defenders of truths forgotten in the political stampede that would turn the world inside out—the stampede that would destroy the distinction between what is private and what is public by insisting, along with the feminists who were rethinking the family, that "the personal is political." Irving Kristol, the father of neoconservatism whom we met in chapter 1, explained this confusion of spheres in 1978: "To begin with, the institutions which conservatives wish to preserve are, and for two centuries were called, *liberal* institutions, i.e., institutions which maximize personal liberty vis-à-vis a state, a church, or an official ideology. On the other hand, the severest critics of these institutions—those who wish to enlarge the scope of governmental authority indefinitely, so as to achieve ever greater equality at the expense of liberty—are today commonly called 'liberals.' It would certainly help to clarify matters if they were called, with greater propriety and accuracy, 'socialists' or 'neo-socialists.'"

From the standpoint of the academic Left, an awareness of race, gender, and/or class in reading any text, whether the U.S. Constitution or a canonical novel from the nineteenth century, was merely a way of deciphering its social origins and cultural effects. It was not a way of avoiding the intrinsic rigor of such texts or of introducing politics into the classroom. Politics had

always been there, in the institutional assumptions that required the reading of this text—say, R. W. Emerson's "Self-Reliance" (1841)—as opposed
to that text—say, Sara Grimke's "Letters on the Equality of the Sexes"
(1838) or Henry Highland Garnet's "Address to the Slaves of the United
States" (1843). It was simply another reading strategy. It was not even a
new strategy. Charles Beard's 1913 book on the Constitution, which showed
that "the people" invoked at the founding were already profuse and plural,
already a contested political category, was probably the first scholarly entry
in the genre. But this reading strategy did violate the idea of the artist or the
author as "a uniquely talented, individual sensibility"—it did treat her as a
condensation of her social origins—to the point where old-school defenders
of the humanities like Roger Kimball claimed that it caused "the eclipse of
the self." The same reading strategy also violated the notion of a literary
canon that, on the one hand, appears to us as naturally national—it is supposed to be the self-evident expression *of* a people—and that, on the other
hand, becomes appreciable as such only through the critical efforts of those
few educated individuals who can explain what knowledge of the canon does
for a people.

Notice the range of violations performed by the mere insertion of race, gender, and/or class into the act of undergraduate reading: artist/author/individual
and canon/nation/people are immediately put at risk, or at least in question, according to both sides in the debate. And notice the dependent relation between
the singular and the collective categories at issue here: it seems that the artist,
the author, or the individual has no stable meaning or function in the absence
of the canon, the nation, or the people, and vice versa—again, according to
both sides in the debate. No wonder the "assault on the canon," as Kimball
defined the relatively minor curricular reforms of the 1980s, looked like an
attack on the nation itself. "For what is at stake in these difficult questions is
more than an academic squabble over book lists and pedagogy," he declared in
a best-selling book called *Tenured Radicals* (1990). "What is at stake is nothing
less than the traditional liberal understanding of democratic society and the
place of education and high culture within it."

The largely left-wing academics who were reforming the college curriculum in the 1980s and 1990s had a similarly excitable view of their purpose in
house, but they didn't believe that changes in required courses and readings
would have huge effects off campus. They, too, were wrong. They started
the skirmishes that became the culture wars of the 1990s. But we should
acknowledge that their emphasis on race, class, and gender in reconsider-
ing the canon was a good-faith effort to open the thing up at both ends, at
the point of production—the intellectual scene of artistic authority—and at

the moment of consumption—the cultural scene of reader reception. What was an author, they asked, and how did one get anointed as such? What was the experience, then the effect, of reading, and how did critical opinion shape them? Was the "authenticity" of slave narratives a problem because their authorial "origin" was a question? Why were women writers and readers— they were the creators and the constituency of modern popular fiction, after all—marginal in the making and the maintenance of "the" canon?

And speaking of slaves and women, didn't they have their own histories? Could it be that they made their own histories? Could it be that the received tradition among American historians—the nonfictional canon, as it were—needed revision from the standpoint of those who had been hitherto excluded from the history book indexes? For example, could you follow the lead of W. E. B. DuBois, a founder of the National Association for the Advancement of Colored People, who claimed in a 1935 book called *Black Reconstruction* that the general strike of the slaves after 1860 was the key to Northern victory in the Civil War? Could you say, in other words, that black folk were political actors and agents in their own right, even under the most oppressive circumstances, even under slavery? Could you rewrite nineteenth-century American history by inserting women into your grand narratives, by asking how they shaped political deliberations without voting, how they determined economic development without owning property? Could it be, then, that "local people," everyday people, were the proper objects of a specifically political history that preceded but somehow resembled the civil rights movement in all its mundane glory? Could it be that the conspicuous individuals who wrote the constitutions and gave the speeches, then as now, were only a small part of a sprawling, sloppy social history that needed telling in terms of identities derived from race, class, and gender? But now that you mention it, aren't identities performed rather than derived from obvious antecedents? And how does sexuality—a dimension, clearly, of gender—figure in such performances, or is it, too, unknown until enacted?

These were the questions that revolutionized the pilot disciplines in the humanities and social sciences—in English, comparative literature, history, political science, sociology, and even economics and philosophy—in the 1970s. They led, in the 1980s and 1990s, toward the invention of new, cross-disciplinary programs like black studies, women's studies, ethnic studies, Jewish studies, and of course cultural studies, where matters of race, class, and gender became central to the curriculum. These questions also opened up whole new scholarly fields within established disciplines, for example, queer theory in English and family/gender/sexuality in both history and political science. Meanwhile they forced every academic to take a stand, to address and accommodate the new questions or be left behind.

Disuniting America?

The "disuniting of America," as Arthur Schlesinger Jr. put it, would seem to be the agenda, if not the result, of such questions and their new institutional apparatus within the universities. For, as he asked, how can anyone speak of the people and for the people across the divisions of race, class, and gender? But we should remember that the late-twentieth-century academic interest in these acquired identities—in groups rather than individuals as the proximate causes of history, politics, even literature—began at least a hundred years earlier. We should also remember that this academic interest is in many ways more inclusive, more conciliatory, than its intellectual alternatives. Even its earnest and clumsy and infuriating sponsorship of political correctness broadened the sociological bandwidth of undergraduate life, making us all more aware of where we didn't come from.

The problem of group identities as discovered and engaged a hundred years ago was the problem of political pluralism. It emerged when the "self-made man," the small producer, the energetic entrepreneur who underwrote the American Dream—he was his own boss, and thus he was an independent, omnicompetent citizen—became an endangered species. That was when the large corporations consolidated their control of productive property and goods production, turning almost everybody into a worker who was dependent on another (on his boss), rather than a proprietor who was dependent only on himself. That was when "the eclipse of the self"—the demise of the self-mastering small producer who was his own man—was first glimpsed by American writers, artists, philosophers, academics, and, yes, politicians. That was when the pioneer individualism of the nineteenth century gave way to cultural pluralism, and group identities became legitimate objects of intellectual scrutiny and political mobilization.

In the early corporate age, these new identities were called social selves, interest groups, sex classes, and ethnic enclaves. Whatever the labels, the point of naming them as such was to understand that the atomic particles of American politics were no longer individuals. They were instead groups, and they were already turning on the axes of race (e.g., the National Association for the Advancement of Colored People), class (e.g., the American Federation of Labor, the Industrial Workers of the World), and gender (e.g., the National Women's Party, the Women's Trade Union League). So the big difference between the early- and late-twentieth-century interest in group identities is not the erosion of academic attention to individualism—"the eclipse of the self" and, accordingly, "the death of the author," were accomplished long before tenured radicals stormed the ivory tower. The big difference is the relatively greater emphasis on ethnicity in the later corporate age, in our own time. The remarkable continuity between these twentieth-century moments resides in the acknowledgment of the simple fact that individuals as the nineteenth century conceived them don't count for much in a culture created and dominated by large corporations, professional associations, and international organizations.

Here is how the president of Harvard University acknowledged this fact:

> The last century has certainly been marked by an apparent increase in the power of corporate, as compared with personal, motives. A hundred years ago democratic theories were individualistic. They treated the state as a sum of equal and independent units. Now we have learned that man is a social being, not only in Aristotle's sense, that he is constrained by his nature to be a member of a state, but also in the broader sense that he is bound by subtle ties to other and smaller groups of persons. . . . We have learned to recognize this; and what is more, with the ease of organization fostered by modern conditions, the number, the complexity, and the aggregate strength of such ties have increased. No one can have observed social life carefully, under any aspect, without seeing that cooperative interests have in some measure replaced personal ones; that in its conscious spirit western civilization has become less individualistic, more highly organized, or, if you will, more socialistic.

These bracing lines were written by A. Lawrence Lowell and published in a book of 1913 called *Public Opinion and Popular Government*. We still inhabit the world he described, but we are just catching up to him; for he treated the decay of the old pioneer individualism as an irreversible historical event—a mere fact—rather than the end of the world or the dawn of the millennium. The resolution of the culture wars might, then, be better negotiated from his standpoint than from any side in contemporary debates on the uses of the university and the purposes of group identities. If we adopted Lowell's standpoint, for example, we would at least be in a position to understand that the eclipse of the self is not a political agenda disguised or illuminated or created by tenured radicals and their academic jargon. We would at last be in a position to understand that "the" self has a history.

We might also be in a position to understand that the group identities derived from voluntary associations are neither threats to anyone's autonomy as an individual nor constraints on anyone's devotion to the American nation as such. In fact, to borrow Lowell's perspective is to see that group identities are the condition, not the negation, of individualism—it is to realize that you come to know yourself as a unique bearer of a distinct personality only insofar as you recognize others as your equals and participate with them in communities of interest. To borrow that perspective is to see, moreover, that the group identities gathered under the ungainly heading of race, class, and gender may well have become the condition, not the negation, of a nationalism or a patriotism that reaches beyond the narrow elites who, once upon a time (and not so long ago), defined it as the passive acceptance of a white, Anglo-Saxon, Protestant culture.

The United States has always been a destination with lots of rough edges and porous borders rather than a unitary nation-state; its inhabitants and citizens have always been orphans, renegades, and castaways who came from elsewhere. This polyglot people have never shared a common racial stock, a linguistic affinity, or a national origin, not even in the seventeenth century. And yet, until the late twentieth century, the dominant culture was undeniably WASPish, perhaps because the national identity was still a function of narratives centered on the founding. As things loosened up in the 1960s and 1970s, due to the civil rights movement, the women's movement, and the mongrel music called rock and roll—the music that both amplified and abolished the color line—the cultural content of the American nation became more complex, more problematic. And so, too, did the question of representation. The plural became political.

Indeed, by the 1980s, "we, the people" became a problem rather than a premise of political deliberation. But those who wanted to emphasize race, class, and gender—or ethnicity—in imagining America had a certain advantage in solving the problem. For it is easier to preserve, protect, and defend a nation you have helped to create than to identify with a political tradition that excludes you. If the history books tell you, for example, that slaves, workers, immigrants, and women were just as important in building America as the educated white men wearing suits—just as important as the conspicuous individuals who wrote the constitutions and gave the speeches and made the fortunes—then the scope of that imagined community, that America, gets broader, and its moral compass spins faster. The mere possibility that is "our America" becomes yours, no matter where you came from. The nation gets bigger, maybe even better, as a result.

Reuniting America?

But the critics of this subdivision had a point in objecting to the centrifugal forces of race, gender, and class. With what were Americans supposed to identify, having validated their claims to a particular, probably ethnic past that did not always intersect with the Western European heritage of the founders—that is, with the legacy of the Enlightenment? As Lynne Cheney, the embattled chair of the National Endowment for the Humanities (NEH), said repeatedly in the late 1980s, there's not much to identify with if the best-selling textbooks emphasize that the enslavement of Africans, the annihilation of Indians, the conquest of Mexicans, the exploitation of workers, the oppression of women, and the reinvention of imperialism were the major accomplishments of the light-skinned sons of Enlightenment. By this textbook accounting, there can be no usable past—only escape routes from a sordid history, only safe distance from all holocausts. But what narrative could certify the Enlightenment, a.k.a. Western civilization, as the idiot sire of human rights, the abusive father of freedom, and the obvious origin of America, all at once?

To put it more plainly, how do you endorse a culture that destroyed indigenous peoples, prospered from slavery, celebrated capitalism—that is, possessive, acquisitive individualism—confined women to the home, tolerated racial segregation, and then made a military mess of the world after 1945? That was the question posed by the controversy over the National History Standards in the early 1990s. These Standards were first developed at the University of California, Los Angeles, with a grant from the NEH and input from scholars around the world, then published in 1994 as two complementary volumes, one for U.S. history, the other for world history. Their most outspoken and effective critic was Lynne Cheney, who in 1993 left her position as chair of the NEH to become the W. H. Brady Jr. Distinguished Fellow at the American Enterprise Institute; there she found enough research assistants to produce a book, *Telling the Truth* (1995), which denounced the Standards and their postmodern sources in the universities.

Cheney was outraged by "oversimple versions of the American past that focus on the negative" and singled out the Standards as "the most egregious example to date" of this "hypercritical" tendency. But she couldn't pose as the Pangloss of the late twentieth century, not after the great transformation of higher education. "We should not, of course retreat into the old myths," she declared, and insisted that "No one is suggesting that we hide our flaws or neglect the achievements of others." Even so, she had two serious concerns about the political implications of the new, hypercritical curriculum. First, it sponsored fundamental change, or at least deviation from the received tradition: "For those intent on political and social transformation, a bleak version of history is better than a balanced one. The grimmer the picture, the more heavily underscored is the need for the reforms they have in mind."

Second, it drained the popular sources of patriotism and, in doing so, it disabled American foreign policy, or at least the application of military power overseas: "As American students learn more about the faults of this country and about the virtues of other nations, . . . they will be less and less likely to think this country deserves their special support." In other words, "they will not respond to calls to use American force." If students understood that "the American system has uniquely nurtured justice and right," by contrast, they might identify with that system to the ideological extent required by its military obligations abroad.

So Cheney was not objecting to the insertion of politics into the classroom—the projection of American power abroad enabled by a more patriotic curriculum is surely a political purpose. She was objecting instead to the particular brand of politics being peddled by a new generation of professors, which promoted radical departures from the past and endangered the national interest in the present. In her narrative, by the 1980s, "a new group of academics was coming into power who viewed the humanities as a political tool, a weapon to be wielded in a variety of causes, but most especially multiculturalism and feminism." This group was clearly in thrall to a postmodern way of thinking that authorized pragmatism, relativism, and deconstruction—"radical skepticism"—by denying the existence of any reality independent of one's perspective on reality. Here is how Cheney summarized the indictment:

> In fields ranging from education to art to law, the attack on truth has been accomplished by an assault on standards. The connection is seldom made clear. Indeed, one of the characteristics of postmodern thought is that it is usually asserted rather than argued, reasoned argument having been rejected as one of the tools of the white male elite. But the thinking seems roughly to be that absent external reality, distinctions of any kind are meaningless. No accomplishment can be judged superior to any other—except as it promotes the interests of desired [sic] groups. Without the objective measures that an external reality would provide, who can really say, for example, that the work of some students is better than that of others?

Let us look more closely, then, at the properties of this postmodern thinking, in which appearance and reality seem to coincide. Doing so will help us decipher the other key words on our list, from pragmatism and relativism to deconstruction and feminism. Then we can decide where the truth really lies.

~

CHAPTER THREE

The Creators and Constituents of the "Postmodern Condition"

The Geographies of the Postmodern

The notion of the postmodern, with all its weird connotations, is powerfully associated with the French philosopher Jean-François Lyotard, whose book of 1979 was written as a "report on the state of knowledge in the Western world" at the request of the provincial government of Quebec (the English translation appeared in 1984 with a foreword by Fredric Jameson, who, as we shall see, had a lot to say about postmodernism long after Lyotard became a mere footnote). For that reason, the very idea of the postmodern has always seemed a dangerous foreign import, an intellectual contaminant from the other shore.

Lynne Cheney spelled out this attitude in *Telling the Truth* by tracing the idea's frightful origins to the theories of Michel Foucault, another French philosopher affiliated with Lyotard and his sources, Gilles Deleuze and Felix Guattari: "Foucault provided a method for continuing revolutionary activity long after American troops had withdrawn from Vietnam. His ideas were nothing less than an assault on Western civilization. In rejecting an independent reality, an externally verifiable truth, and even reason itself, he was rejecting the foundational principles of the West." Alan Bloom thoroughly revised this extra-American genealogy in *The Closing of the American Mind* (1987), yet another best-selling funeral oration on the genteel university that disappeared in the great transformation of higher education—in his view, the "master lyricists" of postmodern academic jargon were two German philosophers, Friedrich Nietzsche and Martin Heidegger, rather than

Foucault, Lyotard, and their French comrades. But he, too, claimed that professors and students alike were driving a foreign import without a license: "Our intellectual skyline has been altered by German thinkers even more radically than has our physical skyline by German architects."

The truth is rather more complicated. In fact, there are at least four ways to argue that the idea of a postmodern condition has undeniably *American* origins. To begin with, Lyotard himself acknowledged that he was introduced to this idea in the mid-1970s while attending conferences in the United States, where "the postmodern" usually meant an impending practical break in the continuum of architectural assumptions, not a theoretical problem. As Ihab Hassan, who applied the term to twentieth-century literature in an influential book of 1971, later noted, "the postmodern debate drifted from America to Europe" in the 1970s. Furthermore, the smoldering intellectual controversy over the durability and reliability of an "external" or an "independent reality"—the heart of the postmodern matter, by all accounts—was rekindled in the late 1950s by Thomas Kuhn, a historian of science at Harvard, not started in the late 1960s by French philosophers inclined to insurrection. What is even more, every question (re)opened by this controversy had been asked repeatedly in the course of the twentieth century, mainly by the American pragmatists, from John Dewey to Richard Rorty, who got their start by reading William James. Finally, the German designers of the contemporary intellectual skyline were themselves indebted, and for the most part consciously so, to these pragmatist antecedents, especially to James.

In his pathbreaking book, *The Structure of Scientific Revolutions* (1962), Kuhn argued that change or progress in science was not cumulative or incremental—old theories did not give way to new ones when "the" facts required it. Instead, theories themselves produced facts that could not be acknowledged or challenged by their rivals. For example, the Copernican revolution of the sixteenth century (the subject of Kuhn's first book) produced different facts about planetary movement than its Ptolemaic predecessor because it took up a different position in observing that movement. As scientific assumptions and models changed in such "paradigm shifts," so too did the observable world and what could be done about it—what had been excluded from view by earlier perspectives was now available for close scrutiny and active manipulation. By the same token, what had once been included was now invisible and unimportant: it was no longer actionable.

The intellectual consequences of this argument are daunting. If there is no body of fact "out there" somewhere, a body of fact that is somehow independent of our assumptions and models—if, as Cheney put it, there are no "objective measures that an external reality would provide"—how do we decide between rival accounts of the same events, the same phenomena, on rational grounds? Do we just give up on reason in adjudicating our political differences and admit that all we have are personal opinions? Absent a fixed, external reality to which all parties can appeal, doesn't relativism reign?

The pragmatists always had good answers to these questions. Rational ground was not reached, they said, when reason threw desire overboard according to the protocols of Enlightenment—reason and desire, fact and value, were inextricably linked. Mind and matter were, too. "Matter is effete mind, inveterate habits becoming physical laws," as an early pragmatist put it. Objectivity could not be obtained by pretending that there was a view of the world from nowhere, from outside the time and space we must inhabit as mortal beings: we can't peek over the edges of our existence as if we're not there, as God or Santa can do if he wants to check on us. So every kind of knowledge is historically situated. What we know is always a function of what we want to know and of what we can know, given our values, purposes, and technological capacities. Certainly there is no fixed, external reality in the pragmatist purview—there is no body of fact independent of our assumptions and models.

How, then, can we decide between rival accounts of the same events, the same phenomena, on rational grounds? Not by appeal to "the" facts, because these change insofar as our assumptions and models change, insofar as our values and purposes and technological capacities change. No, one account is better than another when it includes and transcends its rivals by showing how the questions raised and the facts produced by these rivals cannot be addressed and explained *in their own terms*. The rival accounts always remain, however, as special cases within the new paradigm. For example, Newtonian physics was contained and completed, not obliterated, by Einstein's theories of relativity. Or, to frame it as a social rather than a scientific problem, the older pioneer individualism was not erased by the newer social selfhood—by the new group identities that cultural pluralism and cultural politics recognized—but its cognitive status and political function were profoundly changed.

Notice that this pragmatic approach to the problem of relativism is historical rather than philosophical and that it won't allow opinion to stand in for argument. If you can't show how, why, and when the rival account lost its explanatory adequacy—if you can't tell the story of its intellectual exhaustion—and then demonstrate that your account conserves its significant findings, you haven't staked a claim to anything more than a different opinion. "Objectivity" as Cheney understands it does take a beating here, mainly because external reality becomes fluid and malleable. But then modern science was always based on the pragmatic assumption that if you want to know the truth about external reality—the observable world of objects—you have to manipulate it. Modern scientists (as opposed to alchemists, philosophers, and mathematicians) have taught us that you can't just posit, say, "the music of the spheres" or the existence of a "prime mover" called God, and go on from there to specify, logically, the necessary shape of the universe; you have to go into a laboratory and reproduce the motion of real, physical objects as you believe that motion must happen, and then verify your results. Modern scientists have taught us that the only way to interpret the world is to change it.

The American pragmatists of the early twentieth century were modern scientists in this truly scary sense. They challenged and inspired the European philosophers who would remake the intellectual world of the twentieth century as such—from Émile Durkheim, Alexandre Koyré, Georges Sorel, Jean Wahl, and Alexandre Kojève in France, to Edmund Husserl, Ludwig Wittgenstein, Georg Lukacs, Emil Lask, and Martin Heidegger in Germany—who would in turn challenge and inspire the transatlantic cohort of social theorists that invented the idea of the postmodern condition in the 1960s and 1970s.

Semiotic Subversion

So postmodern thinking is not a foreign import—it is as American as violence or apple pie. But what is its essential content, apart from its skeptical stance on objectivity as conventionally understood (that is, as Cheney understands it)?

There is very little agreement among intellectuals on the chronology of the postmodern, except that—this is important—it always appears as a moment in the twentieth century. Some suggest the revolution in "bourgeois perception" of 1905 to 1915, when relativity, psychoanalysis, and radical empiricism made everything indeterminate; some suggest the 1920s and 1930s, when postindustrial society first emerged; some suggest the 1960s, when pop art adjourned the distinction between high culture (read: priceless European heirlooms) and low (read: commodified American excess); and some suggest the 1970s and 1980s, when the term and its attendants—for example, "deconstruction"—became household words.

But there is substantial agreement on what postmodern thinking accomplishes. It acknowledges an ongoing, incomplete "mutation in Western humanism," as Hassan says, without displacing or renouncing its origins in the Enlightenment (except, of course, at the extremes of the thinking, where angry exiles from the present congregate). In other words, it recognizes the plurality and the plasticity of truth; it remaps the treacherous terrain of "rational grounds," where the "man of reason"—the light-skinned son of Enlightenment—still sets the universal standard; it accepts the eclipse of the old pioneer individualism and the emergence of socialized, multicultural forms of identity; it notices the erosion of sovereignty for both nation-states and individuals, at least as conceived and enforced by modern constitutional law; it celebrates the demise of metaphysics, the philosophical urge to ignore the material causes and historical consequences of mind; and it accordingly welcomes the decay of "metanarratives" like Marxism or liberalism, which narrate the history of the future as progress toward the one true goal of all humankind. Postmodern thinking doesn't deny the possibility of ideas that sediment over time, gradually becoming a kind of external, independent, cultural reality most people can treat as a given fact, a usable past, a universal truth, as in, say, "all men are created equal." The Declaration of Independence makes a difference, as Herman Melville, one of our still-canonical novelists, once said. Postmodern thinking does, however, insist that our differences—the particular and the plural—have been sources of, not deviations from, this unconscious consensus, this common sense we call reality. For example, a whole is not the sum of its parts; it is the contested relation between those parts. Or put it this way: a provisional truth becomes commonsensical, transhistorical, and possibly universal when it begins to explain, not ignore, particular historical circumstances.

Postmodern thinking is then powerfully animated by the more local imperatives we have come to know as deconstruction and feminism. The dreaded and the difficult deconstruction—the handiwork, again, of a transatlantic, cosmopolitan crew originally centered at Yale and the École normale supérieure in Paris—was, and is, the farthest outpost of semiotics, the science of signs invented early in the twentieth century by the American philosopher Charles S. Peirce (the "early pragmatist" quoted above) and the Swiss linguist Ferdinand de Saussure. Their new science offered the fundamental insight that language is not a mirror of nature, a transparent reproduction of external reality; instead, it naturalizes certain things and marginalizes others. By situating us in specific ways, it produces the external reality we take for granted. The form chosen by an author, for example, does not merely reveal the content of her thought—it determines what she can say or write or think. Or, to put it more emphatically, the author's writing *is* the thinking. Concepts, facts, truths, whatever, cannot and do not exist prior to or independent of their expression in language, in narrative, in signs. They're a result of the performances we experience as speaking and writing, and, yes, reading.

The extreme sport of semiotics we know as deconstruction thus directs our attention away from authorial intention and toward readerly expectations. For the text no longer subsists as a complete or closed object with measurable cultural weight, just as the author no longer subsists as an intact or intelligible subject with calculable intellectual bearings. Each is now construed as a field of forces beyond the control of anyone except readers, including critics. The critics' task is then to explain why both text and author are resistant to interpretation because they are not coherent, autonomous entities to be easily, naturally cast in the roles of object and subject. The critics' task is to demonstrate that the relation between subject/author and object/text is an unintentional result of writing, of a kind of performance, not something that existed prior to or independent of its expression in language, in narrative, in signs. Indeed, Jacques Derrida, the French godfather of deconstruction, suggested in a seminal essay called "Violence and Metaphysics" (1964, English translation, 1978) that when you treat this subject/object relation as given, as prior to its production through performance, you have fallen back on the enduring divisions of metaphysics, where particular historical circumstances disappear—where bodies do not matter, where even the face of the Other is obscured by intellectual abstraction—and where, accordingly, violence can be done in the name of those Truths that transcend any time or place or person.

Deconstruction is difficult, confusing, and even threatening because its practitioners appropriate Heidegger's itinerary in *Being and Time* (1927, English translation, 1962) and apply it to texts that, unlike philosophical treatises, persuade without argument—that is, to fiction and poetry, where form is content. Heidegger wanted to demonstrate two propositions. First, the primal scene of modern philosophy and modern science was the confrontation of active subject (inner) and inert object (outer); the inevitable corollary of this staging was the separation of mind and matter, of reason and desire, and so forth. Modernity as such was constituted by these metaphysical theatrics, he argued, even though its intellectual origins were ancient; here his text was the common sense of Western civilization. Second, both philosophy and science were mistaken in positing that primal scene as the self-evident beginning or foundation of thinking, whether philosophical or scientific. The subject/object relation, and with it the very idea of the individual, were the effects of thinking, talking, writing—or acting—rather than their causes. Our inner selves are not the results of retreat from the world; instead, the "objectification" of our desires in that outer world produces what we experience as our subjectivity, our interiority. So human being, what Heidegger called *Dasein*, had a history, and a material one at that. Absent time, it was indecipherable.

These propositions are difficult enough to digest in a long-winded philosophical treatise. They become confusing when they function as unstated assumptions of literary criticism, as they did in the 1980s and after—if you haven't already assimilated Heidegger's agenda, it all begins to sound like noise, like a foreign language you'd like to learn if only you knew where to speak it. These propositions become downright threatening when you realize that they drive nails into the coffin of the modern individual, that they celebrate what Roger Kimball mourns as the "eclipse of the self." No wonder "deconstruction" became a synonym for every kind of academic idiocy in the late twentieth century—it was, in fact, a challenge to every regulative assumption of Western civilization. For it suggests that individuals are not somehow prior to any social contract or political community or linguistic convention; that reason is not the universal intellectual means by which particular desires are suppressed so that all rational individuals can agree on the nature of a fixed, external reality; and that language is not the transparent medium of the truth-tracking capacity we call reason. Deconstruction notes that almost every text is a transcript of a desperate struggle to attain authorial mastery and thus to validate the notion of the authentic, enduring subjectivity whose alias was the genuine self or the modern individual. And deconstruction always decides that this struggle is futile—or at least inconclusive.

The Wingspan of Feminism

But for all its notoriety in the late twentieth century, deconstruction was not a method with a solid purchase on disciplines outside of literature, political theory, and philosophy (and in the latter, it was mainly a local curiosity). Feminism was a different story. It radically reshaped all the liberal arts and social sciences, from anthropology to sociology. At first this meant adding females to the disciplinary mix, as in the pioneering women's history of the 1970s written by Gerda Lerner, Anne Firor Scott, Mary Jo Buhle, Suzanne Lebsock, Ann D. Gordon, Ellen Dubois, Linda Gordon, Alice Kessler-Harris, Bonnie Smith, Lynn Hunt, and Nancy Cott, among many others. By the 1990s, however, a poststructuralist sensibility was becoming the norm of feminist studies across the curriculum, and the social construction of gender began, accordingly, to replace the historical deeds of women as the proper object of scholarly scrutiny. So, once again, identity, personality, and even sexuality—in short, the sources of the individual, the subject as such—were construed as a problem rather than a premise, as a product rather than a presupposition. Here the key figures were Gayle Rubin, Joan Scott, and Judith Butler.

Not to worry about the new "post-ism." Poststructuralism is merely the linguistic form in which a postmodern period of human history gets experienced; it is the medium in which that ongoing, incomplete "mutation in Western humanism" gets transacted in words, images, categories, and characters—that is, in signs. It is no more uniform than the newspaper and the novel, the narrative forms in which the modern period (ca. 1600–1900) was typically experienced. But in all its incarnations, poststructuralism provides credentials, sources, and skills to those who would explain why and how we experienced the twentieth century, particularly its ending, as a new stage of human history. And for feminists, it has been an especially rich vein of theoretical insight and political leverage.

Rubin was still a graduate student when she wrote "The Traffic in Women: Notes on the Political Economy of Sex" (1975), the inaugural event in the development of a specifically feminist poststructuralism. Here she drew on Karl Marx, Claude Levi-Strauss the French anthropologist, Jacques Lacan the French psychoanalyst, and Sigmund Freud himself to outline a theory of kinship that explained the difference between sex and gender. In brief, sex was material or biological; gender was social or cultural. But those social/cultural sources of gender difference and hierarchy were deeply rooted in the most basic taboos and archaic practices—hence the "anthropological" style of the argument.

The incest taboo, by this account, was the enduring device through which daughters were "exported" from their immediate families by fathers with property rights to their bodies. The resulting commercial exchange between families became the basis of a larger kinship system that allowed for political peace and cultural continuity rather than warring clans—a system that allowed, in other words, for society and civilization as such. For the "gift of women" via marriage makes the partners to the exchange blood relations, thus widening the scope of kinship. The modern enforcement of heterosexual marriage and the sexual division of labor within the family were, then, the distant echoes of an ancient prohibition that was still resoundingly successful in reproducing male supremacy. Not even an Equal Rights Amendment could change these fundamental, transhistorical facts of familial life. "The oppression of women is deep," Rubin concluded. "Equal pay, equal work, and all the female politicians in the world will not extirpate the roots of sexism." The public was private, the political was personal: "Feminism must call for a revolution in kinship."

That meant attempting "to resolve the Oedipal crisis of culture by reorganizing the domain of sex and gender in such a way that each individual's Oedipal experience would be less destructive." This resolution sounds utopian, of course, but Rubin assumed that infants and children were naturally bisexual and that the renunciation of their primary attachments to their mothers—what Oedipus could not accomplish—was an emotional catastrophe that had been reproducing gender difference and male supremacy for thousands of years. Like many other theoretically inclined feminists in the late twentieth century, from Jane Flax and Jane Gallop to Susan Suleiman and Kaja Silverman, Rubin wanted to reclaim psychoanalysis, not Freud, the Victorian man who could not have understood her political purposes. For such feminists, the personal was most emphatically not political in the sense that the man's ideas were merely incidents in his autobiography. Instead, they suggested, the personal was political in the more abstract sense that the private, particular sexual dispositions of children had long been systematically converted into public, universal gender differences that validated male supremacy. And so, for their purposes, Freud's theories of infantile development and differentiation became indispensable. As Rubin put it: "Psychoanalysis provides a description of the mechanisms by which the sexes are divided and deformed, of how bisexual, androgynous infants are transformed into boys and girls." Dismissing it because Freud himself was a misogynist "would be suicidal for a political movement dedicated to eradicating gender hierarchy."

Rubin's essay has been cited many thousands of times since its publication more than thirty years ago in a collection of essays entitled *Toward an Anthropology of Women* edited by Rayna Reiter. Its protean force and intellectual reach is comparable to that found in the work of Joan Kelly or Heidi Hartmann, who also tried to suture Marxism and an emergent body of explicitly feminist theory. But Rubin's essay has sparked much more debate and discussion among American feminists, largely because it raised questions that could be addressed only by understanding and then rewriting the theoretical backstory of her argument.

Certainly that is what Joan Scott set out to do in a paper presented to the American Historical Association in 1985 and published a year later in the *American Historical Review* (*AHR*) under the title of "Gender: A Useful Category of Historical Analysis." Scott's career is a calendar of the changes caused by the rise of the women's movement in the 1960s and 1970s, on the one hand, and by the articulation of a specifically feminist poststructuralism in the 1970s and 1980s, on the other. She started out as a more or less Marxist labor historian affiliated with *Studies on the Left*, the signature journal of the early New Left. Her first book was *The Glass Workers of Carmaux* (1974), a study of skilled artisans turned into machine herds by French industrialization. Soon after, Scott collaborated with Louise Tilly, a sociologist, on an influential book called *Women, Work, and Family* (1978), which blended their mutual interest in class formation with the new agenda of family history to argue that women suffered at least as much as male workers when industrialization emptied the home of its economic functions. In 1980, she became the director of the Pembroke Center for the Study of Women at Brown University, thus completing the transition from historian of labor, where class is the operative category, to historian of women, where gender was quickly becoming that category.

The *AHR* essay marked two other transitions, Scott's move from Brown to the Institute for Advanced Study in Princeton—which gave feminist scholarship a new intellectual cache—and her emblematic embrace of poststructuralism as a theorist of gender rather than a historian of women. She wrote the essay on the assumption that the early promise of women's history to redefine "traditional notions of historical significance" was still unfulfilled; for the category of gender, like that of race, did not yet have the elaborate theoretical infrastructure that sustained the scholarly study of class across the curriculum. Her task was then to draw up the blueprint and see if the thing could be built.

In a more programmatic sense, her task was to end the "continuing marginal status" of women's history in the discipline by demonstrating how gender was a crucial component of every field, even those given to reporting on what presidents and prime ministers said to each other about where next to go to war. But this seemingly modest, "synthetic" project had implications for every discipline because the challenge posed by the "separation or dismissal" of women's history was not empirical: "It has not been enough for historians of women to prove either that women had a history or that women participated in the major political upheavals of Western civilization." Only a new paradigm for empirical research on gender as such would change all the facts: "The challenge posed by these responses [to women's history] is, in the end, a *theoretical* one."

The theoretical alternatives available to scholars interested in gender were all of recent vintage, Scott noted, because classical social theory, from the eighteenth to the early twentieth century, from Adam Smith to Max Weber, never developed a way of thinking about sexual relations as social systems: "Concern with gender as an analytic category has emerged only in the late twentieth century." This absence explained both the incoherence of honest attempts to enlist classical social theory in the analysis of gender and the emergence of the very word gender "at [the] moment of great epistemological turmoil" in which poststructuralism came of age.

As theoretical things stood in the early 1980s, there were only three alternatives to a poststructuralist approach. One was to study the persistence of patriarchy by focusing on reproduction and sexuality; this tended toward the anthropological attitude that treated male supremacy as a transhistorical attribute of all civilizations and gender difference as a natural, unmediated dimension of every society. Another was to adapt Marxism to the task at hand and argue that "families, households, and sexuality are all, finally, products of changing modes of production"; this was to accept the nineteenth-century formulas of Frederick Engels as the last word on the subject. And another was to adapt psychoanalysis to the analysis of gender; but this, at least in the Anglo-American context, was to settle for the "object relations" school supervised by Nancy Chodorow and Carol Gilligan, who treated gender difference as a function of child-rearing habits or posited a social ethic specific to a separate "women's culture."

Scott proposed to historicize the schematic psychoanalysis of the object relations school by using Jacques Lacan's poststructuralist emphasis on language in creating the unstable subject of modernity: "This kind of interpretation makes the categories of 'man' and 'woman' problematic by suggesting that masculine and feminine are not inherent characteristics but subjective (or fictional) constructs. This interpretation also implies that the subject is in a constant process of construction." Like many other feminists, she had some doubts about Lacan's applicability to the local knowledge of discrete historical events. But she insisted that his poststructuralist approach to symbolic systems—"to the ways societies represent gender"—was indispensable: "Without meaning, there is no experience; without processes of signification, there is no meaning (which is not to say that language is everything, but a theory that does not take it into account misses the powerful roles that symbols, metaphors, and concepts play in the definition of human personality and human history)." And this approach harbored decidedly deconstructionist purposes: "We need a refusal of the fixed and permanent binary opposition [between male and female], a genuine historicization and deconstruction of the terms of sexual difference."

Scott's own definition of gender realized these theoretical imperatives by evacuating the anthropological premises Gayle Rubin had rented in writing her feminist address. Gender has been "a constitutive element of social relationships based on perceived differences between the sexes," Scott declared, and, even more provocatively, it has also been "a primary way of signifying relationships of power." It isn't merely a function of family, household, or kinship, and it isn't a relic of archaic taboos, as Rubin had claimed. Instead, it has organized and amplified every symbolic system, including those that have permitted the idea of individualism and the collective identity of class; the history of subjectivity and the history of work, which between them include almost all of human history as such, would, according to this theoretical program, now require the study of gender difference. Gender could not, then, be foreign to "politics and power in their most traditionally construed sense." For the legitimacy of state power and military force is a linguistic problem rather than a logistical matter—laws and armies and wars must eventually be justified in words, no matter who fights them. So their success must depend on the legibility of the gendered metaphors that statesmen, jurists, and diplomats have always deployed to explain their decisions.

Scott's concluding trespass on the terrain of traditional political history clinched her theoretical case and opened up a whole new way of writing diplomatic as well as social, cultural, and intellectual history. It got her into some trouble, too, mainly with her empirically minded colleagues in departments of history, sociology, and political science, for whom the actual deeds of women mattered more than their representation as females in the discourse of their disciplines. But regardless of your discipline, Scott's essay still stands as the bridge you must cross if you want to map the connection between the theory and the practice of gender.

Gender Trouble

Judith Butler's enormously influential work of the 1980s and 1990s—it is impossible to exaggerate her impact on every academic discipline—is built upon the specifications of Joan Scott's design for a new theoretical infrastructure of feminism. But it redraws the bridge in crossing. Butler's first book, based on her doctoral dissertation, was *Subjects of Desire: Hegelian Reflections in Twentieth-Century France* (1986). Here she traced the recuperation of G. W. F. Hegel's *Phenomenology of Spirit* (1807) by the French philosophers Alexandre Kojeve, Jean Hippolyte, and Jean Paul Sartre, then turned to the recent revolt against the Hegelian "dialectic of desire" in the works of Foucault, Lacan, Derrida, and Deleuze. As she tells us in the preface, she was not yet prepared, in 1985, to treat these revolutionaries with the same care she had taken with their predecessors. Even so, the intellectual sources of her next book, published three years later, can be found in that last chapter, called "Hegel and Contemporary French Theory."

Another crucial source of the incendiary new book, *Gender Trouble* (1990), was the Gender Seminar assembled under Joan Scott's direction at the Institute for Advanced Study in the 1987–1988 academic year, which included two other prominent scholars, Donna Haraway and Evelyn Fox Keller, who, as accomplished feminist historians of science, were then asking, "Is sex to gender as nature is to science?" Butler, like Scott, Haraway, and Keller, was looking for a way to "denaturalize" gender by interrogating the relation between bodies and identities, between subjectivity and agency. In conducting this search, her working hypothesis was the guiding assumption of modern feminism—to wit, the important differences between males and females, apart from reproductive capacities, are historically determined cultural conventions and, as such, are the proper objects of intellectual scrutiny, social movements, and public policies.

So the personal was definitely political; for Butler's book was a profound critique of "the" subject presupposed by modern philosophy and modern science. Indeed, it recalled Heidegger's excavation of the same subject, perhaps because it, too, designated Friedrich Nietzsche as its philosophical antecedent. But her concern was that women recently liberated from male supremacy would merely imitate "Man" in the era of the ego. That is why she asked, "Do women want to become subjects on the model [of Man] which requires and produces an anterior region of abjection?" Her answer explained the political connotations of her project: "We may be tempted to think that to assume the subject in advance is necessary in order to safeguard the *agency* of the subject. But to claim that the subject is constituted is not to claim that it is determined; on the contrary, the constituted character of the subject is the very precondition of its agency. . . . [And] if we agree that politics and power exist already at the level at which the subject and its agency are articulated and made possible, then agency can be *presumed* only at the cost of refusing to inquire into its construction."

As the political theorist Adam Przeworski claimed in 1985 that class consciousness is the product of struggle (thus annulling sociological definitions of class), so Butler claimed that the gendered subject and its agency are the results, not the origins, of actions (thus annulling sociological definitions of gender). That subject was neither imposed on nor determined by the inert externality of sex or nature—it was performed, and so it was always and already a historical event to be treated as such by historical methods. She cited a Nietzschean warrant for this antiphilosophical claim: "The challenge for rethinking gender categories outside of the metaphysics of substance [a reference to the sublime object of deconstructionist critique] will have to consider the relevance of Nietzsche's claim in *On the Genealogy of Morals* that 'there is no "being" behind doing, effecting, becoming: the "doer" is merely a fiction added to the deed—the deed is everything.'" And having assessed the warrant, she allowed the search: "There is no gender identity behind the expressions of gender; that identity is performatively constituted by the very 'expressions' that are said to be its results."

"No ideas but in things," as the pragmatist poet William Carlos Williams put it early in the twentieth century. By insisting that an inquiry into the construction of agency (hence identity) was the political purpose of feminism, however, Butler made some significant enemies. At least she started some important arguments. For example, two political theorists, Seyla Benhabib and Nancy Fraser, both feminists trained in the school of critical theory, worried that Butler's account of gender formation robbed women of their political capacities. Benhabib asked, "If this view of the self is adopted, is there any possibility of changing those 'expressions' that constitute us? If we are no more than the sum total of the gendered expressions we perform, is there ever any chance to stop the performance for a while?" She concluded that "the very project of female emancipation" was simply unthinkable from the perspective Butler proposed: "What follows from this Nietzschean position is a vision of the self as a masquerading performer, except of course we are now asked to believe that there is no self behind the mask." Fraser was less combative but equally critical of Butler, especially of her "deeply antihumanist" language—that is, of a language so far "removed from our everyday ways of talking and thinking about ourselves [as] to require some justification." She recommended a return to nineteenth-century notions of subjectivity and agency as the antidote to a performative theory of gender and identity.

Notice that these worries were conveyed by committed feminists, women of the Left who nonetheless sound very similar to Roger Kimball—the man who saw the eclipse of the self in the great transformation of higher education and its corollary, the demise of the humanities as conceived in the nineteenth century. Notice, too, that these debates about identity and agency were conducted on the Left , by the Left, in remarkably strident terms. In view of these weird facts, is it possible to say that the so-called culture wars began when liberals and leftists started disagreeing about the nature of the self, the function of the family, and the pliability of reality?

Culture Wars on the Left

Well, yes, it is possible. That was a rhetorical question. Kimball himself said in 1998 that "the real battle that is now shaping up is not between radicals and conservatives but between radicals and old-style liberals." So let us examine some other outstanding examples of left-wing frustration with the "linguistic turn" of poststructuralist, postmodernist thinking in the late twentieth century. Having examined them, we will be in a position to understand that the so-called culture wars were domestic squabbles—they were in-house arguments about the future of liberalism—until the very end of the century, when they spilled out into party politics, when the private became public, when the personal finally got political.

Our first example is from 1995, when Alan Sokal, a physicist from New York University (NYU), embarrassed the editors of the cutting-edge left-wing journal *Social Text* by writing a hilarious parody of poststructuralist prose for a special issue on the "social construction of nature" (one of the editors was Andrew Ross, also of NYU, who, as Lynne Cheney noted with disdain, labeled himself an "assassin of objectivity"). The day the issue came out, Sokal revealed his hoax in *Lingua Franca*, a popular new magazine devoted to the cultural politics of academia (a good indication, by the way, that the headquarters of the larger culture was higher education). Like Mrs. Cheney, he believed in a fixed external reality governed by scientifically proven laws of motion—and like the editors of *In These Times*, a socialist newspaper published in Chicago, he believed the academic Left had lost its way when it made the linguistic turn and decided, following Charles Peirce's semiotic lead, that "matter is effete mind."

As a dedicated activist who lent his time and money to many left-wing causes, Sokal wanted to show that the academic Left was wasting its time on esoteric, trivial pursuits insofar as it was not concentrating on the material realities of poverty at home and abroad. He wanted to show that what passed for serious thinking on this strange new Left was merely jargon. It was a convincing performance, but it begged the questions that founded the journal and animated the particular issue—what can objectivity mean in a world that can take Thomas Kuhn's conclusions for granted, and what can subjectivity mean in a world that can't assume the position of a white, male, bourgeois proprietor of himself?

Our next example is from 1997, when Harvard University Press published three lectures by Richard Rorty under the title of *Achieving Our Country: Leftist Thought in 20th-Century America*. Rorty was one of the most important public intellectuals in the United States, and by most accounts he was our most distinguished pragmatist philosopher (the only competition would be Hilary Putnam of Harvard, who invited him to Cambridge to give those lectures). Certainly he led the revival of pragmatism on this side of the Atlantic during the 1970s and 1980s, mainly by participating in the poststructuralist linguistic turn that derived from the rediscovery of semiotics. As a "red-diaper baby"—his father James was briefly affiliated with the Communist Party of the United States of America in the 1930s—and a bona fide liberal who has always wanted to tax the rich and educate the poor, Rorty had solid left-wing credentials. But his lectures were a withering critique of the Left that had taken over the universities.

Like many right-wing critics of this same political tendency, he called it the Cultural Left, but the story he told was a tale of decline and fall from the glory days of the New Deal, when the Old Left—a coalition of labor unions and intellectuals like Rorty's own father—invented the welfare state. First the New Left of the 1960s repudiated these predecessors; then its constituents went to graduate school, became professors, and taught students how to hate their country. This Cultural Left of the universities had nothing to say about the economic sources of poverty and inequality because it was interested only in the return of repressed ethnic identities: it spent "all its time talking about matters of group identity, rather than about wages and hours." It lacked "American national pride" because, unlike the Old Left, and even the New Left—which had, after all, fought for the civil rights promised by the Declaration and inscribed in the Constitution—it did not believe that the original promise of American life could be redeemed.

The wonderful irony in Rorty's best-selling performance was his prior sponsorship in philosophy of the linguistic turn that produced deconstruction, among other novelties of scholarship. Like the influential literary critic Richard Poirier, he had often compared the American proponents of pragmatism, from Emerson to James, with the French proponents of poststructuralism, from Lacan to Derrida, and had declared them obvious affiliates of the same solution to both the philosophical problem of situating the self in the world and the literary problem of explaining oneself to the world. Rorty called this solution "postmodernist bourgeois liberalism," but it was just as dangerous to Mrs. Cheney's conventional notion of objective truth as Michel Foucault's rendition of reason. Meanwhile, however, Rorty's call for a renewed "national pride" and a reinvigorated individualism offended almost everyone in the pilot disciplines of the American university system—almost everyone, that is, on the Cultural Left.

Yet another example of left-wing culture wars is from 1999, when the eminent philosopher and ardent feminist Martha Nussbaum went after Judith Butler in the pages of *The New Republic*, the wonky weekly that has taken itself too seriously since 1914. Here again the issue was the evasion of "material realities" and the erasure of individual agency supposedly navigated by the linguistic turn of poststructuralism. Nussbaum's blistering attack on Butler recalled the remarks made almost a decade earlier by Benhabib and Fraser, but its angry emphasis on "material realities"—the phrase is used eight times in a seven-page piece—finally makes it sound like a parody of the vulgar Marxism once peddled by Communist Party hacks. And again, it begged the very question raised by Butler's theoretical position: to wit, what is the residence of agency if we cannot answer by writing the address of the old pioneer individualism? Or ask the same question another way: what if the agency of an individual is something like a linguistic capacity? People learn to speak a language by adapting themselves to inherited social conventions they choose not to avoid because they want to be understood—they are constituted as speakers, if you will, by inserting themselves into the language they are learning, playing by its rules. But isn't there plenty of room for innovation, variation, and deviation in any individual's facility with the language being learned? As Butler herself answered in another setting, "the constituted character of the subject is the very precondition of its agency."

Let us consider one final example of left-wing doubts about the linguistic turn of poststructuralism in the 1980s and 1990s. The three most influential Marxists of the late twentieth century were Fredric Jameson (a founding father of *Social Text*), Frank Lentricchia, and David Harvey—two literary critics at Duke and a geographer from Johns Hopkins by way of Oxford. All three were both intrigued and disgusted by the phenomenon of postmodernism, which they associated with what they called "late capitalism" or "consumer capitalism" as per Ernest Mandel's specifications; Jameson went so far as to announce that this sorry stage of civilization represented "the purest form of capital yet to have emerged." And all three were appalled by the "humanist fantasy" of poststructuralism because it sentenced them to the "prison-house of language," where—you guessed it—those fundamental "material realities" were unavailable for critical scrutiny. They never diagrammed an escape route from this obscure site, but they did arm many academics against its stifling enclosures.

The critique of "tenured radicals" was, then, an intramural sport on the left in the late twentieth century. It was most definitely not a vast right-wing conspiracy—but it was in many ways conservative because it sought to rehabilitate nineteenth-century notions of individualism, agency, and objectivity. There was, in fact, a right-wing critique of academic excess, but its producers lived in a state of exile, far from the debauched ivory tower and in protest against the reckless hedonism of the larger society; this self-imposed distance made their complaints always sound like they were radically distorted by the wrong amplifier. For example, Robert Bork, the outspoken jurist we met at the end of chapter 1, claimed in 1996 that the only conceivable explanation for a progressive income tax was envy; that gun control laws were the cause of violent crime because they disarmed the law-abiding population (if criminals knew everybody carried a gun, they would be deterred from using their own); that the Declaration of Independence was a big mistake because, by enfranchising the insane individualism of the Enlightenment, it ignored the problem of social order; and that—oops—Western civilization was to blame for what happened in the abominable 1960s.

No, really. Here is what Bork sincerely stated in *Slouching Towards Gomorrah: Modern Liberalism and American Decline* (1996):

> This [the shrinking number of required courses in college curricula after 1914] confirms a pattern repeatedly suggested in this book: trends slowly moving through an area of life, in this case higher education, until the Sixties when those trends accelerated rapidly. This [antecedent unknown] suggests, as noted earlier, that we would in any event have eventually arrived where the Sixties took us but perhaps two or three decades later. Which [antecedent absconded] in turn suggests that we are merely seeing the playing out of qualities—individualism and egalitarianism—inherent in Western civilization and to some degree unique to that civilization.

Bork probably should have let Lynne Cheney read the manuscript, especially since they overlapped at the American Enterprise Institute in the early 1990s. She could have warned him off this alarming attack on the pillars of Western civilization. The world-weary William Bennett, Ronald Reagan's secretary of education, then George Bush's "drug czar," and then Bill Clinton's scold–in–chief, could have, too. In a 1992 book, Bennett, like Cheney, insisted that "we must study, nurture, and defend the West"—that is, Western civilization—in large part because "the West is good." In the same book, he praised Judge Bork as "perhaps the finest legal mind in America." Yet he chose to endorse Bork's doubts about both the egalitarian imperatives of the Declaration and the individualistic premises of Western civilization. Indeed, Bennett's paperback blurb for *Slouching Towards Gomorrah* makes it sound like a masterpiece of either social history or pornography: "A brilliant and alarming exploration of the dark side of contemporary American culture."

The culture wars inflamed by such determined combatants were fought, for the most part, on a battlefield controlled by the Left—that is, on campus, in the new public sphere of higher education. Did the larger culture give the same homefield advantage to the Left? We begin to address that question in the next chapter by going to the movies.

CHAPTER FOUR

~

"Signs of Signs"
Watching the End of Modernity at the Cineplex

Reading for the Ending

Robert Bork and William Bennett—Mrs. Cheney, too—were of course rail-
ing against a culture that reached beyond the campuses. Their purpose was
to reform (or debunk) the university and thus to redeem that larger culture.
But the evidence suggests that Americans needed no prodding from tenured
radicals as they moved in the 1980s and 1990s toward acceptance of equity
between races, classes, genders, and sexual preferences, on their way to be-
mused tolerance of almost anything, including animal rights.

To be sure, education as such remained the object of cultural critique from
self-conscious conservatives. Pat Robertson, for example, the televangelist
and presidential contender—he participated forcefully in the Republican
primaries and debates of 1988—claimed that the public school system in the
United States was "attempting to do something that few states other than
the Nazis and Soviets have attempted to do, namely, to take the children
away from the parents and to educate them in a philosophy that is amoral,
anti-Christian and humanistic and to show them a collectivist philosophy
that will ultimately lead toward Marxism, socialism and a communistic type
of ideology." Jimmy Swaggart, another televangelist, was more succinct:
"The greatest enemy of our children in this United States . . . is the public
school system. It is education without God."

Even so, the larger culture exhibited unmistakable signs of rapid, irreversible, and enormous change. The educators themselves, high and low,

were being educated by that change. How, then, should we summarize that change—how should we gauge its symptoms?

One way is to import Samuel P. Huntington's notion of a "clash of civilizations" as the characteristic divide of the late twentieth century. Huntington was the Harvard political scientist who made his political bones back in the 1960s by planning "forced draft urbanization" in Vietnam—if the peasants aren't out there in the countryside helping the guerillas (the Viet Cong) because you have removed them to existing cities or concentrated them in newly constructed "urban centers," he surmised, you can then stage direct military confrontations between American soldiers and communist insurgents. In keeping with his policy-relevant duties in the aftermath of Vietnam, he suggested in a 1995 book that impending global conflicts would turn on cultural (read: religious) divisions rather than the older divisions of political economy, which had placed capitalism and socialism at the opposite extremes of diplomatic decisions and developmental options. The domestic analogue would be the so-called culture wars, which dispensed, for the most part, with arguments about economic arrangements and instead engaged the problems of moral values, civic virtues, and familial integrity—"cultural indicators," as Bennett called them in a flurry of articles and books.

Another way to summarize the same great divide is to enlist Daniel Bell and to propose that the "cultural contradictions of capitalism," as he calls them, reached their apogee in the early 1990s, when the so-called culture wars got formally declared. In the sequel to *The Coming of Post-Industrial Society*, Bell argued that the American social structure—the mundane routine of work, family, and daily life—"is largely bourgeois, moralizing, and cramped," the arid domain of "traditional values" but meanwhile the culture "is liberal, urban, cosmopolitan, trendy, fashionable, endorsing freer lifestyles, and permissive." In other words, the bourgeois values inherited from the nineteenth century became problematic if not merely obsolete in the postindustrial rendition of twentieth-century consumer capitalism. To borrow the terms invented by Raymond Williams, the residual (bourgeois) culture was still committed to deferring gratification, saving for a rainy day, and producing character through hard work, whereas the dominant (capitalist?) culture was already animated by a market-driven hedonism—a "consumer culture"—in which such repressive commitments seemed quaint.

But notice that the Cultural Left ensconced in the universities was aligned with the bohemian values validated by a postindustrial consumer capitalism, whereas the New Right enfranchised by the churches and the think tanks was opposed to these same values. In this sense, once again, conservatism in the late twentieth century was not a blanket endorsement of what free markets make possible; like the radicalism of the same moment in American history, it was a protest against the heartless logic of the market forces created and enforced by consumer capitalism.

From either standpoint, however, Huntington's or Bell's, we witness a nineteenth-century version of self, family, and nation competing with a twentieth-century version. From either standpoint, bourgeois society struggles to survive against the global tentacles of postindustrial consumer capitalism. Perhaps the impending conclusion of this struggle, the impending extinction of bourgeois society, is what we mean—and is all we can mean—by the end of modernity. The modern world, the "era of the ego" was, after all, created by bourgeois individuals eminently capable of deferring gratification.

But most Americans were not reading Huntington or Bell in the 1980s and 1990s. Nor were they using Judith Butler's poststructuralist vocabulary to understand what was happening to them. How then did they experience and explain the end of modernity? The question can be asked in more specific ways. Were these academic theorists just making it up? Or were they making sense of new realities—of fundamental changes? Was there a colloquial, vernacular idiom in which these changes were anticipated, recorded, codified? To answer, let us revisit some hugely popular movies of the late twentieth century—let us see what they require us to experience and explain—and then, in the next chapter, turn to some equally popular cultural forms, TV and music.

Big Movies, Big Ideas

To begin with, let us have a look at *The Matrix*, *Terminator II*, and *Nightmare on Elm Street*, each a part of a movie "franchise" in which increasingly intricate—or ironic—sequels retold the same story from new angles. The preposterously complicated plot of the original *Matrix* (1999) is almost beside the point. But for those of you who haven't seen it, here goes. In a postholocaust future that resembles the scorched earth of the *Terminator* movies, machines have taken over the world: technological hubris has finally put an end to progress. Human beings have been reduced to dynamos whose metabolism is converted into the energy the machines need to—what?—go about their evil business. These benighted human beings just think that they're going to work on those familiar city streets (the "city" looks like Chicago). In fact, they're only holograms projected by the machines to keep their energy source happy. As in the *Nightmare* franchise, appearance and reality are identical, at least in the beginning.

But an underground movement exists to wake these unwitting creatures up by bringing them out of the Matrix and teaching them how to fight the power on its own holographic terms. This movement recruits Neo, a young blank slate of a man—played of course by Keanu Reeves, a young blank slate of a man—onto whom the underground leader has projected his millennial ambitions. Neo (his screen name) turns out to be the "chosen one" after all; he quickly surpasses his teacher, the leader, and becomes a virtual martial artist who kicks virtual ass.

Neo learns to enter and disable the Matrix, thus revealing the awful reality beneath the normal, hopeful images that sustain the physical life of the dynamos down on the energy farm. The assumption here is that human beings can't stay alive without hopes and dreams: if they knew that they were merely cogs in a vast energy-producing machine, they would surely die. By the same token, if they lived in a perfect world, they would know from their experience of Western religion—which insists that you can't get to heaven until your body expires—that they were dead. In both settings, they would be unhappy, but their hopes for a brighter future that is somehow different from the abiding present would keep them alive; the evil designers of the Matrix introduce imperfection into the grid when they realize this simple truth of human nature.

In *The Matrix*, the artificial finally overpowers the real, or rather the natural; meanwhile, the expectation of an end to the illusions of the holographic world finally becomes a religious urge that displaces any residual pretense of science fiction. The monstrous agents of the Matrix are shape-shifting, indestructible machines that inhabit and impersonate human beings. But Neo has no oppositional force or effect against them unless he's "embodied" as a slice of computer code and inserted into a holographic "reality"—until he's "embodied" in recognizable human form as a part of a machine. And his triumph over these agents of dehumanization is a result of his belief in himself as the messiah (the "chosen one"), which requires first a consultation with "the Oracle"—a woman who, by the way, inhabits the Matrix, not the scene of resistance—and then the loss of his corporeal form. At any rate, the laws of gravity and mortality no longer apply to our hero by the end of this movie: he has become a godlike creature who can soar like Superman.

Terminator II (1998; the original was in 1984) has no less of an appetite for biblical gestures and sacrificial rites. But the cyborg from the future who helps save the world from the bad machines isn't an immaterial, possibly immortal presence like Neo. He's always embodied. And even though he's mostly machine—his apparent humanity is only skin-deep—he's a better father to young John Connor, the leader of the coming rebellion against

"Skynet," than anyone else in view. "This machine was the only thing that measured up," his mother, Sarah, says while watching the son and the cyborg do manly, mechanical things under the hood of a car.

In the original installment of the franchise, Sarah Connor is impregnated by a soldier sent back from the postapocalyptic future to protect her from the cyborg intent upon killing her; somehow everybody knows that her offspring will some day lead the rebellion against the machines. In *Terminator II*, the stakes are even higher. Sarah wants to abort the apocalypse, and her son pitches in with the help of the same model of cyborg that, once upon a time, came after his mother. In doing so, she is of course relieving her son of his heroic duties in the dreaded future—in the absence of real fathers in the flesh, after all, mothers have to do what's right.

The apocalypse is finally aborted in three strokes. The Connors and their protector destroy the computer chip from the original cyborg of *Terminator I*, which has fueled research and profits at the malevolent corporation that invented Skynet, the digital universe of knowledge to be captured by the bad machines on August 29, 1997. Then they defeat a new, more agile and flexible cyborg sent back to kill young John by dipping the thing in molten metal—the end of the movie is shot in what looks like a cross between a foundry and a steel plant, both throwbacks to an imaginary, industrial America where manly men worked hard and earned good pay (Freddy Krueger stalks his teenage victims in a strikingly similar dreamscape, as if what haunts them, too is an irretrievable and yet unavoidable industrial past). Finally, the old, exhausted, even dismembered protector cyborg lowers himself into the same vat of molten metal that had just dispatched his robotic nemesis, thus destroying the only remaining computer chip that could restart the train of events that led to Skynet.

So the narrative alternatives on offer in *Terminator II* are both disturbing and familiar: Dads build machines—or just are machines—that incinerate the world, or they get out of the way of the Moms. Like the cowboys and outlaws and gunfighters of the old West, another imaginary landscape we know mainly from the movies, such men might be useful in clearing the way for civilization, but they probably shouldn't stick around once the women and children arrive.

The endless sequels to the original *Nightmare on Elm Street* (1983) follow the trajectory of the *Terminator* franchise in one important respect—the indomitable villain of the 1980s evolves into a cuddly icon, almost a cult father figure, by the 1990s. But the magnificent slasher Freddy, who punctures every slacker's pubescent dreams, always preferred the neighborhood of horror, where apocalypse is personal, not political: it may be happening right now, but it is happening to you, not to the world.

Here, too, however, the plot is almost irrelevant because it turns on one simple device. It works like this. The violence and horror of your worst nightmares are more real than your waking life; the dreamscapes of the most insane adolescent imagination are more consequential than the dreary world of high school dress codes and parental aplomb: welcome to Columbine. Freddy teaches us that the distinction between appearance and reality, the distinction that animates modern science—not to mention the modern novel—is not just worthless, it is dangerous. If you don't fight him on his own postmodern terms, by entering his cartoonish space in time, you lose your life. If you remain skeptical, in the spirit of modern science or modern fiction, you lose your life.

The enablers of every atrocity in sight are the parents and the police (the heroine's father, for example, is the chief of police), who are complacent, ignorant, and complicit, all at once. They killed the child molester Freddy years ago when he was freed on a legal technicality—or at least they thought they killed him—and so his revenge on their children seems almost symmetrical: the vigilantes in the neighborhood are now victims of their own extralegal justice. And their hapless inertia in the present doesn't help the kids. In fact, their past crimes have disarmed their children. The boys on the scene aren't much help either—they're too horny or too sleepy to save anybody from Freddy's blades, even when the girls explain what will happen if they don't stand down, wake up, and get right with their bad dreams.

The Cultural Vicinity of *The Matrix*

So what is going on in the cultural vicinity of these hugely popular, truly horrific scenarios? At least the following. First, representations are reality, and vice versa. The world is a fable, a narrative machine, and that's all it is. The directors of *The Matrix* make this cinematic provocation clear by placing a book in the opening sequences—a book by Jean Baudrillard, the French theorist who claimed a correlation between finance capital and the historical moment of "simulacra," when everything is a copy of a copy (of a copy), not a representation of something more solid or fundamental. At this moment, the reproducibility of the work of art becomes constitutive of the work as art: nothing is unique, not even the artist, and not even you, the supposed author of your own life. Everything is a sign of a sign. The original *Nightmare* had already proved the same postmodern theorem with more gleeful ferocity and less intellectual pretensions, but it performed the same filmic experiment and provided the same audience experience. *Terminator 2* accomplishes something similar by demonstrating that the past is just as malleable as the future: again, the world is a fable waiting to be rewritten.

Second—this follows from Baudrillard's correlation of finance capital and the historical moment of simulacra—the world is, or was, ruled by exchange value, monopoly capital, and their technological or bureaucratic offspring. The apocalypse as conceived by both *The Matrix* and *Terminator II* is a result of corporate-driven greed (in the latter, the war that arms the machines is fought over oil). An ideal zone of use value beyond the reach of the market, a place where authentic desires and authentic identities are at least conceivable, is the coast of utopia toward which these movies keep tacking. The movies themselves are of course commodities that could not exist without mass markets and mass distribution, but there is no hypocrisy or irony or contradiction lurking in this acknowledgment. Successful filmmakers understand and act on the anticapitalist sensibilities of their audiences—none better than Steven Spielberg. Even so, they know as well as we do that there's no exit from the mall, only detours on the way.

Third, the boundary between the human and the mechanical, between sentient beings and inanimate objects, begins to seem arbitrary, accidental, inexplicable, and uncontrollable. *Blade Runner* (1982) and *RoboCop* (1987), perhaps the two best movies of the 1980s, are testaments to this perceived breakdown of borders, this confusion of categories: the good guys here are conscientious machines that are more human than their employers. That these heroes are both victims of corporate greed and street gangs does not change the fact that, like the tired old cyborg of *Terminator 2,* their characters and missions were lifted directly from the Westerns of the 1930s and 1940s—they're still figuring out what it means to be a man while they clean up Dodge City, but now they know that machines, not lawyers, might do the job better. Again, the artificial overpowers the natural and remakes the world. A fixed or stable reality that grounds all representation and falsifies mere appearance starts to look less detailed and to feel less palpable than the imagery through which we experience it; or rather the experience is the imagery. So the end of Nature, conceived by modern science as an external world of objects with its own laws of motion, is already at hand, already on display. The world has been turned inside out.

That is why the eviscerated world on view in these movies seems "posthistorical": technological progress can no longer look like the horizon of expectation, not even for the citizens of the most advanced capitalist nation on the planet. Even here the machines are taking over, downsizing every sector, but particularly manufacturing, making good jobs in the factory or the foundry—or for that matter in the back offices—a thing of the past.

When the machines do everything, the prospect of getting a better job than your father (if you have one) becomes unlikely, and the prospect of human civilization looks no better than bleak. Put it another way. If the future of Man doesn't look so good because the difference between sentient beings and inanimate objects has become arbitrary, accidental, inexplicable, and uncontrollable, the future of men looks even worse.

Fourth, the self, the family, and perhaps the nation are at risk in a world ruled by simulacra—that is, where you can't specify the difference between appearance and reality, between machines and men, or when you realize that everything, maybe even your own self, is a sign of a sign. We have already noticed that John Connor's adoptive father is a cyborg; and we've noticed that the parents in the original *Nightmare* are a big part of the problem our pubescent heroine faces.

We should also notice that only two of the small band of heroes which recruits Neo to the cause have been born outside the Matrix—you can tell because they don't have metal inserts in their necks and arms—but there's no explanation of who Mom and Pop are, except that, like the leader, they're African American. This is a family? We must assume so, because these two are designated as "brothers." Meanwhile the others are trying to figure out where they begin and the computer code ends (we in the audience are as well, especially when the traitor decides he wants to go back into the Matrix and eat virtual steak). Their creaky old craft—it, too, looks like a remnant of industrial America—is named *Nebuchadnezzar* after an ancient king of Babylon who had conquered Judaea in accordance with a cranky God's wishes, but the key to their survival is "Zion," the mainframe that unites the resistance.

This naming of the thing that keeps them together is significant because it is shorthand for a nation that is imminent but not extant—it's an idea whose time has not yet come, as in the "promised land." The question it raises is, how are we to imagine a productive relation between these three categories (self, family, nation) now that we have put them at risk, that is, in motion, in cyberspace, where the weakened condition of a fixed, external reality loosens all ties?

Generic Panic

So the end of modernity was not the intellectual property of academics isolated in their ivory tower, lacking any connections to the "real world." It was deeply felt and widely perceived in the popular culture organized by film (and by TV and music, of course, which we'll get to later). One way to measure the breadth of this feeling, this perception, is to notice how it informed really bad movies as well as really good ones and how it reanimated—in the most literal sense—the politics of cartoons. Or, to put it in the terms proposed by Carol Clover, the brilliant analyst of horror films, one way to measure the widespread panic induced by the end of modernity is to watch how the thematics and sensibilities of truly awful movies entered and altered the mainstream.

Let's begin with the panic.

Many historians and critics have pointed to the profound sense of an ending that permeated American film of the 1970s, 1980s, and 1990s. But it was not just the American century that was waning in Oscar-winning movies like *The Deer Hunter* (1978), which dramatized the military defeat of the United States in Vietnam as a crushing blow to American manhood. The fin-de-siècle feeling built into the approach of a new millennium was compounded and amplified by realistic reports—and hysterical fears—of pervasive criminality, random yet universal violence, maybe even ineradicable evil; by the decline of patriarchy, which accompanied the decomposition of the traditional nuclear family and the deindustrialization of the American economy; by the rise of the new "postfeminist" woman whose bodily integrity, moral capacity, and sexual autonomy were validated by the Supreme Court in the *Roe v. Wade* decision of 1973, then contested by the emergence of the Religious Right; by corporate malfeasance and government corruption—incessant scandal, public and private—from Watergate to Gary Hart on toward Iran-Contra and the dangerous liaisons of the Clinton years; by damning revelations of the uses to which American power had been put during and after the Cold War from Iran to Chile to Nicaragua, where revolutions in the 1970s were designed to discredit and disarm the Great Satan, the Whited Sepulchre based in Washington, D.C.; and by the public, determined, sometimes flamboyant display of homosexual affection and solidarity in the name of gay rights, a movement both complicated and magnified in the 1980s by the eruption of a deadly new sexually transmitted disease, HIV/AIDS.

When everything—law and order, manhood, fatherhood, womanhood, family, heterosexuality, even national honor—is ending, the apocalypse is now. At any rate that is the feeling that permeates the atlas of emotion etched by American culture in the late twentieth century. To illustrate this feeling, let us take a look at what happens generically in American film from the late 1970s to the late 1990s.

Probably the most important trend is the ascendance of the horror genre, in all its weird permutations (slasher, possession, occult). It remained a low-brow, B-movie genre from the early 1930s into the 1970s, but then, with the rapid expansion of the *Halloween* (1978) and *Friday the 13th* (1980) franchises in the 1980s, it became the stuff of blockbuster box office. As Mark Edmundson and others have noted, when *Silence of the Lambs*, a tasteful, muted, sublimated—almost stuffy—slasher film won the Oscar for Best Picture in 1991, horror had become the mainstream of American film. It had meanwhile reshaped every other genre, even Westerns, for example, Clint Eastwood's *High Plains Drifter* (1972).

Another important trend is an integral part of the ascendance of the horror genre. Where once female protagonists were hapless victims of violence unless they could rely on their fathers, husbands, and brothers—or the law—to protect them from the slashers, psychopaths, and rapists, they now take the law into their own hands and exact a new kind of revenge on a world of pervasive criminality coded as male. Here the thematic movement "from the bottom up," from truly awful to pretty good movies, is unmistakable. A terrifically bad movie called *I Spit on Your Grave* (1976) first installs the female victim of rape in the role of single-minded avenger, for example, and it thereafter presides, in spirit, over more polished, upscale films like *Silence of the Lambs*.

Yet another important trend in late-twentieth-century movies is the hypothesis that the family as such is dysfunctional, perhaps even destructive of social order and individual sanity. As Robin Wood has argued, the horror genre is the laboratory in which this indecent hypothesis has been tested most scientifically, from *The Texas Chain Saw Massacre* (1974) to *The Omen* (1976) and *Poltergeist* (1982), all movies about families permeated or penetrated by unspeakable evil—families confused by the modern liberal distinction between private and public spheres. But the return of the repressed gangster, begun by *The Godfather* cycle in the 1970s, magnified in the 1983 remake of *Scarface* (the original appeared in 1931), and completed by *The Sopranos* on cable TV in the late 1990s, also demonstrated, in the most graphic terms, that strict devotion to family makes a man violent, paranoid, and finally unable to fulfill his obligations to loved ones.

If all you inhabit or care for is your family, both these genres keep telling us, you are the most dangerous man alive. At the very least you'll forget your loyalties to a larger community, contracting your commitments until they go no further than the boundary of your own home; at that point, you will have destroyed your family and broken the rules that regulate life out there where everybody else lives. But how do you situate yourself in relation to a larger community—to the state, the nation—in the absence of this middle term, the family? It was an urgent political question in late-twentieth-century America, as the decomposition of the traditional nuclear family accelerated, and it was raised most pointedly on screen, by a culture industry supposedly out of touch with "traditional values."

A fourth important trend in the movies of the late twentieth century is an obsession with the ambiguities and the consequences of crime. Film noir of the 1940s and 1950s was predicated on such ambiguities and consequences, of course, but the sensibility of that moment seems to have become a directorial norm by the 1980s. The difference between the good guys and the bad guys is at first difficult to discern in the battle between the criminals and the deputies staged by Arthur Penn in *Bonnie and Clyde* (1967), in part because it is clear from the outset that our heroes are deranged. It gets more and more difficult in the 1970s and 1980s, when Clint Eastwood's *Dirty Harry* franchise makes the detective less likable than his collars; when drug dealers, pimps, and prostitutes become lovable characters in "blaxploitation" movies (*Sweet Sweetback* [1971], *Shaft* [1971], *Superfly* [1972]); when gangsters become the unscrupulous yet dutiful bearers of the American Dream (*The Godfather* [1972]); when Custer's Last Stand becomes a monument to imperial idiocy (*Little Big Man* [1970]), even as the Indians become the personification of authentic America (*Dances with Wolves* [1990]); when the origin of civic renewal is a crime that appears as both domestic violence and foreign policy—it begins as incest and ends as the colonization of what was once exterior to the city fathers' domain (*Chinatown* [1974]); and when the assassination of a president becomes comparable to the "secret murder at the heart of American history" (*JFK* [1991]: this is the district attorney talking to the jury!).

That not-so-secret murder is of course the American Dream itself—the dream that allows you to become father of yourself, to cast off all the traditions and obligations accumulated in the "Old World," to treat the past as mere baggage. If you are father to yourself, you don't have a father except yourself: you don't have a past to observe or honor or, more importantly, to learn from. But when you're on your own in this fundamental sense, as Americans like to be, you lean toward radical visions of the future and radical resolutions of problems inherited from the past. As D. H. Lawrence noted in his studies of classic American literature almost a hundred years ago, the masterless are an unruly horror.

And when you know that every cop is a criminal—and all the sinners saints—sympathy for the devil becomes your only option as a viewer of movies. The lawful and the unlawful intersect in startling ways in this social and cultural space. So do the natural and the supernatural, as witness Quentin Tarantino's easy transition from *Reservoir Dogs* (1992) and *Pulp Fiction* (1994)—movies about the redemption of the most callous criminals—to the vampire flick written with Robert Rodriguez, *From Dusk Till Dawn* (1997), a movie that mixes so many genres it seems as contrived as a cocktail invented in SoHo. Witness as well the epidemic of celestial messengers, angry demons, impossible conspiracies, and talented witches on TV after Tony Kushner, an avowed Marxist, won the 1993 Pulitzer Prize for his two-part Broadway play *Angels in America*. *Buffy the Vampire Slayer* was waiting in the wings, state left. *The X- Files* entered earlier, stage right.

One more important trend, which tracks the other four quite closely, is the remarkable increase in spectacular violence done to heroes, victims, and villains alike. The analogue of video games is not very useful on this score, however, because the recipient of excruciating violence in the movies of the late twentieth century is typically a female who then exacts revenge (*I Spit on Your Grave*, *Ms. 45* [1981]) or a male who revels in the physical torture he's "taking like a man," presumably because this debilitating experience equips him with the moral authority he will later need to vanquish the enemy without ceremony or regret. The *Rocky* (1976) and the *Rambo* (1982) franchises sponsored by Sylvester Stallone are the founding fathers of the latter movement, in which masochism finally becomes unmistakably male.

The *Lethal Weapon* (1987) franchise animated by Mel Gibson's jittery impersonation of Norman Mailer's "White Negro"—Gibson's cop character has to teach his African American partner (Danny Glover) how to live in the moment, how to be existential if not suicidal—is the parallel film universe in which guys get crazy because they have to, because the world has excluded them from the theater of good wars and good jobs, where boys once learned how to be men. *Fight Club* (1999) is the final solution to this fear of male irrelevance and the apogee of male masochism at the movies. In its moral equivalent of war, men keep trying to mutilate themselves, but we know it's okay because they use their bare hands: until the ugly and inexplicable ending, they're purposeful artisans, not mindless machine herds.

Experience and Explanation at the Cineplex

Let us work backward in this list of filmic trends of the late twentieth century to see if we can make historical sense of them, to see if they have anything in common. The increase of spectacular violence at the movies has of course been explained as a result of the recent decline in the median age of the audience—adolescents it is said, have always experienced the onset of their pubescence and then their reluctant graduation to adulthood in the unholy images of dismemberment. More scenes of carnage, more rivers of blood are what these hormone-fueled maniacs need and what Hollywood gladly delivers. It is an argument that works pretty well until you realize that adults still buy more tickets than the teenage crowd and that the violence on view increased exponentially in every genre toward the end of the twentieth century, to begin with in Westerns and war movies—for example, *The Wild Bunch* (1969), *Apocalypse Now* (1979), *Platoon* (1986), and *Saving Private Ryan* (1998)—where teenagers did not tread unless accompanied by their parents.

The better arguments are offered by film theorists who suggest that the extreme fury inflicted on the human body in the movies since the 1970s should be understood in terms of a general unsettlement of subjectivity—of selfhood—and who suggest that by the late 1980s, the signature of this unsettlement had become male masochism. In *The Philosophy of Horror*, a groundbreaking book of 1990, Noel Carroll suggests that the ever more elaborate violence visited upon the characters of his favored genre constitutes an "iconography of personal vulnerability." Horror as such, he insists, is "founded on the disturbance of cultural norms." The late-twentieth-century festival of violence in movies is, then, a visual depiction, a pictorial externalization, of the anxieties necessarily attached to the end of modernity, when "an overwhelming sense of instability seizes the imagination in such a way that everything appears at risk or up for grabs." But the crucial cultural norm in question is the father of himself—the modern individual, the American Adam.

That is why Carroll correlates the "death of 'Man'" postulated by postmodern theory with the "demotion of the person" expressed by the extraordinary violence of a recent horror film—the popular, colloquial, vernacular version of academic elocution can be seen at the Cineplex, he suggests, long before (or after) you are forced to read Foucault and Derrida by your demented professors. Carroll summarizes his argument as follows: "What is passing, attended by feelings of anxiety, is the social myth of the 'American' individualist, which, in the case of horror, is enacted in spectacles of indignity, [and is] directed at the body." What is passing, right before our very eyes in the artificial night of the local theater, is that remnant of the nineteenth century, the bourgeois proprietor of himself. It is a violent business, this cinematic execution of our former self, and it can never be finished. No wonder we want to prolong the agony on screen.

What is also "passing" in the torrent of violence that floods every genre in the late twentieth century is manhood as it was conceived in the "era of the ego," circa 1600 to 1900, as it was then embalmed in the canonical novels and the literary criticism of the 1920s—Ernest Hemingway and Lewis Mumford come to mind—and as it was reenacted in movies, mainly Westerns, of the 1930s, 1940s, and 1950s. The strong, silent types who inhabited that imaginary American space west of everything give way, by the 1980s and

1990s, to male leads who are anything but. All they want is to talk about their psychological afflictions, as if we—the audience—can cure them. Tony Soprano is the culmination of this cinematic species. And it is no accident that the backstory informing every episode is Tony's search for meaning in a world turned inside out by race and gender ("Woke up this morning, the blues [that is, the blacks] moved in our town," as the song goes over the opening credits). For it is here, in the world of therapy and thus the language of psychoanalysis, that the problem of male masochism at the movies becomes visible and, in the most old-fashioned sense, remarkable.

Kaja Silverman and Carol Clover are among the accomplished film theorists who have deployed the language of psychoanalysis to interpret the systematic abuse and abjection of males in late-twentieth-century movies (by then, a film theorist who did not trade in the currency of psychoanalysis was an anomaly, something like a chaperone at a bachelor party; Noel Carroll resisted the urge and found a voice by falling back on the Marxoid rhythms of Fredric Jameson). Like their counterparts—David Savran and Barbara Creed are probably their best contestants—both Silverman and Clover rely on two famous essays of 1924 by the founding father, Sigmund Freud, in which masochism is defined as the psychological space that permits, maybe even demands, male experimentation with an imaginary femininity.

In all the clinical/case studies Freud cites, it is men who are being masochistic, but the passivity that allows their penetration, laceration, and so forth, is coded as female. "In the case of the girl what was originally a masochistic (passive) situation is transformed into a sadistic one by means of repression, and its sexual quality is almost effaced," he declares. "In the case of the boy," on the other hand, "the situation remains masochistic." For he "evades his homosexuality by repressing and remodeling his unconscious phantasy [of being beaten, penetrated, by his father]; and the remarkable thing about his later conscious phantasy is that it has for its content *a feminine attitude without a homosexual object-choice.*" In these psychoanalytical terms, masochism on screen looks and feels like men trying to be women—men trying to identify as women—but without cross-dressing and without coming out of a closet to renounce heterosexuality. Again, it is the psychological space in which an imaginary femininity becomes actionable.

At any rate, it is the cultural space in which the mobility—the increasing instability—of masculinity can be experienced. Clover has shown that the predominantly male audience for crude horror films like *I Spit on Your Grave* is not indulging its sadistic fantasies by identifying with the rapists, as pious mainstream critics would have it; instead, that male audience is placing its hopes and fears in the resilient character of the Last Girl Standing, the young woman who ignores the law because she has to, the gentle female who comes of age by killing the slashers and the psychopaths. Violence is the cinematic medium in which this transference, this out-of-body experience, gets enacted. Violence is the cinematic medium in which male subjectivity gets tested, in other words, and is finally found wanting except as a form of emotional solidarity with the female character who outlasts her tormentors.

So male masochism at the movies looks and feels bad—it is hard to watch, particularly when Mel Gibson's William Wallace is getting tortured in *Braveheart* (1995), when Sylvester Stallone's *Rocky* is being beaten to a pulp, or when Brad Pitt is begging for more punishment in *Fight Club*—but it accomplishes something important. Its violent sensorium lets us experience the end of modernity as the dissolution of male subjectivity and the realignment of the relation between what we took for granted as feminine and masculine (keeping in mind that this realignment may well prove to be regressive and destructive). Freud was on to something, then, when he suggested that by way of male masochism, "morality becomes sexualized once more [and] the Oedipus complex is revived." Translation: the identities we discovered as we detached ourselves from a primal, physical, emotional connection to our parent(s)—as we worked through the Oedipus complex—are perturbed and perplexed, perhaps even reconstructed, by the horrific experience of masochistic violence at the movies. These identities now become fungible, divisible, negotiable, recyclable—in a word, scary.

The criminal element of late-twentieth-century film is of course related to the increase of spectacular violence done to heroes, victims, and villains alike. The American fascination with crime runs deep because rapid change is normal in this part of the world—here "crisis becomes the rule," as a famous philosopher, John Dewey, once put it. His admirer Kenneth Burke explained that "any incipient trend will first be felt as crime by reason of its conflict with established values." It's hard to distinguish between criminals and heroes because they both break the rules and point us beyond the status quo, and they're always urging us to expect more (the heroes of sports are heralds of this type, from Bill Russell and Mickey Mantle to Michael Jordan). They're like the revolutionaries of the college textbooks—Max Weber's "charismatic" leaders—but they're more rooted in everyday routine, in what we call "practice." They're more visible, more approachable, more likable than, say, Lenin, Mao, Castro, or Che, because they don't want to change the world, they want to change the rules.

So crime, like violence, is as American as apple pie. But the late-twentieth-century filmic rendition of criminal behavior departs from its antecedents, especially in depicting gangsters. Where such felons were once represented as deviations from a norm of manhood and domesticity, and thus as a threat to the peace of the city and the integrity of the nation—think of Paul Muni, Jimmy Cagney, and Edward G. Robinson in their founding roles of the early 1930s—by the 1970s and 1980s, Gangsters R Us. By the 1990s, accordingly, crime as committed at the movies became the origin and insignia of everything American. This is a useful notion, mind you. It forces us to acknowledge that the Western Hemisphere was not a "new world" when Europeans invaded America and that the idea of original sin still has explanatory adequacy. At any rate, it lets us know that our country was not born free: it is no exception to the rules of history, no matter who—whether Marx or Freud or Weber—wrote them up as the laws of motion that regulate modernity.

It also lets us know that the private space of contemporary home and family is not exempt from the public atrocities of the political past. *Poltergeist* and the remake of *The Haunting* (1999) suggest, for example, that the extermination of Indians on the frontier of American civilization and the exploitation of child labor during the Industrial Revolution cannot be forgotten, not even by the most ignorant individuals and the most insulated, intimate, social organisms of the present—they suggest that the return of the repressed is always already underway from within the family. The political is personal in the late-twentieth-century United States. Otherwise it is almost invisible.

The "traditional" family was, after all, breaking down in the late twentieth century, and crime rates were, in fact, climbing in the 1960s and after: for many observers, such as George Gilder and Charles Murray, the relation between these two phenomena was clearly and simply cause and effect. And the extrusion of women from the home—from familial roles and obligations—looked to them like the proximate cause of the cause. Feminism signified "sexual suicide," in Gilder's hysterical phrase. It takes on new meanings in the context of awful yet rousing movies like *I Spit on Your Grave* and *Ms. 45* Here the female protagonists, young professional women who are victims of brutal and repeated rape, decide to kill the perpetrators instead of waiting on the law made by their fathers, husbands, or brothers. In doing so, they broaden the scope of their vengeance to include male supremacy itself. They're carefully killing off the idea that men should have control of women's bodies. So the figurative mayhem on view is not suicide but homicide—it is patricide, the adjournment of the law of the father, the inevitable result of giving women the weapons they need to protect themselves against violent men.

And that brings us back to where we began, to the ascendance of the horror genre, wherein violence, crime, and family are typically represented, and sometimes rearranged, by the suffering of women at the hands of men. What links our five filmic trends of the late twentieth century, in this sense, is gender trouble—that is, "the disturbance of cultural norms" which derives from the social (and thus political) problem of the new, "postfeminist" woman and which redraws the perceived relations, the effective boundaries, between males and females.

Cartoon Politics

A similar disturbance, a similar problem, meanwhile recast the politics of cartoons. In the next chapter, we'll get to the excremental visions of *Beavis and Butthead* and *South Park* and to the liberal tilt of *The Simpsons*. There we will note, once again, that even in these small-screen suburbs of Hollywood, popular culture in the United States kept moving to the left after Jimmy Carter, after Ronald Reagan, after George H. W. Bush, and, yes, after Newt Gingrich, leaving the learned scribes and earnest scolds from the New Right to wring their hands until the second coming of Bush in 2000. For now, to conclude this chapter, we'll look at *The Little Mermaid* (1990), *Beauty and the Beast* (1992), and *Toy Story* (1995) on the big screen—for these were the movies that woke Disney Studios from its long artistic slumber and reminded us of the possibilities residing in the comic abstractions of animation.

Females are never very far from the leading roles in Disney's feature-length productions: the studio's memorable hits before the 1960s and 1970s, when it began cranking out musical extravaganzas starring dogs, cats, and mice, were *Snow White and the Seven Dwarfs* (1937) and *Sleeping Beauty* (1959), both driven by their female leads' search for true love in a world dominated by incestuous envy or anonymous violence (and what you remember about *Bambi* [1942] is the death of the mother). The character of Cruella de Vil in *One Hundred and One Dalmations* (1961) affirms this precedent, but she has no human content or counterpart—she's all cartoon. Something new happens in *The Little Mermaid*, a movie produced with the computer technology and political sensibility promoted at Disney by Jeffrey Katzenberg, a young visionary who, like Matt Groening over at FOX TV, wanted to make comics that mattered.

The questions they kept asking in the 1990s were, What are the functions of families if females have been freed from an exclusive preoccupation with domestic roles (as wives and mothers)? What can we do with a past we've outgrown? What are parents good for, anyway? And where's Dad? In Disney films, however, as in fairy tales, these familiar antecedents are never given by the past—they're not just there because they happened in the past, because they somehow preceded and produced us. Instead, they get created by fantastic narratives that erase them, reinstate them, and reinvent them at inappropriate times, according to the bizarre but rule-bound logic of contradiction that regulates cartoons (to wit, every category or distinction sustained by common sense is now subject to violation by the principle of plasticity). They're always there, in short, only not so that you would notice. They're mostly missing, like absent causes or like real parents who can't seem to show up when it counts but who shape your lives anyway.

Ariel, the little mermaid, is the "postfeminist" woman par excellence: she has Promethean curiosity and energy and ambition. "What's a fire," she asks, "and why does it, what's the word, burn?" She wants to escape from the fluid, formless, watery world where the everyday objects that signify modern human civilization—things like eating utensils—have no name and no purpose and where fire, the origin of civilization as such, is impossible. She wants the forbidden knowledge available only to the people who walk around on land and use wooden ships to skim her ocean. Above all, she wants freedom from her father's stifling supervision—she wants to be the father of herself.

Ariel introduces her agenda of desires by singing about all the things she's found in the shipwrecks she explores. She calls this stuff treasures, wonders, gadgets, gizmos, whose-its, what's-its, thingamabobs. She doesn't understand what any of it is for—how or why it gets used by people "up there"—but she's sure that all of it somehow fits together in a way of life that is very different from hers. When Ariel calls herself "the girl who has everything" (she's using a phrase common in the 1980s), she's really complaining that by themselves, as simple objects, her things don't have any significance. So when she goes on to sing "I want more," she doesn't mean more stuff. What she wants is the way of life in which the stuff makes sense.

That's why she doesn't sing about the stuff in the rest of the song. Ariel sings instead about seeing, dancing, running, jumping, strolling—about walking upright as the prerequisite of "wandering free." What would I give, she asks herself, "if I could live out of these waters?" But it's obvious that she can wander more freely in the water than anybody her age can on dry land. So she must have some ideas about freedom that involves more than moving about in space. She makes those ideas clear in the next part of the song. "Betcha on land," she sings, "they understand—bet they don't reprimand their daughters." She's singing about how her father has scolded her, has tried to keep her in her proper place, under water, where nothing seems to matter. Then she identifies herself with all the other ambitious girls who don't want to stay in that same old place where men get to make all the decisions: "Bright young women, sick of swimmin', ready to stand." Ready, that is, to stand up to their fathers (and husbands and brothers), to face them as equals on their own two feet.

Ariel's agenda is eventually contained by her devotion to the human being she falls in love with (yes, he's a handsome prince) and learns to want to marry. All the dangers of her proposed departure from her undersea world—all the sexual tensions and fears this departure from her family, this deviation from her father's wishes, might create—are eventually tamed by the idea of marriage. When Ariel is paired off with the prince, the possibilities of her ascent become familiar: her goal becomes the start of a new family that marriage symbolizes.

But this use of the familiar let Katzenberg and his animators take chances with their mermaid story without offending or troubling their audience, which of course included millions of unsophisticated children as well as educated adults. The movie did contest the common sense of its time—it did contest the related notions that women should not want what men do and that women are so naturally different from men that equality between them is unimaginable. Even so, it ends up suggesting that marriage is the way to answer all the questions raised by those "bright young women" who were, then as now, "sick of swimmin'" under the direction of their fathers (and husbands and brothers). And that is a way of suggesting that the important questions of our time can be answered from within the family.

You may have noticed that Ariel seems to have no mother—no one to help her father, Triton, the king of the oceans, decide what's best for her. But look closer. The only character in the movie who is the king's equal is Ursula the Sea Witch (she's the devil who gives the girl legs in contractual exchange for her voice, thus putting her on land in range of the prince, but also casting the little mermaid—that would be the teenager—as the Doctor Faustus of the late twentieth century). Ursula competes directly with Triton for control of Ariel's future, as if she were the mermaid's mother. And in her big number, she shows this "daughter" how to get the man she wants. She's the closest thing to a mother Ariel has.

Now Ursula seems simply evil because what she's really after is the power of the king—she used to live in Triton's castle, she tells us in passing, and she wants to move back in. So it's clear that, once upon a time, just like the devil himself, she challenged the king's powers from within his own home, his own castle, and got kicked out as a result. No matter where we look in the movie, then, it seems that females, both mothers and daughters, have to leave the castle if they're going to stand up to the king as his equal. This departure is either cause or effect of conflict with the father who rules that castle, but it happens to both Ariel and Ursula.

Yet we're supposed to be able to tell the difference between them, apart from the obvious differences of age, size, shape—and species (the devil is a huge octopus). We're supposed to know that Ariel is good and Ursula is evil. So we have to ask, what does Ursula want that makes her evil? What makes her rebellion so awful? And why is Ariel's rebellion acceptable in the end, when Triton relents and uses his powers to give his daughter legs and a human husband? Both stand up to the father. But one is killed by Ariel's husband-to-be; the other is rewarded with entry into the enlightened world of men on earth. One is driven out of the castle; the other chooses to leave. One tries to challenge the inherited ("normal") relation between father and mother; the other wants to re-create this relation in a new family. One breaks the law of the father by defying him; the other upholds it by doing the same thing. How so?

If we read this movie as a comic retelling of the ancient Oedipus cycle, we can see that the law of the father still works only if Ursula's rebellion gets punished by death. Only if the sea witch is removed can Ariel pair off with the prince by calling on her father's great powers. But remember that Ursula is in effect the mermaid's mother. And remember that she is killed by the prince—the future son-in-law of the father, the king—with the bowsprit of the shipwreck Ariel found at the very beginning of the movie. Everybody is cooperating, in the end, to aim this shaft, this phallic device, at the belly of the beast; everybody is cooperating to kill the mother, to remove her from the scene she's tried to steal. By doing so, they preserve the law of the father and let Ariel ascend to earth.

That is what must happen if we believe that the important questions of our time can be answered from within the family—something's got to give if we're confined to this small social space. *The Little Mermaid* suggests, accordingly, that either the law of the father or the mother herself will give way. All those "bright young women" still "sick of swimmin'" need new ground to stand on, but if that ground can be found only within the family, father or mother must go. No wonder single-parent households were the fastest-growing demographic of the late twentieth century.

Where's Dad?

Beauty and the Beast was the politically correct sequel to *The Little Mermaid*. It solidified Disney's reputation as the place to be if you wanted to experiment with computerized animation—Pixar soon lined up with everybody else—but the movie was a boring love letter to the narcissistic nerds, the high school geeks, who wrote it as their revenge on the athletes who, once upon a time, got the girl. Here the female lead rejects the dumb jock and chooses the hairy intellectual with the big library, all in the name of her hapless father, the absentminded professorial type who invents useless, even dangerous machines. He's the mad scientist without portfolio, without purpose—he's the father figure who, like Homer Simpson, remains benign because he has no power, no purchase on the world. His inventions explode like fireworks, not like bombs.

So the law of the father still works in this monotonous movie, disabling the cartoon principle of plasticity by presenting as given, as frozen, the categories that were at issue, in question, in motion, in the larger culture. The first Pixar contribution to the new Disney mix of the 1990s, *Toy Story*, won't stand for that kind of authentic abstention and its cynical attendant, resignation from the world as it exists. Like *The Simpsons*, it forces us to play with the idea of the father as an absent cause of everything that's both funny and sad at the end of the twentieth century.

In any event it makes us want to ask, where's Dad? Mom is in plain sight from the standpoint of all the toys who open the movie by planning a parallel birthday party for her son, their beloved Andy. Dad is invisible from beginning to end unless we read their story, the toys' story, as a treatise on how to reinsert fathers into the family romance of our time. His absence is the premise of the movie, in other words, but the writers don't leave it at that; they urge you to believe that Toys R Us by suggesting that Woody and Buzz, the cowboy and the astronaut who compete for the son's undivided attention, are the father we all need.

Woody (Tom Hanks) is the distant echo of the Western hero who resists progress and fears the future because he knows they mean the eclipse of his independence, his unique and self-evident position in a fixed moral universe. He recalls Sebastian the Crab from *The Little Mermaid*, another unwitting opponent of development, who wants Ariel to stay down under "de water" because up there on dry land, they work too hard: "Out in de sun, dey slave away." But Woody also stands at the end of a long line of white-collar middle managers who crowded TV screens in the 1950s and 1960s, pretending that "father knows best" (think of the staff meeting that Woody holds before Andy's birthday party). So he represents a hybrid of male images drawn from film and TV, the characteristic cultural media of the twentieth-century United States.

Buzz (Tim Allen) is Thorstein Veblen's engineer, Vince Lombardi's shoulder-padded poet, and Tom Wolfe's astronaut rolled into one—he's the ex-jock with the right stuff who hates the past and believes almost religiously in the technological armature of progress. He wants to go to the moon and thinks he already has the equipment he requires. He represents "the machine," the favorite metaphor of American writers in the twentieth century, but he reminds us of cheesy Saturday-morning cartoons, too, and not just because he recognizes himself in a TV commercial.

Together, and only together, Woody and Buzz are the missing father the son needs. At the outset, Woody is simply afraid of the future—he might be displaced by a new toy—and Buzz is just contemptuous of the past, when space travel was science fiction. By itself, neither side of the modern American male can make the family whole again by restoring the father to his proper place at its head. And each, by himself, is vulnerable to Sid, the nasty boy next door who captures them.

This boy is another mad scientist, a young Frankenstein, but he means business—he's perverted modern technology to the point of absurdity if not criminality by turning beloved toys into ugly and malevolent machines. Like the folks who are exploring the human genome, he takes things apart and reassembles them as if he's trying to invent brand-new species (think of the disfigured baby doll's head glued to Erector Set spider legs). He scares everybody, including his sister, but mainly he scares the parents in the audience, who still like to think they're the origin of the next generation.

For this kid's goal is to downsize Dad by dividing him up and dispersing his parts among many new contraptions. Sid represents the hard side of Microsoft—he's bound for glory in Silicon Valley by depriving dads of the good jobs they had when baby boomers were dutiful sons. Like the audience, and like dads everywhere, Woody and Buzz experience this threat as dismemberment, perhaps even as impending castration. No kidding. Susan Faludi's best-selling book of 1999 quotes Don Motta, a middle-aged middle manager laid off by McDonnell Douglas in 1992, as follows: "There is no way you can feel like a man. You can't. It's the fact that I'm not capable of supporting my family. . . . I'll be very frank with you. I feel I've been castrated."

Only by joining forces, only by coming together and trading on each other's strengths, can Woody and Buzz—the two sides of American manhood (thus fatherhood)—defeat the perversions of technology and familial relations that Sid represents. Only then can they resurrect the mangled toy soldiers, the heroic fathers from World War II, who were buried by Sid in the sandbox—buried that is, in the post-Vietnam memories of their postwar children. Only then can they reappear, courtesy of old-fashioned rocket science, at their son's side, just as his family reaches the horizon of no return.

So Toy Story was a great deal more complex and frightening than another parable of "more work for mother" or another evasion of the question, where's Dad? This movie spoke directly and productively to the sense of loss—the loss of jobs, the decomposition of "traditional" families, the fear of the future—that permeated American culture back then. The sequel did not.

In *Toy Story 2*, Woody still fears the future in which Andy will outgrow his favorite fatherly toy. He fears it so much that he had decided to retire to a museum of TV memorabilia, the cartoon equivalent of a nursing home, where he won't have to beg for attention. Buzz understands Woody's fear, but he's willing to let go, even to be put on the shelf where childish things languish and get forgotten until the garage sale—he's willing to let this son grow up and decide for himself what's worth keeping and caring for. Before Woody can leave for the museum, however, he gets kidnapped by a crazed antique dealer. Buzz then leads the other toys on a successful rescue mission that ends with Woody's return to the familial fold, just in time for Andy's return from summer camp. The newfangled father apparently knows best, even though his purpose is merely to retrieve the wanderer, to keep Woody where he belongs, in the bosom of his—or is it the?—family.

The original *Toy Story* taught us that a usable model of fatherhood and family—of selfhood as such—can't be imagined by committing ourselves to the past or the future, as if these are the terms of an either/or choice. It taught us that we exile ourselves from the present and from our families when we try to stay in the past along with Woody or when we try to flee the past along with Buzz. In the end, these two understood that each had to adopt an attitude toward history which allows for both previous truth and novel fact—an attitude that lets each of them change the other and so makes their cooperative effort, their unison, greater than the sum of its parts. They taught us that the point is to keep the conversation going between the past and the future, not to choose between them. The point is to live forward but understand backward.

So the sequel is less hopeful, more elegiac (more funereal, more nostalgic) than the original. It spoke directly, but not very productively, to the sense of an ending that our strange millennial moment afforded us. For it suggests that you can't teach an old toy new attitudes. All you can do is get older and watch as your kids grow up, move out, move on. And pretty soon you'll be on the shelf like your own father, downsized not by technology but by time—by the growing gaps of memory you share with the people who say history is bunk.

Such weary resignation probably seems realistic as the baby boomers start thinking about how to finance their retirements. Even so, *Toy Story 2* inadvertently advertises another and more useful truth. It goes like this. Only when our attitudes toward history become fixed do the past and the future look the same, that is, impervious to change. When those attitudes are unhinged by watching the end of modernity, when we understand that the world is a fable waiting for our editorial revisions, we know better.

You might now ask, Ye gods, how and why did cartoons become so serious and so central in American culture at the end of the twentieth century? Good question. We start with a tentative answer in the next chapter.

~

CHAPTER FIVE

"Angels in America"
Technologies of Desire and Recognition

Cartoon Politics, Again

At the end of the twentieth century, American thought and culture became increasingly cartoonish. That is neither a criticism nor a complaint. It may even be a compliment. For cartoons are strident abstractions from the particularities of ethnic, racial, and sexual experiences, the stuff of identity politics. These abstractions reverse the typical moves of the classical Hollywood cinema, which rendered great social issues—for example, class struggle—as biography, and in doing so turned the public and the political into something personal (think of *It Happened One Night* [1934], *Pretty Woman* [1990], or *Maid in Manhattan* [2002]). These new cartoon abstractions move the other way, turning the world inside out by rendering what seems personal as something public and perhaps political. They attract our attention because the "characters" in cartoons don't look or sound like anybody we have ever met—and they never have to change over time.

Cartoon characters don't have inner lives—they're allegorical figures, all surfaces. So they're a blank screen onto which we can project ourselves, no matter what our origins might be. They're "elemental," as Norman Klein puts it: "The character is supposed to be empty, to be filled with the audience's sensibility." Here's a visual demonstration drawn from Scott McCloud's brilliant book *Understanding Comics* (1994):

EACH ONE *ALSO* SUSTAINS A CONSTANT AWARENESS OF HIS OR HER *OWN* FACE, BUT *THIS* MIND-PICTURE IS NOT NEARLY SO VIVID; JUST A SKETCHY ARRANGEMENT... A SENSE OF SHAPE... A SENSE OF *GENERAL PLACEMENT.*

SOMETHING AS *SIMPLE* AND AS *BASIC*--

--AS A *CARTOON.*

THUS, WHEN YOU LOOK AT A PHOTO OR REALISTIC DRAWING OF A FACE--

--YOU SEE IT AS THE FACE OF *ANOTHER.*

BUT WHEN YOU ENTER THE WORLD OF THE *CARTOON*--

-- YOU SEE *YOURSELF.*

I BELIEVE THIS IS THE *PRIMARY CAUSE* OF OUR CHILDHOOD FASCINATION WITH *CARTOONS,* THOUGH OTHER FACTORS SUCH AS *UNIVERSAL IDENTIFICATION, SIMPLICITY* AND THE *CHILDLIKE FEATURES* OF MANY CARTOON CHARACTERS ALSO PLAY A PART.

THE CARTOON IS A *VACUUM* INTO WHICH OUR *IDENTITY* AND *AWARENESS* ARE *PULLED...*

...AN *EMPTY SHELL* THAT WE INHABIT WHICH *ENABLES* US TO TRAVEL IN *ANOTHER REALM.*

WE DON'T JUST *OBSERVE* THE CARTOON, WE *BECOME* IT!

THAT'S WHY I DECIDED TO *DRAW* MYSELF IN SUCH A SIMPLE *STYLE.*

WOULD YOU HAVE *LISTENED* TO ME IF I LOOKED LIKE *THIS*??

McCloud comic. *Source*: Page 36 from *Understanding Comics* by Scott McCloud. © 1993, 1994, by Scott McCloud. Reprinted by permission of HarperCollins Publishers.

In this chapter, we'll be visiting TV, music, and computer culture—maybe a novel or two, just for fun, but just in passing—as a way of verifying these cartoonish claims. The argument here is pretty simple. Toward the end of the twentieth century, Americans learned to live with real differences by blurring them, abstracting from them, in the postrealistic, almost fantastic settings of TV, music, and computer culture.

You have surely noticed that American art, all pictorial art, got more and more abstract in the twentieth century, as Cubist and surrealist sensibilities penetrated and reshaped every kind of painting and sculpture. The big exception was performance art, a new genre created mainly by women, beginning in the 1970s. But even here the world was turned inside out by artists like Karen Finley, who wanted you to know that the brown stuff she was eating and smearing on her body could be the real thing, genuine shit. Then what? What's inside anymore? "We are what we eat," but *twice*, once as food and then again as what our bodies have already expelled?

Cartoons, comics, and movies—the last is the distant echo of the first two—tilt the world differently. They are a way of rejoining what had been severed by the modern world we recognize in the coming of the codex book. Words and pictures parted company in the sixteenth century, during the Reformation, when people learned to read the Bible for themselves instead of just listening to the priests, when worship became a matter of words, without any visual distractions in the form of pictures or statues or stained glass. According to the Protestants, nothing but "plain speech" was needed to save the souls of the sinners.

The distance between words and pictures was never hard and fast—there were always illustrated books for children—but it kept growing so that by the eighteenth century it seemed unbridgeable, perhaps because realism was gaining on other narrative forms, both here and in Europe. Cartoons and comics closed that distance at the very end of the nineteenth century, reuniting words and pictures in startling ways that led straight to motion pictures.

Now you might wonder how the Reformation is relevant to the cartoonish quality of late-twentieth-century American thought and culture. It is, in the following strange sense. The original Protestants didn't trust Reason because it was just another human faculty corrupted by sin (hence their fervent belief in faith as the condition of redemption); their distrust of Reason marked, but also complicated, the relation between higher and lower culture, or between educated and popular culture. The comics and the cartoons—and the movies—of the early twentieth century completed that weird complication to the point of erasing the line between high and low culture.

Or, rather, those early comics and cartoons and movies waited patiently until the late twentieth century, when the graphic novel and Pop Art finally validated their postmodern complication of the relation between words and pictures. Will Eisner, Roy Lichtenstein, and Andy Warhol ended this long waiting period in the 1960s by making cartoons the stuff of stirring narrative and fine art. When Art Spiegelman won the Pulitzer Prize in 1994 for *Maus*, a two-volume story about a troubled Holocaust survivor and his son—rendered as figures who remind us of Mickey Mouse, if only Mickey had a shrink—the graphic novel suddenly acquired a new respectability. All these artists were nonetheless borrowing from the visual conventions of cheesy comics from the 1950s and even earlier.

Rock and roll had a similarly commercial, cheesy genealogy and a similar effect. By the 1970s it, too, was the cultural mainstream. But then disco and punk rock fought it out, and neither won, much to our current relief—unless we think of heavy metal as the angry offspring of these unlikely parents. We'll ask that genealogical question later, when we get to the music of the end of the twentieth century.

For now, let's look at the cartoons, the real deal on TV. Of course they started as shorts that introduced feature-length movies—we've all seen the scrawny Mickey Mouse, just a line drawing in motion, steering that steamboat at the dawn of Disney studios—but they came of age on television, as the Saturday morning absurdities that taught the baby boomers how to understand surrealism and maybe even Situationism, yet another bastard child of Cubism.

That was long before *The Simpsons*, *South Park*, and *The Family Guy*. That was back when Bugs Bunny, clearly a new version of the Trickster who permeated African American folklore (think of Br'er Rabbit), and when Wile E. Coyote, Sisyphus reincarnated as a dog chasing the same bird unto infinity, remade the cartoon imagination. Back then we knew that Elmer Fudd, the supposed human, wasn't going to kill the Wabbit because Bugs was too shifty, too cool, and we knew that the serious scientist, the existentialist hero—that would be the coyote whose every contraption mangled its own inventor—wasn't going to catch the Road Runner (beep-beep), the embodiment of natural athletic talent. But we kept watching, we suspended our disbelief because we knew, somehow, that these endlessly reiterated episodes had something to do with our real lives, with our own fantasies and frustrations.

Did we know, somehow, that Bugs Bunny announced the advent of a new racial regime in which the silly, sometimes angry white man with the gun would finally be outsmarted by the Trickster? Did we know, somehow, that Wile E. Coyote couldn't build a machine that could contain or destroy the natural energies of the athletes and the animals among us? Did we know that big science was kind of a joke because the atomic bomb had only amplified the Cold War? Maybe. In any event, let us consider the cartoonish character of late-twentieth-century American culture with such questions in mind. In doing so, we might see a political agenda in the making.

Consider, to begin with, *The Simpsons*, the longest-running situation comedy on television, which is brought to you by FOX TV, the cable network that has carved out a unique niche for itself by being blatantly conservative. The series was created by Matt Groening, a starving artist whose previous credentials were confined to venues like *The Reader*, a free weekly, and *In These Times*, a socialist newspaper, two fugitive journals published in Chicago. By now the show has of course attracted the talents of innumerable Ivy League graduates who want to write smart dialogue for TV, but we should remember that it started out as a parody of *The Wonder Years*, a sappy sitcom with "real" characters that revisited the 1950s and 1960s from the standpoint of a boy who wanted to know why nothing about his world—the "outside" world tattooed on his family's every gesture—made sense.

At the outset, in the first three years or so, *The Simpsons* reproduced this standpoint, watching a world turned inside out by the idiocies of parents and siblings—where seemingly private transgressions became public scandals, and vice versa, because no one could keep a secret or a job long enough to let some personal interiority develop, because everything was out there, everything was written on the surfaces of the population on screen. Then something happened, and Homer, the hapless father, replaced Bart, the cynical son, as the lead character of this perverse and yet productive homage to *Ozzie and Harriet*, the sitcom that ruled the airwaves in the 1950s, and *The Honeymooners*, another sitcom from the same period that deleted all the children—and all the furniture—to focus on the bizarre relation called matrimony.

In both *Ozzie and Harriet* and *The Honeymooners*, the nuclear family of the postwar suburbs and the outer boroughs is lampooned by watching as the leading man stumbles (Ozzie) or stomps (Ralph) through life without a clue as to what is happening inside or outside the home over which he is supposed to preside as husband. In the third or fourth season of *The Simpsons*, Homer became a hybrid of these "real" characters and the focus of the series, weekly addressing the questions raised at about the same time by Disney's *Toy Story I* and *II*, not to mention Susan Faludi's prize-winning book on the end of American manhood (*Stiffed: The Betrayal of the American Man* [1999]).

The familiar questions (we asked them in the last chapter) go like this: Where's Dad? What is his function here in this small tribe we call a family? Can I count on him? Or has he been downsized to the point of an endangered species? And if he has, what happens to the family as such? Then as now, father did not know best, but we kept asking the questions.

Where both *Toy Story I* and *II* tried to restore the father to his proper role at the head of the family—you can go back and read about these movies in chapter 4 of this book—and where Faludi (and many other writers) tried even harder to revive the ailing patriarch, *The Simpsons* says, enough already—we don't need fathers of the kind that haunt our familial imagination and keep us rowing, boats against the current, toward the place we never were. Groening & Co. tell us that families, those small tribes where the children try to grow up and the parents try, too, are hilarious, even ridiculous devices that do not need fathers who function as patriarchs. *The Family Guy* tells us the same thing, to be sure, and yet, as funny as it is—talk about surrealism—it is by now a parody of a parody: it's a copy of *The Simpsons*, but with no affection for the past that is reanimated by Homer, his family, his neighbors, and his employers in Springfield.

The Family Guy does erase the boundaries determined by realism. Just like *The Simpsons*, it does turn the world inside out by identifying the infant and the dog as the only believable, that is, reliable, narrators, and this in accordance with longstanding cartoon practice. Even so, it also erases the boundary between the past and the present, so the laughs it gets are cheaper than the ones Homer earns by inhabiting and reexamining the social roles he thinks he has inherited. The fathers in both families are impervious to the cartoon realities that surround them, but Homer is at least nostalgic for the past in which the breadwinner was the head of household.

Excremental Visions

South Park is a very different cartoon genre, although it certainly borrows from MTV—from, say, *Beavis and Butthead*. For its creators have gone to the extreme of animation and rendered every character as a little round cutout with eyes and a mouth, a circle that moves like a stage performer who is always face front, as if the world is a chorus line made of buttons. The differences between the figures on screen are made of voice and color and hats, so there's not much point in watching the "performance"; but if you listen in, you'll get the joke, especially when Chef, the black voice of authenticity, speaks (performed by the late Isaac Hayes, who made his bones writing music for blaxploitation movies in the 1970s and who hosted an R & B radio show for a New York radio station). So the extremity of this abstraction, this conscious abstention from the possibilities of visual representation in comics and cartoons—from the possibilities Disney and Pixar provided—makes *South Park* a kind of radio show, almost all sound. It's a television show for the blind.

But there's something happening here that is worth remarking, and its name is shit. This show is the most amazing study in anality since Jonathan Swift, or maybe Martin Luther, and it marks a moment in what we have come to know as globalization. We know that its creators are close readers of globalization because they made a feature-length movie, *Team America* (2004) using marionettes, the antirealist halfway point between film noir and Disney animation, to debunk the so-called war on terror and to ridicule the larger contours of U.S. foreign policy. We also know that they are obsessed with how the world elsewhere always intrudes on the small-town life of their cartoon population (in this they follow the lead of *The Simpsons*). But this intrusion is famously depicted as an anal probe from outer space organized by aliens who are always those oblong skulls that appear on guitar picks, cartoon figures we somehow recognize. That intrusion from elsewhere is also depicted as Father Christmas from the sewer, the Santa (scramble the letters and you get Satan) who makes the once-sacred holiday—when was that?—an excremental, that is, commercial, vacation from reality. And it is similarly depicted as a loquacious turd that gets its fifteen minutes of fame as the subject of an interview. Is it your imagination, or do the microphone and that piece of shit have the same shape?

Now, we could dismiss the scatological investments of *South Park* as the backward, frat-boy humor of the creators, who do, in fact, indulge every adolescent idiocy available to them. In other words, we could say that their indefatigable anality has nothing to do with the culture they interpret and nothing to do with their aesthetic purposes and results—it's something to be ignored or explained away, it's unimportant, it's just there. But what if they're onto something? What if their otherwise inexplicable popularity is, like Luther's, a function of a new anality determined and organized by the universalization of exchange value—of finance capital—we call globalization?

We can't answer the question without recourse to psychoanalysis. At any rate, our answers will be more interesting if we treat Freud as we did in the last chapter, while pondering the spectacle of male masochism at the movies—as a theorist of culture rather than a psychotherapist. Notice that in using psychoanalysis in this way, we are participating in as well as reporting on the intellectual history of the late twentieth century, when the macroeconomic materialism of Marx ("the economy is determining in the last instance") gave way to the bodily materialism of Freud. That was when the differences between males and females became a practical question because equality between males and females became a political purpose—when gender trouble and its attendant, an "imaginary femininity," reorganized our thinking about everything. At that moment, Freud's scandalous invention became an indispensable device in the tool kit of cultural criticism; for as Jacqueline Rose has observed, psychoanalysis "can in many ways be seen entirely in terms of its engagement with this question of feminine sexuality."

Psychoanalysis helps to decipher *South Park* and its cultural traction from a different (but related) angle on sexuality. Here Freud's general theory of sublimation and specific studies of "anal erotism" are immediately relevant and consistently productive. Sublimation happens, he argued, insofar as particular bodily experiences are repressed and translated into the more accessible symbolic resources made available by the culture at large. Words and less complicated visual icons are the crucial symbolic resources in this sense, for we situate ourselves in the world beyond our bodies by talking or writing (or drawing), by depicting and changing the world with words and icons that others can understand. We feel and communicate our original experiences as bodily states or desires because as infants we can make sounds, but we have no intelligible words or icons. We grow up, then, as we grow out of our bodies by means of linguistic abstractions—we sublimate and sanitize those original experiences as we rise above our bodies by replacing sounds with words and icons. But of course the body's urges always remain as ingredients in the mind's eye.

Money is the only symbolic resource that is comparable in scope to language. It is the universal commodity that works like a primal metaphor, thus allowing us to recognize and negotiate difference by equating unlike things (reducing a whole person, for example, to a bodily orifice, as in "he's a real asshole," or acknowledging the equivalent values of an expensive car and a cheap house). Psychoanalysis follows the lead of anthropology, however, in treating money not as the epitome of economic utility but as the extremity of irrationality. In Freud's terms, money is the sublimated, sanitized equivalent of shit. In other words, our desire for money—wealth in the abstract—is the enduring residue of the emotional attachment to excrement that comes with the anal-sadistic phase of infantile development, before the bodily sources of the child's sexual pleasure are "elevated" and confined to the genitals by the rigors of the Oedipus complex.

The child's feces are originally experienced and perceived as a detachable part of his body, as the first thing he can control with muscular effort and the first object he can give away, as a gift—by the same token, it is the first approximation of his property, a separate, tangible, and fungible asset he owns outright. No wonder anal erotism organizes his infantile being: his feces are the material evidence of his differentiation from himself and from the external world, but they also measure his mastery over his body, which is all the identity he knows. As he inevitably learns to rise above the bodily pleasures of playing with the fecal masses he produces, that is, as he sanitizes the urge to accumulate and allocate more of his own shit, he gradually transfers his emotional attachment to other separate, tangible, and fungible assets, like collectibles, coins, and eventually less solid forms of money.

By this accounting, the anal-sadistic urges are transhistorical dimensions of human being, but they remain as recessive symptoms of infantile development, as signs of childishness or deviance, until the advent of a money economy validates them as necessary, rational, even admirable character traits of adults. At that point, the anal-compulsive personality becomes normal; for when money mediates all social relations outside the family, no one can avoid the urge to accumulate—to abstain is to suffer poverty and social disgrace, perhaps even to starve to death.

Let us now restate the question that was the occasion for this methodological manifesto: What if the creators of South Park are onto something, what if their otherwise inexplicable popularity is, like Luther's, a function of a new anality determined and organized by the universalization of exchange value—of finance capital—we call globalization? What if the desublimation of money, which requires the return of the repressed infantile experience Freud named anal erotism, is both the means and the end of their cartoon abstractions?

In the sixteenth century Martin Luther explained that "money is the word of the Devil"—this Evil One was the modern Protestant version of the ancient and medieval Trickster—so that bondage to the new world of capitalism meant surrender to the demonic. The Devil and commodity fetishism always go together, as Norman O. Brown and Michael Taussig have more recently demonstrated. Like Luther, they also explained that since money was more or less excrement—in dreams and in archaic cultures, money always appears as some kind of shit—this surrender to the demonic was a way of dredging human beings in their own feces. If the world is ruled by the Devil, as Luther insisted it was, everyone is unclean. But the Protestants' revolt against the complacency of Catholicism—you'd better understand that your very soul is at risk, they kept saying, don't trust the priests—was also a way of making the anus the central organ of waking life, thus inverting Dante's specification of the afterlife, the last circle of Hell, where the worst sinners keep writhing in the Devil's asshole.

This new, angry attitude toward the demonic monetary forces of globalized capitalism is what the unconscious Protestantism of South Park accomplishes. We are all awash in our own feces, it tells us—suburban Americans are no less subject to the financial forces driving globalization than Mexican peasants—and in this sense the cartoon series is a primitive, antirealist rendition of Karen Finley's equally excremental vision of a world turned inside out. Neither *South Park* nor Finley is stuck in an anal stage of infantile development—neither are the rest of us in their audiences—no, we respond to their extreme anality because we can feel in our bodies, in our bones, the universalization of exchange value that goes by the name of globalization.

For there is no such thing as progress from one infantile stage of development to another; all of them remain as the residue of your individual reality, and each of them is differently elicited by the larger cultural reality. In the case of *South Park*, that larger reality is something we can all feel as a world reshaped by the mysterious, demonic, excremental forces of capitalism without borders. If everything has a price, no matter where you are on earth, then everything has turned to shit. No brand of authenticity is any longer available. The question *South Park* makes us ask is, so what? Darkness falls on our brightly painted suburbs—the excremental Other invades; "the blues moved in our town," as the Sopranos theme song puts it—but we're going to laugh about it anyway. This tragedy may well look like comedy before we're through. Keep watching, Cartman says, keep laughing. Maybe Chef will save you, too.

The questions that remain about *South Park* center on the allegorical function of the oracular Chef, the surreal voice of reason who is the only black character. Is he the Trickster whose advice makes no sense to the literal-minded children who attend the school where he cooks? Is he the demonstration of the demonic—the Trickster and the Devil are always linked, and their connection is always commerce—and if so, does that explain why he is black? Is he Br'er Rabbit's Tar Baby, that gooey, fecal mass, all grown up and growling at us? He looks and sounds like the Other, a voice from another time and place, but he's not one of those aliens from outer space. Where then does he come from? Does he represent the desublimation of money accomplished by the insistent anality of the series? Is he in this sense the figuration, the caricature, the shape, the presence, of globalization? Again, is that why he's black? Ask the question another way: If Bill Clinton was "the first black president," as Nobel Laureate Toni Morrison put it—he knew all those hymns by heart—is Chef the last racialized Other, the comedic version of the dream that has haunted the American imagination since 1607?

There are more questions to be asked about *South Park*, of course, and the even greater number of answers shouldn't end with yes or no. So let us now turn to other cartoons, always asking why every medium became less and less realistic toward the end of the twentieth century, when angels and vampires and seers and cyborgs convinced us that a "posthuman future" had arrived. That would be a future in which the borders between heaven and earth, mortality and immortality, life and death, machine and man, fact and fiction, or, for that matter, between human and animal, have somehow been erased. Miracles abounded back then, in keeping, perhaps, with the approach of the new millennium, with all its mechanical promises and technological horrors.

Apocalypse Now?

For example, Anne Rice became a best-selling author writing realistically, although always adverbially, about Lestat the vampire, who descended, somehow, from the ancient pharaohs of Egypt and hung out in modern-day New Orleans. Tim LaHaye, the evangelical firebrand, and his coauthor, Jerry B. Jenkins, a cheerful journeyman, meanwhile created a twelve-volume novel series called *Left Behind* (1995 and following), which has sold over fifty million copies. Here we begin with *The Rapture*, the end of days when Jesus yanks the righteous out of their seats, places them in heaven, and leaves the rest of us hardworking stiffs to fight the Antichrist over at the United Nations—in a reversal of a PG movie rating, everybody twelve and under gets to go to the fun place. This odd idea and its equally odd demographic become the Pentecostal premise for interminable dialogue about getting right with God.

The novel is clearly an attempt to reproduce the narrative antics of John Bunyan's great work of 1678, *The Pilgrim's Progress*, the most popular book among nineteenth-century Americans outside the Bible. *Left Behind* has a cast of thousands, however, led by the small, agile, middle-class Tribulation Force, the faithful, fanatical A-Team that finally leads everyone to the promised land of life as death, the place where you go to die so you can meet your maker and reunite with your family. But unlike the filthy, funny Protestantism perfected by John Bunyan—a big fan of Luther—in *The Pilgrim's Progress* and again on angry display in *South Park*, this urgent and yet boring, fiction is all dressed up with no place to go.

For in the postironic world of *Left Behind*, everybody has to "earn his salvation" and thus teach us how to get back to the discipline of real work—it's the fictional, evangelical equivalent of Newt Gingrich's "Contract for America," the manifesto that brought the Republicans back to power in 1994, at least in the Congress, by insisting on a transparent relation between effort and reward or, alternatively, between crime and punishment (this is also how *Law & Order*, the Nixon slogan of 1968 and the Dick Wolf TV franchise, got revived, first as farce, again as tragedy).

And then there is *Buffy the Vampire Slayer*, the cult classic of 1990s TV, a show written, produced, directed, and otherwise managed by Joss Whedon, who was the screenwriter for the movie of the same name that bombed in 1992. Irony abounds in these televised parts because Whedon wants to know why good and evil are so thoroughly imbricated, so constantly entwined—why and how they wear the same face. In his narrative neighborhood, on the other side of town from Mr. Rogers, the vampires are as clueless and hilarious as the worried high school (then college) students who arm themselves to fight the products of the "Hellmouth" underneath good old Sunnydale, California. Notice that the demonic rules this world, just as Luther claimed it did. You can't escape evil because you're always already part of it, Whedon insists, but you can fight it without being a conscientious parent or a principled counselor or a crusading principal.

You don't have to be a well-educated adult or someone who can afford good books and good works, in other words; you just have to know that you can't abstain from this struggle. You're up to your ears in the stinking effluvia of life on earth, mingling every day with insufferable assholes. It is a very Protestant position in the old-fashioned, excremental, Lutheran sense. So it is no accident that the Trickster in the famously operatic episode of the last season—it's all song and dance, and it explains how Buffy's friends unknowingly retrieved her not from death but from heaven, thus returning her to hell on earth, the world ruled by the Devil—is a well-dressed black man with horns. This correlation is not racism in action, not any more than Chef is the blackface echo of minstrelsy in *South Park*. It is instead the condensation of modern cultural history since Luther, which reminds us that when the Trickster who is the Devil makes the contracts, we must make the payments. Your money or your life, he keeps saying. Either way, you lose because everything has turned to shit—that is, to money. Everything is now a moment in the impossibly complex cultural system we call globalization, for everything is part of its price system. And maybe that's not such a bad thing—maybe it's a good thing. Maybe our attempted abstentions from the commodity form and consumer culture are worse than pointless.

But the series has a postmodern edge because it contemplates the impending catastrophe that is our posthuman future. What if we can live forever, like vampires Whedon asks—and why shouldn't he, in view of cloning, artificial insemination, and the rest of the big science that will soon make us immortal? What then? Does a life that stretches across centuries, not mere decades, accrue meanings not available to us mere mortals? His answer is No, in thunder, like Hawthorne's as Melville once heard it. Whedon's vampires are desperate to return to the state of longing we call human nature, where we hope for the embodiment of our love, where we hope to commit ourselves to someone who will outlive us—a child perhaps—and to devote ourselves to some cause that will outlast us. For him, such hope for an ending is the reason to write, and it is also what drives his vampires back toward the finitude of human nature we call this mortal coil.

What does the Slayer teach us, then? Buffy teaches us, first, that the fear or the love of nonhuman forms of life is another way of hoping. It's like the fear or the love of God, only better, because it requires the fear and the love of your neighbor, the vampire, who can get pretty ugly and pretty angry if provoked. The Golden Rule that culminates in the Declaration of Independence ("all men are created equal") now scans the horizon of sentient beings who might not be human: they might be animals, they might be cyborgs, they might be vampires; they're not anything like you, but you should be paying attention, and they may be your equal. Do unto others as you would have them do unto you, that it's the rule. But now the Others are not your kind, so be careful.

She teaches us, second, that women are extraordinary athletes who need a coach (*The Watcher*) but not a father or a husband, not even when the coach wants to graduate to fatherhood, as Giles, the Watcher, so poignantly does. Title IX is clearly at work in Buffy's extracurricular activities—this federal statute creating equity in school funding for women's athletics must be the origin of her mandate—because everyone knows her skills are superior but everyone also knows that exterminating all those dangerous creatures is a team sport.

She teaches us, third, that a girlish infatuation with the bad boy and the class clown and the most valuable player—he's the matriculated vampire—could be deadly; indeed it could destroy civilization, so maybe the girls should get over this kind of high school attachment, maybe get with the nerds, or maybe just give up on boys altogether, as Willow, Buffy's best friend, learns to do by becoming a lesbian. And finally, she teaches us, season after weary season, that there's no way beyond this tedious world with all its tiresome, almost rural idiocy. Big science surrounds us, superheroes are among us, but we won't get out alive. Maybe the vampires will survive the fire next time. The rest of us will be dead, sooner or later, and that is probably a good thing because the uniquely human knowledge of impending death—we're all waiting to die, we just don't know how it will happen—keeps us thinking about what should endure when we're gone. If you're immortal, you can't care that much about what will last among human beings because you know that all of it will decay and that you'll always be there to watch it die. If you're not immortal, these things matter.

The Limit of Realism

Now the question becomes, what accounts for this outbreak of antirealist television toward the end of the twentieth century—a visual world in which not even the law of gravity holds, in which the chosen one, the Slayer, is a woman? What explains the increasingly cartoonish quality of American culture? Stupidity, some say, derived from a lack of good books and rigorous education, which results in an inability to understand the real world as it exists. Others say, no, it's not stupidity, it's the need to escape a real world constituted by inequality, imperialism, and war: we need entertaining diversions from the gross realities of our time. Either way, the real world looks like an inert, external thing rather than a prospect, a horizon of expectation, created by the discourse—the words and images—of TV.

There is a better answer residing in the American literary/artistic tradition, which has always resisted realism, the urge to photograph the world as if the camera has no bearer. Or, rather, that tradition, from Charles Brockden Brown to Toni Morrison, from Marsden Hartley and Stuart Davis to Will Eisner, has always tried to include Gothic and romance forms, and commercial vernaculars, in the reproduction of the real—and this attempted inclusion still happens in visual media like TV and motion pictures as well as novels. For example, speaking of novels, it happens in Don DeLillo's *White Noise* (1985), which convinces us that the only reality worth thinking about is the thinking we do about reality; and in William Gibson's *Neuromancer* (1984), which convinces us that our bodies are not our selves; and in Toni Morrison's *Beloved* (1987), which convinces us that ghosts are always gathering to remind us of what we'd better not forget. Realism has never been the mainstream here, not even when William Dean Howells and Mark Twain were the twin pillars of the literary establishment in the late nineteenth century, not even when Ernest Hemingway tried to reinvent it in 1926 with *The Sun Also Rises*.

There is no adequate designation for this antirealist tradition. Some might call it literary naturalism, but the naturalists themselves, for example Frank Norris and Theodore Dreiser, knew they were drawing on the romance forms perfected by the American Renaissance of the 1850s (Hawthorne's "castles in the air"). Some might call it the North American version of "magical realism," the Latin American genre perfected by Gabriel García Márquez, in which realist specifications of time, space, cause, and effect become irrelevant to the telling of the story. But let's just call it natural supernaturalism, following M. H. Abrams, without reducing or equating it, as he does, to romanticism. Then we can see that all those angels congregating in late-twentieth-century America, not to mention the demons and the vampires, are figures capable of reminding us of the possibility of redemption—they are a way of telling us that we have good reasons to hope rather than retreat. Like the love-struck angel played by Cary Grant in *The Bishop's Wife*, a movie of 1947, or by Nicholas Cage in *City of Angels*, a movie of 1999, they are a way of telling us that this life, in this body, right here and now, is not probation for an otherworldly heaven. It's all we've got.

The world elsewhere is close by, so be patient, they all say. If you watch carefully, they say, you might see that heaven and earth, God and Man, are not that far apart. Certainly Tony Kushner, the avowed Marxist who won the Pulitzer Prize in 1993 for *Angels in America*, his two-part allegory about HIV/AIDS, said so. In this theatrical, postrealist world—it made it to TV thirteen years later in a highbrow production directed by Mike Nichols—the sacred and the profane are inseparable, and everyone is redeemable, even Joe McCarthy's monstrous sidekick. But if that is true, if Kushner is right, if faith and love are active dimensions of our everyday lives, then even a world teeming with monsters becomes a more malleable place. That is the principle of hope kept alive by the strange allegories of late-twentieth-century television—in the cartoon universe of Springfield and in the "as if" suburb of Sunnydale.

Musical Endings

The same principle also abides in the music of that end-of-century moment, from disco to punk to heavy metal, on toward the hip-hop nation. Even country music got more edgy, more angry, back then in the 1980s and 1990s, as it became the mainstream of American music as such, at least on the radio.

There's an American music as such? Isn't that something like positing an American culture rather than an ethnocultural riot of difference? The answer to both questions is yes. American music was born in the brutal collision of European and African forms as mediated and modified by Caribbean styles. It was always an Atlantic hybrid being passed along from slaves to planters to Scots-Irish yeomen, and then back again, creating a circle of culture that we call either the blues or country music. The basis of almost all African and Celtic music was the pentatonic scale that reduced the classical seven-note scale to five notes—so the slaves and the Scots-Irish of the antebellum South always had something in common. By the 1920s, the hybrid noises built on this scale were sorting themselves into what we now hear as black and white, as the blues and country music, when the blues moved toward a minor key version of the pentatonic by adding intermediate notes that were neither major nor minor and when country music left the minor keys behind.

Rock and roll was supposedly the reunion of these musics, but the blues as such makes a point of blurring the distinction between minor and major keys—those "blue notes" are neither/nor—so it's always audible in country as well as rock. The difference between these two genres is by now only lyrical. But the blues has endured as the foundation of twentieth-century American music by forging the template of a secular, commercial, improvisational dance music. The blues, like every other American music, specializes in transformation by repetition, by singing the same thing over and over again, only differently. It borrows the European tonal-harmonic structure of I-IV-V, root, tonic, subtonic, and so on—blues in the key of E normally goes E, A, B—but it superimposes an African sound, the pentatonic scale and a call-and-response pattern, on this basic structure. In doing so, the blues makes the color line audible but also moveable. It enunciates the difference between Europe and Africa but doesn't leave it at that; both aural regions are changed by the mixture of their musical conventions.

For example, the blues guitar is always answering the stated chord, sometimes with a pentatonic "fill" that complicates the sound of the fading chord, sometimes with a lead that completes (or challenges) the melody heard in the vocal. The second verse in a twelve-bar blues is almost always an answer to the first because it repeats the words but usually changes the chord—it sounds different, so it is different, even though it's an exact lyrical repetition of what has come before. The third verse is typically a response to the first two, which changes their original meanings by converting the tragedy marked there into comedy, by converting despair to hope. "It has optimism that's not naïve," as Wynton Marsalis, a student of Albert Murray, puts it. "You accept tragedy and move forward." The tonal-harmonic tension created by playing the V chord is resolved by the return to the root (the I chord), but that musical resolution is both amplified and questioned by the lyrical conclusion.

The foundational American music is, then, the exemplar of what Harold Cruse called "a black aesthetic" and what he defined as the real promise of American culture. The "Negro group," as he named it, from which this aesthetic sprang was, however, a hybrid of European, African, and Indian strains, so it contained most of America as such. Its music—our music, America's music—was, and is, secular, commercial, and technologically driven. In the twentieth century, it was never a folk music produced by people who could afford to stand outside the market and play for fun. Its habitat was the club or the street, not the church, and, then as now, it thrived on the mechanical reproduction permitted by the phonograph and the records the machine could play. It was always electric, even before T-Bone Walker hooked his guitar up to an amplifier in 1939—recording technology required microphones as well as phonographs in the 1920s. So this technology was not a formal apparatus that was somehow external to the music; instead, it infused the sound, it determined the content of the music we now take for granted.

American music in the twentieth century is, then, always a commercial, technological phenomenon, but it comes and goes—rock and roll, for example, died out between 1958 and 1963—and when it returns it usually arrives as the renewal of rhythm, timbre, voice, and dance, in other words, as a restatement of the black aesthetic. Disco, in these terms, did not announce the death of American music, by then codified as rock and roll, but rather the early, awkward sign of its rebirth. In the early to mid-1970s, rock had become esoteric, even enervating FM music, all soaring lyrics and poetic effects. It meandered so earnestly through major scales and masculine themes that it got boring.

Disco cured us of this affliction by returning us to the dance floor—that is, by making rhythm the central element of the music and by restoring sexuality to its proper place in American music as such. But this time around, heterosexuality was in question. Disco was the music of a new, more open, more playful gay America, and everybody understood that, especially the yahoos who gathered to burn records in defense of "real" rock and roll at Comiskey Park, on the South Side of Chicago, in 1977. Disco propelled Michael Jackson's early solo career in part because it restored rhythm and dance—movement and style—to the foreground of song, in part because we knew as we watched him that there was a new identity in the making here, something neither black nor white, maybe even something neither male nor female. MTV's videos helped, of course, but our assumption that dance is an integral part of the singer's performance, which we now take for granted unless we're listening to Tony Bennett or Johnny Cash, owes everything to the rise and fall of disco in the 1970s and 1980s.

Punk rock was another kind of restoration. Its urgent attempt to get back to the doctrines and the practices and the attitudes of the founders—this ain't rocket science, this is three-chord rockabilly!—produced a brand new music, just as the Protestants' urgent attempt to get back to their roots produced a brand new theology. Unlike disco, the pretend simplicity of punk, particularly the British version, often sounded angrily masculine, and so its gender-bending functions were disguised unless you saw the performers in action or saw the picture of the band on the album cover. Then you knew this music was dangerous.

One of the telltale signs of the impending danger is the simple fact that three women are the memorable "front men" of punk rock in the 1970s—Deborah Harry of Blondie, Chrissie Hynde of The Pretenders, and Patti Smith, the hypochondriac poet turned muse for Robert Mappelthorpe. Not to mention the material girl, Madonna, who kept refusing any version of authenticity and, as a result, kept us wondering about our own identities. She wasn't exactly a punk rocker, to be sure, but she bent the music of the 1980s and 1990s with her "feminine endings," as Susan McClary puts it—Madonna's songs, which she was typically a cowriter, were "about staying in motion for the sake of survival," always suspending or delaying tonal-harmonic resolution.

Another telltale sign of the danger—the gender trouble—that punk brought to our world was the New York Dolls, a leering, androgynous, trash-rock, glam band with remarkable musical knowledge, background, and skills. In high heels. This band took over the Manhattan music scene in the early 1970s and became the touchstone of punk rock for the rest of the century. Like the Ramones, but unlike the Clash, the Dolls embodied the future of rock and roll, the future in which authenticity became obsolete. As a contemporary journalist wrote in *Crawdaddy*, a lowbrow magazine about popular music, "While these groups and their fans on this burgeoning scene profess to be parodying or 'camping on' various sexual styles (bisexuality, transvestitism, sadomasochism), it is difficult to say where affectation ends and reality begins." Indeed. The world was turning inside out as male and female traded places and hard rock began to look softer—or at least more feminine in its appearance, its performance.

Another indication that gender trouble was the regnant mode of musical arrangement at the end of the twentieth century is, of all things, heavy metal, a genre supposed to be by, for, and about angry white men who have enough stamina to hoist huge triangular guitars and scream for hours about evil, suicide, and such, meanwhile watching as large male bodies pass through the mosh pit, pointing themselves toward deliverance. In fact, metal was, like punk, a stage for experimentation with the newly various meanings of masculinity in terms of dress, style, voice, and sound. The great difference between the two genres was not the increasingly insistent androgyny of the performers, from Ozzy Osbourne to Poison to White Snake and, yes, Kiss, all in high heels and mascara like the New York Dolls—Robert Plant, Iggy Pop, and David Bowie sported very similar wardrobes in the 1970s—no, the great difference was heavy metal's self-conscious reanimation of classical music, even of Bach, and its consequent departure from the blues idiom of other popular American musics.

To be sure, Eddie Van Halen and Randy Rhoades were admirers of the blues and always used it as a point of departure, but their guitar work, which inspired a whole generation of heavy metal musicians, was based on classical modes, sequences, riffs, and virtuosity. The very sound of metal, as it constantly sinks into the dark Aeolian mode and the Baroque note cycles it copies, amplifies, and distorts, is, as Robert Walser explains, "archaic, directional, and thus fateful." The unfamiliar harmonic progression (it typically goes VI-VII-I as against I-IV-V) prepares us for a resolution that we expect but may not want; it produces a sexual politics that is at least risky. For in heavy metal, you can hear the ending of the era of the ego—if you listen closely enough, you may even hear the end of male supremacy.

Hip-Hop Nation

But the signature sound of the end of the twentieth century was, as we all know, hip-hop, from the Sugar Hill Gang to NWA to Ice-T and on unto P. Diddy and Queen Latifah. Everyone listened in as urban renewal became the project of the objects, the goal of the ghetto itself, not the program of the local government—that is, as young black men and women decided to reinvent their lives, their streets, their neighborhoods, and their nation through music, dance, clothes, and, not least, subway graffiti. As Tricia Rose put it long ago, "hip hop style *is* black urban renewal," national liberation from the bottom up. The South Bronx, once the scene on which Ronald Reagan could compare this part of the United States to a ravaged Third World country, pulled itself up by its own musical bootstraps and changed America as well as every other place on the planet.

It wasn't just Public Enemy that had a more or less nationalist agenda of racial solidarity and suspicion of the powers that be (particularly the police). All rappers appealed to the same "Cop Killer" code that Ice-T perfected in 1992 because they knew that a colonized people, no matter where it is found, must try to protect its own with the weapons at hand—as Malcolm X always said. They also knew that parity between the races could be a function of cultural segregation rather than a result of equal rights for individuals regardless of race, as Booker T. Washington, Marcus Garvey (a favorite of The Last Poets, who were the inspiration for Chuck D. of Public Enemy), and, yes, even W. E. B. DuBois proposed. In this sense, S. H. Fernando Jr. is right to insist in *The New Beats* (1994) that hip-hop culture signifies the "rebirth of a Nation."

But whose nation? Why do white boys from the suburbs dig this music, and how did they make it the mainstream of American culture if it's the chorus of a black nation? Good questions. Here are some tentative answers. It's a music of decolonization, a way of asserting the black aesthetic as the voice of the nation as a whole, just as the Harlem Renaissance of the 1920s could be the anthem of the "New Negro" and the fulfillment of the promise of American life as such. That aesthetic and that promise are neither black nor white, so the nation conjured by the music can be inhabited and honored by anybody, of any race, just like the Fourteenth Amendment says. If the black aesthetic speaks to and for all of us, our country has finally come of age. Perhaps it came of age in the 1990s, when Michael Jordan's aesthetic changed the way basketball got played and perceived, when five black starters became commonplace in the NBA, even as its TV audience swelled, and when the Chicago Bulls became America's team.

Hip-hop is also an answer to the downsizing of Dad, a way of reasserting, restating, and reconfiguring masculinity—or manhood. Andrew Ross has explained how this musical debate works. On the one hand, we hear the falsetto tones of the Motown ballads in which apologies and pledges organize a fragile, possibly equal relation between males and females and, on the other hand, we hear the strident bass lines and angry vocals of hip-hop, which reorganize this sexual relation as hierarchy, as male supremacy personified by the Gangsta. But not quite supremacy—the Gangsta was, and is, both an appreciation and an exaggeration of the new anxieties attached to the meanings of manhood at the end of the twentieth century.

When William James worried in "The Moral Equivalent of War" (1910) about how to reinstate the "masculine virtues" in the presence of structural unemployment and the absence of real work, and, not incidentally, in the face of impending world war—violence on a scale never seen—nobody accused him of ignorance. Nor should we accuse the early rappers of ignoring the reality of their neighborhoods, of tarrying too long with the negative, of worrying too much about the fate of black manhood. They had good reasons to fear the future, just as James did, but they reasoned in music. Their reasoning still makes sense.

The age of hip-hop is, after all, the age of the "war on drugs," which created incarceration rates in the United States higher than any other so-called developed country and which not incidentally, put almost one in every five black men in jail, even as rates of violent crime plummeted in the 1990s. The filmic gangster was born in the 1920s as the early war on drugs called Prohibition got started, and he matured very early in the 1930s, in the astonishing characterizations of Edward G. Robinson (*Little Caesar*), James Cagney (*Public Enemy*), and Paul Muni (*Scarface*). Like the sonic Gangsta of rap music, he was a meditation on the kind of manhood available to American males who had no recognizable function, no place in the mode of production authorized by the law and the government. Unlike the hero of Western movies, however, that strong, silent type who talks mainly to the horse, the early gangster couldn't stay still and wouldn't be quiet—he would not wait for redemption. He was determined to disturb you.

So, too, will the sonic Gangsta of hip-hop, the man who makes his own laws in homage to the Corleone family of *The Godfather*. But look at the hip-hop nation's heir apparent in Brian De Palma's remake of *Scarface* (1983)—he speaks broken English, but he's clearly Michael Corleone reborn as a Cuban refugee—and what you see is an Oedipal drama in which the son is cast as the father, the immigrant original. It's as if we have've been invited to a remake of *The Godfather, Part 2*, but Marlon Brando and Robert DeNiro have somehow been replaced (erased?) by Al Pacino. The patrimonial succession, the generational order of things that made sense even in the violent world of *The Godfather*, has somehow been disturbed by the insertion of the new immigrant from an inarticulate elsewhere, from outside the United States: this man is foreign, and yet familiar; he turns the world inside out just by going about his business. Like the first Tony Carmonte (Paul Muni), who also seemed to come from another world, this man can't stay still, he won't be quiet, and he is not waiting for redemption.

As a later would-be Gangsta, 50 Cent, put it, he's going to "get rich or die trying." He's the embodiment of the American Dream: he's breaking the rules out on the new frontier of the inner city; he's outside the law, but he loves his country; he wants a family, and he can provide for it. So the sonic Gangsta of hip-hop is the transformation by repetition of the filmic gangster who got his start in 1931, just as Brian De Palma's *Scarface* is the transformation by repetition of Tony Carmonte's career. Sexuality, masculinity, and the meaning of success on the American scene are crucial issues in every rendition of this man on the make. For him, manhood is always in question, or, rather, a question that has no definitive answer.

Hip-hop completes, or at least consolidates, the black aesthetic—and thus the American nation—in three other ways. First, it amplifies the imperative of transformation by repetition. It constantly "samples," that is, it treats already recorded phrases as the raw materials of its compositional urge by removing them from their original contexts so that you are forced to recognize the old even as you hear the new; the original is not displaced, but it acquires a new function, a new meaning, in its new musical setting. The either/or choice between past and present, between previous truth and novel fact, is thereby adjourned—precedent is honored by its incorporation in the sound being produced right now, in this improvisational moment but it is also changed by its insertion in that sound. Second, hip-hop returns us to the dance floor by reinstating rhythm, timbre, timing, rhyme, and style as the key elements of American music as such. This restoration is more important than it may seem at first glance. For it transformed every genre, even country, as its propulsive beats became the bottom line of popular music.

Third, and most important, hip-hop reminds us that recording technology is the content, not merely the form, of modern American music. It is the culmination of the age of mechanical reproduction, as Walter Benjamin named the twentieth century. Rap music is the culmination of that historical moment when reproducibility became constitutive of the work of art—think of film, ask yourself, where's the original? and then try, who's the author?—and when machines made it hard to distinguish between the producer and the consumer of the work. Hip-hop is unimaginable in the absence of the microphone, the turntables, and the vinyl, the apparatus of twentieth-century American music. These devices are not mere vehicles for delivering a certain sound that could exist outside of them; they determine the sound itself—that scratching sound is just noise, except now it functions as a manic rhythm section. Again, the technology is the content of the music, not merely its electric form.

The dissolution of the distinction between producer and consumer of such industrialized music derives from the same recording technology. Rappers compose by listening, they produce by consuming, that is, by placing already recorded music in new settings, making it new by resituating it, by amplifying it, by changing its place in the scheme of things. In this sense, they are members of the intellectual avant-garde that forced us, at the end of the twentieth century, to question the difference between active subject (the producer) and passive object (the consumer)—just like the poststructuralist and postmodernist professors did. Again, the rappers reasoned in music, but as a result their cultural effect has been greater than that of the professors.

The Technology of Desire

The technological sources of this cultural effect—that is, the adjournment of the subject-object distinction that has animated Western philosophy since Plato and his footnotes—cannot be exaggerated. Not that technology is a set of inert machines, mere matter absent human purpose or presence, which somehow causes cultural change, as if Louis Althusser, an influential French theorist of the 1970s, had returned from the grave to refurbish the vulgar Marxist notion of base/superstructure (economy/ideology). No, technology is a social movement, a social process, through which we express ourselves in material realities and come to know ourselves in that embodiment of our mostly irrational purposes. Charles Peirce, the original pragmatist, got it right in 1893: "Matter is effete mind, inveterate habits becoming physical laws." Or as Donna Haraway put it more recently in her *Manifesto for Cyborgs* (1986), "It is not clear who makes and who is made in the relation between human and machine."

Haraway's bass line was her constant citation of "high-tech culture." She was pretty sure that it had displaced all the dualisms (e.g., subject/object, mind/body) invented by Western civilization, which, as the deconstruction-ists always insisted (see chapter 3), reinforced hierarchy among humans. Here is how she put it in that bizarre and profound manifesto: "To recapitu-late, certain dualisms have been persistent in western traditions; they have all been systemic to the logics and practices of domination of women, people of colour, nature, workers, animals—in short, domination of all constructed as others, whose task is to mirror the [white man's] self. Chief among these troubling dualism are self/other, mind/body, culture/nature, male/female, civilized/primitive, reality/appearance, whole/part, agent/resource, maker/made, active/passive, right/wrong, total/partial, God/man. . . . High-tech culture challenges these dualisms in intriguing ways."

But what exactly is high-tech culture? We all experience it, every day and almost every hour, as we sit at our "personal" computers looking up the most esoteric information, even Googling ourselves from time to time, or watching cable TV via satellite, or visiting the ATM down the block, or text-messaging on our cell phones. We write and receive e-mail, we're surprised when someone we know calls us on the land line—that thing is for fund-raisers—and we take for granted the extreme abstraction called the Internet, the once-distant geography of cyberspace.

We should remember, however, that it was only toward the end of the twentieth century that we could begin to inhabit or apprehend the whole world in this way, as something close by, not next door but right there in the room with us, bright, blaring, invasive. We did not have to experience that invasion as an anal probe or as the Tar Baby from hell, to be sure, but we knew it was something that was having an effect on our interiors. The "personal" computer was then, and is now, the technology of globalization, just as it is the device that forced us to confront, or clarify, or adjourn the difference between machines and men, outside and inside, them and us. In the next chapter, we'll get to the foreign policy implications of these newly imagined differences. For now, let us ask how computers changed the way we think about, and feel in, the world that is no longer elsewhere.

Once upon a time, a computer was a huge machine housed at the Pen-tagon or IBM; it filled entire rooms, it spit out millions of perforated cards that were not supposed to be bent, folded, or mutilated on pain of death; it counted everything except your calories. And then, that big, imposing, quasi-public thing became "personal," by way of Texas Instruments, Apple, Microsoft, and other strange companies, in the 1980s. So almost everybody went out and bought a computer and a printer (it usually weighed about eighty pounds) and started word processing. "Electronic mail," once the property (also the invention) of U.S. intelligence agencies and the Defense Department, meanwhile became available to the declassified among us, causing local epistolary outbreaks of sincere and useless prose, all of which will someday be understood as the inarticulate beginnings of the blogosphere. Then, in the last decade of the twentieth century, e-mail became the norm of interpersonal communication. By 1998, words printed on paper and delivered in an envelope began to look either quaint or threatening—it was probably a phone bill.

How then did the personal computer and cyberspace change us? In at least three ways. First, as Richard Lanham has brilliantly demonstrated, they reunite words and images, sound and color, and thus revolutionize what he calls the "economics of attention." Like comics, cartoons, and movies, they move us away from the attitude of "sensory denial" that makes us read the book for the ending and search the author for his intention—the attitude in which we are always trying to look through the style and the rhetoric to get at the substance buried somewhere else, under layers of the annoying ornament we know as language. In that sense, the cultural effect of computers is comparable to the graffiti that adorned the surfaces of New York subway cars in the 1970s, for both create a new "alphabet that thinks," or, rather, a set of letters—every one another abstraction—that makes us think differently about the purposes of words, which are already icons.

Now we can look *at* the performers as well, as if style, movement, rhythm, timbre, and grace matter as much as the words they utter or sing—again, as if the form they adopt determines as well as reveals the content of what we can see and hear when they perform. On the laptop in the airport, Surfaces R Us. If you want to go deeper, that's fine; just remember that your computer and its artificial intelligence have made the distinction between surface and depth, or outside and inside, or machine and man, or style and substance problematic. This technological effect has the same import as the poststructuralist urge in academia to dispense with "the" subject who was the "man of reason" in the era of the ego.

Second, the personal computer disperses power, it lets us all participate in the debates of our time, and it makes electoral politics almost an afterthought, a footnote to the blogosphere. Cultural and identity politics become the norm, so the goal of political activism is no longer to rewrite the party platform but to rethink subjectivity itself. The demographic decline of the three TV networks that once organized political discourse became almost pathetic in the 1990s, but meanwhile, "news," understood as both means and end—in the newsroom you now report on the reporting of events and on the reporters themselves—became much more important at the end of the twentieth century. Cable television had emerged from obscurity, probably because all those retired folks who watched Dan Rather on CBS could not wait for the next word on the weather in the middle of the day, when they were contemplating the possibilities of a walk with the dog or the spouse.

Meanwhile the Internet had also emerged as a constant stream of information, news of a kind, to which you could respond, not merely watch. The democratic, interactive character of these developments should not be exaggerated. But neither should it be dismissed. Newspapers as such are now in deep financial trouble, in part because almost everyone gets his or her daily reports on the world from elsewhere: "online," in a space that can't be inhabited except virtually, marginally, anonymously, and also urgently, in a "place" where sentences matter more than they do on the printed page, a place where sounds, motion, and images have both changed and enhanced the significance of words.

Third, orality, literacy, and the larger sensory regime in which these capacities of communication get stored and developed are transformed by our deployment of the computer's artificial intelligence. Once upon a time, knowledge was stored and transmitted in song, in epic verse, in stories, in gossip, because the people who could read and write were few and far between—they were priests, scribes, monks, men who claimed exemption from the necessities of this world. Mass communication happened in speech or song or not at all (and this is why rhetorical or musical skill was so important). Then the codex book came along, and everything changed—well, almost. Everybody started reading the Bible in the sixteenth and seventeenth centuries, or tried to, but until the end of the eighteenth century, speech and song were still the media in which knowledge was conveyed and stored.

Now, if speech and song are knowledge as such, then reciprocity is the rule. You'd better be listening closely and responding physically to the sounds and the gestures of the person who's talking or singing. Either you situate yourself in a relationship to the speaker or the singer, or you are ignorant. Hearing was more important than seeing under this sensory regime. But when the printed word—the codex book, the pamphlet, and the newspaper—became the principal means of conveying and storing knowledge, the sense of sight attained a new privilege, a new command, over all others and reorganized them accordingly (note that our bodies, our selves, were thus changed). This new sensory regime made distance and withdrawal from others—from the objects of our scrutiny—both possible and necessary. It enabled modern individualism.

The personal computer allows abstraction, just like cartoons, but it troubles, and perhaps disables, modern individualism. Here's how. It restores sound and lets us, even forces us, to respond to the more complicated, reciprocal world where we can hear those voices and see those simultaneous responses that disappeared into the codex book. It completes cartoons and comics; it is video when you want it and feedback when you don't , but the sound track is, in this sense, always present, always audible. That new, computerized "orality"—the word comes from Walter Ong, the great scholar of literacy—makes a social, public self more available, more plausible to users of the Internet than it can be to advocates of the codex book. So it complicates the meaning of individualism; it promotes a social self as against the private self that is prior to society, language, political traditions, or communities. As Will Eisner noticed in 1985, "Historically, technology has always had the effect of expanding the artists' reach while challenging their individuality. With the arrival of machines (computers) capable of generating artwork, rather than simply reproducing it, came a new impact on individuality." At least the personal computer keeps us moving between the opposite extremes of individualism, one private and the other public—it keeps us guessing as to where the boundary between them lies. It keeps us toggling, as Lanham puts it.

In these terms, the "personal" computer is anything but. It allows anyone an identity that can be anonymous and yet perceptible so that the performance of the self on screen is its only significance—the doer behind the deed or prior to the sentences and the sounds is irrelevant to understanding the deed, the sentences, and the sounds. Those nicknames, or "handles," that everybody adopts are enactments of this performative principle; they say, "As I speak in this voice and this venue, I step outside myself, but as I do I make myself by asking you to recognize me as the sum of my affect and my utterance, not my origins." In these terms, the personal computer is the physical, palpable, technological embodiment of the intellectual innovations specific to the late twentieth century, when Friedrich Nietzsche's rendition of the end of modernity became commonplace—when the "man of reason" passed away. And in its insanely various and strangely productive usages, we might detect the revolution that is contained, in both the inclusive and the exclusive sense, by American thought and culture at the end of the twentieth century.

Steamboat Willie. The first incarnation of Mickey Mouse, just a line drawing in motion. As Mickey fleshed out, so did the backgrounds, until his world looked as real as ours. Source: *Walt Disney Pictures/Photofest.*

Angels in America. *The Prior Walter Benjamin's Angel of History, played by Emma Thompson in the highbrow PBS production of* Angels in America, *Tony Kushner's Pulitzer Prize-winning "Gay Fantasia," a two-part allegory of HIV as a modern plague. Is she facing backward when she addresses the audience?* Source: *HBO/Photofest.*

Buffy the Vampire Slayer. *In Joss Whedon's narrative neighborhood, on the other side of town from Mr. Rogers, Buffy teaches us that there's no way beyond this tedious world with all its tiresome, almost rural idiocy. Big science surrounds us, superheroes are among us, but we won't not get out alive. Maybe the vampires will survive the fire next time; the rest of us will be dead, and that is a good thing.* Source: The WB/Photofest.

Bugs Bunny. Clearly a new version of the Trickster who permeated African American folklore. Did we know, somehow, that he announced the advent of a new racial regime in which the silly, sometimes angry white man with the gun would finally be outsmarted? Or did we see a cartoon version of Clark Gable, the fast-talking, carrot-chomping hero of It Happened One Night? *Source:* Warner Bros./Photofest.

Donna Summer. She worked hard for the money, honey. Like funk, disco signaled the renewal, not the demise, of American popular music by returning us to the dance floor and making rhythm tracks the central element in the musical scene. It also did so by expressing and advertising a new, more open gay culture. Source: *Photofest.*

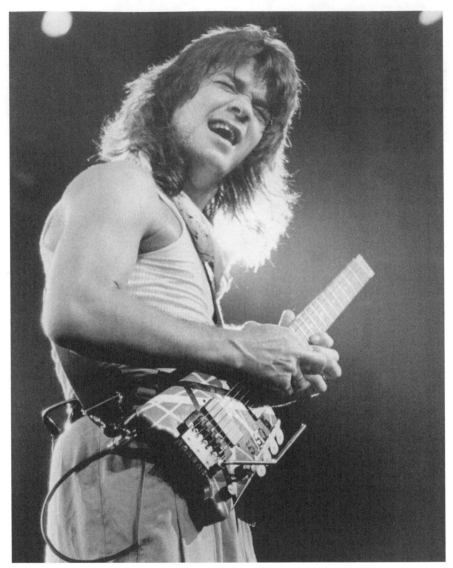

Eddie Van Halen. The rock star as virtuoso steeped in classical music. Another indication that gender trouble was the regnant mode of musical arrangement at the end of the twentieth century was, of all things, heavy metal, a genre supposed to be by, for, and about angry white men who have enough stamina to hoist huge triangular guitars and scream for hours about evil, death, suicide, and such. Source: *Photofest.*

THIS WOMAN HAS JUST
CUT, CHOPPED, BROKEN, and BURNED
FIVE MEN BEYOND RECOGNITION...

BUT NO JURY
IN AMERICA
WOULD EVER
CONVICT HER!

I SPIT ON YOUR GRAVE

...AN ACT OF
REVENGE!

JERRY GROSS presents "I SPIT ON YOUR GRAVE"
A CINEMAGIC PICTURES PRODUCTION
A MEIR ZARCHI FILM
starring
CAMILLE KEATON · ERON TABOR · RICHARD PACE · ANTHONY NICHOLS
produced by JOSEPH ZBEDA · written & directed by MEIR ZARCHI
DISTRIBUTED BY THE JERRY GROSS ORGANIZATION   Color By METROCOLOR ®

R   RESTRICTED
UNDER 17 REQUIRES ACCOMPANYING
PARENT OR ADULT GUARDIAN

I Spit On Your Grave *(1976). Outside of* Trolls III, *this is quite possibly the worst movie ever made, but it is no less important for that. The victims here include not only the four men who gang rape the heroine, but male supremacy itself.* Source: *Cinemagic/Photofest.*

The Little Mermaid *(1990)*. *Ariel wants to leave her fluid, formless, watery habitat, where human artifacts have no proper names and no real functions, where work is unnecessary and obedience to the Father is the primary rule. "Betcha on land, they understand—bet they don't reprimand their daughters! Bright young women, sick of swimmin', ready to stand."* Source: *Buena Vista Pictures/Photofest.*

Freddy Krueger, from A Nightmare on Elm Street. *The gleeful Slasher who adjourns the distinction between appearance and reality by bringing a childish dream world to life, thus ending our allegiance to a world governed by reason, science, or adults.* Source: *New Line Cinema/Photofest.*

Public Enemy. This was taken soon after Spike Lee's hit movie Do the Right Thing *(1988) had made them a mainstream sensation. The group was named after one of the original gangster movies. Chuck D., the rapper (right front), was inspired by the Last Poets, a group of proto-rappers formed in 1968 that was, in turn, inspired by Marcus Garvey and Malcolm X, both popular spokesmen of race pride and black nationalism.* Source: *Photofest.*

RunDMC. According to the New York Times, *this was hip-hop's first "crossover" group, but Run (Joe Russell) and D. (Darryl McDaniel) dressed in hoodies and jeans to keep it real, and their samples of rock music (in their case, Aerosmith) followed long-standing precedent among DJs. Source: Photofest.*

Scarface *(1931). Paul Muni's performative blueprint. Unlike the hero of Westerns, that strong, silent type who talks mainly to the horse, the early gangster couldn't stay still, and he wouldn't be quiet—he was determined to disturb you. Like the sonic Gangsta of rap music, he was a meditation on the kind of manhood available to males who could find no place in the mode of production authorized by the law. Source: United Artists/Photofest.*

Scarface (1983). Every successful intruder on the American scene was once an immigrant or a criminal: Al Pacino's manic homage to Paul Muni, which soon became the representational reality of the sonic Gangstas who were "gonna get rich or die tryin'," erases the family romance that was The Godfather and reinstates violence as the American anthem. Source: Universal Pictures/Photofest.

The Simpsons. *Where's Dad? By the third or fourth season, Homer took over from Bart, the son, as the central character in TV's longest-running sitcom, thus dispensing with all our Oedipal expectations and forcing us to the conclusion that fathers are vestigial beings who nevertheless keep us laughing.* Source: *Fox/Photofest.*

South Park, the boys. The minimalist extremity of animation: every character is rendered as a little round cut-out with eyes and a mouth, a circle that moves like a stage performer who is always face front, as if the world is a chorus line made of buttons. This conscious abstention from the possibilities of visual representation makes South Park a television show for the blind. Source: Paramount/Photofest.

South Park, Mr. Hankie. There is something happening here that is remarkable, and its name is shit. This TV show is the most amazing study in anality since Jonathan Swift or maybe Martin Luther—Father Christmas comes from the sewer, anal probes come from outer space, and loquacious turds get their fifteen minutes of fame—but why? Source: Comedy Central/Photofest.

South Park, Chef. Is he the Trickster, a surreal yet benign demonstration of the demonic? Is he Br'er Rabbit's Tar Baby, that gooey, fecal mass, all grown up and growling at us? Is he the comedic version of the racial dreams that have haunted the American imagination since 1607? Source: Comedy Central/Photofest.

Robert DeNiro in Martin Scoresese's Taxi Driver. *Are you talking to me? In 1976, Times Square was not a tourist destination unless your purpose in coming was pornographic. Travis Bickle understood that and knew what to do about it. Source: Columbia Pictures/Photofest.*

Toy Story. *Where's Dad? In its first feature, Pixar answered the question by putting him right in front of you, but not so that you'd notice. Woody is the Western hero who fears the future; Buzz is the man of action who hates the past. If they don't come together and combine their attitudes toward history so that each modifies the other, they'll be downsized by the mad scientist next door and unable to help Andy, their son.* Source: *Walt Disney Pictures/Photofest.*

The Spirit. *The artist behind this syndicated comic strip, Will Eisner, is the founding father of the graphic novel and perhaps the first theorist of how the visual space and conventions of comics form the analogue of the "sequential art" we call movies.* Source: *Warren Publishing/Photofest.*

The New York Dolls. The touchstone of punk rock, and, no offense to Jon Landau or his client, the future of rock and roll. A leering, androgynous, trash-rock glam band with remarkable musical knowledge, background, and skills. As Crawdaddy *put it in reporting on New York's punk scene: "It is difficult to say where affectation ends and reality begins." Source: AP/Wide World Photos.*

Ronald Reagan in the South Bronx. At the very moment that hip-hop made urban renewal the project of the objects, the goal of the so-called ghetto itself, Ronald Reagan appeared to bemoan the decay of the South Bronx. Little did he know that young black men and women were already reinventing their lives, their streets, their neighborhoods, and their nation through music, dance, clothes, and, not least, graffiti. Source: AP/Wide World Photos.

art spiegelman

MAUS

A SURVIVOR'S TALE

I

MY FATHER BLEEDS HISTORY

Spiegelman. Source: *Book Cover from Maus I:* A Survivor's Tale/My Father Bleeds History *by Art Spiegelman copyright © 1973, 1980, 1981, 1982, 1984, 1985, 1986 by Art Spiegelman. Used by permission of Pantheon Books, a division of Random House, Inc.*

Warhol. Source: © 2009 The Andy Warhol Foundation for the Visual Arts/ARS, New York.

Lichtenstein. Source: *Roy Lichtenstein estate.*

CHAPTER SIX

~

The Ending
of the "American Century"

The American Century Revisited

The historian Martin J. Sklar has called the "American Century" a twice-told tale: one that got started in the very early twentieth century, another that got going in the 1940s, when the United States finally became the indispensable nation because it won the Second World War. Almost all other historians think of this imperial phenomenon as something that began in the throes of that war, right around mid-century, when Henry Luce, the editor of *Time* magazine, announced its advent. Here is how Luce characterized it in a famous essay for *Life* magazine: "Once we cease to distract ourselves with lifeless arguments about isolationism, we shall be amazed to discover that there is already an immense American internationalism. American jazz, Hollywood movies, American slang, American machines and patented products, are in fact the only things that every community in the world, from Zanzibar to Hamburg, recognizes in common. Blindly, unintentionally, accidentally, we are already a world power in all the trivial ways—in very human ways. But there is a great deal more than that. America is already the intellectual, scientific and artistic capital of the world."

Luce was right, of course. He published this essay, called "The American Century," in 1941. But follow Sklar's lead and listen now to Frank Vanderlip, the vice president of the National City Bank of New York, the origin of what we know as Citcorp—probably the source of your credit card—speaking in February 1902 at the Commercial Club of Chicago about "the Americanization of the world." This phrase was neither a promise nor a threat nor a fact.

The man was merely quoting the title of a book by the British editor of the *Review of Reviews*. "The twentieth century is America's century," Vanderlip said, and then quoted another English journalist to prove the point: "The century which has just closed is Great Britain's. The century which has just begun is yours."

Vanderlip understood the impending superiority of the United States as an economic phenomenon driven by the large corporations that had erupted from the wreckage of late-nineteenth-century market crises in the great merger movement of 1898 to 1903. On the one hand, "America's century" was a matter of "industrial progress," "commercial invasion," "growth, development, the conquest of markets"—not a Pax Americana signified and enforced by military power. On the other hand, it was the result of the new corporate-industrial social order: "I believe in the great corporation," he said. "I believe there is no more effective way for us to impress ourselves on the trade situation of the world than through these great industrial units that can project into the world's markets the strength of their commercial position with irresistible force."

Frank Vanderlip was not a diplomat with credentials from the State Department when he visited the United Kingdom and returned home to announce the advent of a century in which the American idea of enterprise would reshape the world. But as Sklar notes, and as other historians such as Walter LaFeber and Lloyd Gardner have demonstrated, this banker—Vanderlip was once a journalist, then a Treasury Department bureaucrat—"personified an intersecting of the spheres of intellect, government, and modern [corporate] business." In this sense, he already spoke the language of U.S. foreign policy in the twentieth century. Or, rather, he was one of its inventors, and then again one of its architects, because he stood at the heart of the changes that happened at the turn of the last century.

Let us now revisit the principles of U.S. foreign policy as they were enunciated once upon a time, just two years before Vanderlip spoke in Chicago, so that we can interpret his prophetic language and decide accordingly whether our current policy-relevant vocabularies need improvement. When our language skills are good enough, we can decide whether, or how, things changed at the ending of the savage moment we call the twentieth century. And even if we can't decide, we'll know we have a good argument going one way or the other.

The Economic Logics of Globalization

The Open Door Notes that founded twentieth-century U.S. foreign policy were circulated in 1899 and 1900. They were written by John Hay, who had begun his career as Abraham Lincoln's secretary and who became William McKinley's secretary of state in 1897. Hay was not their singular "author," however—he was part of a political and intellectual scene that included Frederick Jackson Turner, the theorist of the American frontier; Alfred Thayer Mahan, the influential historian of empires and sea power; Theodore Roosevelt, the supposed Rough Rider who, like Turner, believed that the idea of new frontiers had somehow become the American Dream; Woodrow Wilson, Turner's roommate in graduate school at Johns Hopkins; and sophisticated businessmen like Frank Vanderlip.

These men understood that the United States was an inherently expansionist nation. It had developed by displacing indigenous peoples and conquering (or buying) territory, so that by the 1860s it was already a continental polity. "Extend the sphere," James Madison had urged his fellow patriots in 1787—if you keep incorporating more factions, interests, peoples, states, and territories into the constitutional fabric of American politics, majority rule becomes more difficult but more durable. But now what? In the 1890s, it was clear that a frontier defined by territorial expansion was over (this was Turner's special insight, but everyone also knew that Mexico and Canada were not ripe for military conquest). How to preserve the dynamism of American life in the absence of that frontier?

The related question was, where do we sell our goods? By the 1890s, it was clear that American industrial capacity was more than sufficient to supply the entire continental market; prices and profits had been falling since the 1870s. Would overseas markets offset this deficiency of demand, raise prices, and restore profits? If not, persistent economic crisis might deform the political system by making class conflict look normal. Arthur T. Hadley, the president of Yale University (he was an influential economist who also served on the finance committee of the Pennsylvania Railroad), explained the difficulty this way in 1896: "A republican government is organized on the assumption that all men are free and equal. If the political power is . . . equally distributed while the industrial power is concentrated in the hands of a few, it creates dangers of class struggles and class legislation which menace both our political and our industrial order." At the end of the nineteenth century, then, "an entirely new era in national life," as Vanderlip put it, was dawning. Americans had reached another verge.

Meanwhile, the European powers were carving up the world into exclusive "spheres of influence"—that is, colonies. France, Germany, and Great Britain were already scrambling in Africa and Asia to create new outposts of their business enterprises, from which the trade and investment of other countries would be barred. The German thinking on the issue was especially interesting because, as articulated in the intellectual agenda of *Mitteleuropa*, it proposed to reproduce both the American experience of the nineteenth century—let's conquer the whole continent!—and the Napoleonic dream of an empire that would encompass the entire Eurasian land mass. This intellectual agenda animated German diplomacy from the 1870s to the 1940s and produced two world wars.

The turn-of-the century moment when *Mitteleuropa* squared off against the Open Door was the culmination of the second great stage of globalization (that's right, globalization didn't begin in 1989). The first stage began in the sixteenth century, with the rise of joint-stock companies and the colonization of the Western Hemisphere by European powers. Trade rather than direct investment—rather than the transfer of technology—was the medium of globalization in this period. The second stage began in the 1870s, when France and Germany started acquiring new colonial possessions in the hope of challenging Great Britain for control of the world's resources; the United States became a participant in 1898 with the Spanish American War. In this second stage, surplus capital, that is, direct investment, became the medium of globalization, but it flowed mainly into extractive industries (mining, for example) or plantation agriculture. The extraordinary economic growth it fueled came to an abrupt halt in 1914 with the start of World War I; the volume of world trade and investment did not recover until the 1960s.

In the third stage, our own time, the medium of globalization is the financial integration of world markets enabled by the collapse of the Soviet Union and the new purchase of "free trade" on the imaginations of policymakers everywhere. It is driven by massive transfers of technology ("outsourcing") that export manufacturing plants—thus jobs—from the United States to less developed countries. This of course is the kind of direct investment that downsized Dad in the late twentieth century. From his standpoint, globalization is not such a good thing: the North American Free Trade Agreement may be dangerous to his health.

At the height of the second stage of globalization, the collision of two realities—the new importance of world markets for American enterprise and the aggressive new colonialism of the Great Powers—happened in China, and thus became the occasion for Hay's Open Door Notes of 1899 to 1900. The so-called Boxer Rebellion, the 1899 uprising of the Chinese people against the Great Powers and their colonial ambitions (it was the prelude to the revolution that officially began in 1911, something like what started in Russia twelve years before the Bolsheviks seized power in 1917), looked like a real crisis from the standpoint of the State Department. For it confirmed that colonized peoples—impoverished peoples held in subjection by superior military force—will just keep rebelling.

More important, their rebellions will disrupt the world's markets by creating political upheaval, thus impairing the confidence of traders and investors. And so that disruption will probably lead, in turn, to war between the Great Powers over access to diminished markets. As Woodrow Wilson asked on September 5, 1919, in a speech in St. Louis, "Why, my fellow citizens, is there any man here or any woman, let me say is there any child here, who does not know that the seed of war in the modern world is industrial and commercial rivalry?"

At any rate this was the economic logic at work in Hay's notes. The Open Door world he proposed in them was the outline of an anticolonial imperialism. Like other contributors to the doctrine and citizens of the world it would turn inside out, Hay did not shrink from the idea or the enactment of imperialism; he knew the United States itself was originally conceived as a "mighty empire" to be realized by the acquisition of an entire continent. Charles Conant, the most important theorist of American empire, explained in 1898 that the labels didn't matter very much because the development of "decadent nations" by means of imperialism was not a matter of choice; the countries with a surplus of capital had to export it—the alternatives he posed were foreign wars, outright socialism, or state spending for welfare—and the countries with a shortage of capitalism as well as capital had to import it.

> New markets and new opportunities for investment must be found if surplus capital is to be profitably employed. In pointing out the necessity that the U.S. shall enter upon a broad policy, it need not be determined in just what manner that policy shall be worked out. . . . Whether this policy carries with it the direct government of groups of half-savage islands may be a subject of argument, but upon the economic side of the question there is but one choice—either to enter by some means upon the competition for the employment of American capital and enterprise in these countries, or to continue the needless duplication of existing means of production and communication.

In other words, if the world's markets were crucial to the future of the American experiment, as Conant, Vanderlip, and almost everyone else believed, the United States had to intervene in the ongoing contest among advanced nations for access to those markets; only the form of that intervention was in question. But Hay did propose to dismantle the exclusive spheres of influence the Great Powers had created, and in doing so he was redefining imperialism as such. This redefinition would shape U.S. foreign policy until the very end of the twentieth century.

The Open Door World

The assumptions and imperatives built into the Open Door world Hay out-lined went approximately as follows. First, the growth of world income was the key to world peace. If the volume of world income grew consistently, no nation would have to increase its share at the expense of others by military means, by conquering peoples, creating colonies, or going to war over access to resources (as happened regularly in the seventeenth, eighteenth, and nineteenth centuries). Other things being equal, the best way to grow the world's income was to allow for the free flow of capital and finished goods across international borders—tariffs and exclusive spheres of influence (colonies) were the principal obstacles to economic growth so conceived. An Open Door world, "a fair field and no favor," was, then, the necessary condition of world peace.

Second, national sovereignty or self-determination, even for the most backward of peoples, had to be acknowledged and enforced. China, which had been systematically dismembered by the Great Powers, was Exhibit A, but there were many other parts of the world ruled by the lawless whims of imperial, exploitative purpose. The Belgian Congo was just the worst case; French Indochina was almost as bad. The regulative assumption here cut two ways, both determined by close study of American historical experience. On the one hand, the United States had been able to absorb enormous amounts of foreign capital in the nineteenth century without becoming a colonial appendage of a Great Power because its political integrity, its national sovereignty, had been secured by the Revolution and the Constitution. On the other hand, the rebelliousness and backwardness of the American South after the Civil War had been reanimated by military conquest and occupation. The tentative conclusions to be drawn from the study of this historical experience were simple but profound—maybe military conquest is not the prerequisite of imperial success, and maybe world power need not wear a uniform.

Third, trade was less important than investment, or, to put it in contemporary parlance, the "transfer of technology" from more advanced to less developed countries was the path to a future in which all nations might share the benefits of growth. Trade between countries can, in fact, contribute to the underdevelopment of the more backward party to the bargain—just as "dependency theory" and liberation theology in the late twentieth century claimed—because the goods being exchanged cost the less developed country more of its current, available labor time; by contrast, the value of the goods exported by the more advanced country include the past labor embodied in its fixed capital, its technology, so more of its population can be doing something other than producing raw materials for export. Adam Smith, one of the founding fathers of modern political economy, clearly understood this asymmetry as a result of free trade. Here is how he explained it in *The Wealth of Nations* (1776):

> The revenue of a trading and manufacturing country must, other things being equal, always be much greater than that of one without trade or manufactures. . . . A small quantity of manufactured produce purchases a great quantity of rude produce. A trading and manufacturing country, therefore, naturally purchases with a small part of its manufactured produce a great part of the rude produce of other countries; while, on the contrary, a country without trade and manufactures is generally obliged to purchase, at the expense of a great part of its rude produce, a very small part of the manufactured produce of other countries.

The American architects of anticolonial imperialism believed that direct investment—transfers of technology—could change this dynamic by equipping everyone with the tools of industrial development. At any rate, they were convinced that changing the rules of trade in raw materials or finished goods could not address the real question, the real problem—that is, how to invest surplus capital in the less developed countries. Here is how Conant characterized this problem in 1901: "The benefit to the old countries in the control of the underdeveloped countries does not lie chiefly in the outlet for consumable goods. It is precisely to escape the necessity for the reduplication of the plants which produce the goods, by finding a field elsewhere for the creation of new plants, that the savings of the capitalistic countries are seeking an outlet beyond their own limits." That Conant worked for every administration from William McKinley to Woodrow Wilson, from 1899 to 1915, that he put the Philippines on the gold standard—the banknotes circulated thereafter were called "Conants"—and that he meanwhile published five books on modern banking and modern imperialism might suggest how widely shared such an idea was in the policymaking circles of the time.

But if you assume that investment is more important than trade and that transfers of technology compose the path to a peaceful future, you must believe that development is the property of all people. You must believe that there is no disqualification residing in race, or in religion, or in any other cultural artifact. You must believe that every person, every civilization, is capable of turning toward modernity and finding its possibilities compelling. You must also believe that the continuum of civilization is mostly a matter of economic development, and you will act accordingly, as if racial differences and religious disputes are real but artificial, as if they can be smoothed, if not erased, by the growth of world income an Open Door policy permits and requires. "Civilization follows material development," as William Howard Taft, the future president and former civil governor of the Philippines, explained in 1901 to a congressional committee.

But go ahead, put the proposition more pragmatically—even if you are a racist (as Taft was according to our standards), you know you cannot conduct foreign policy in racial terms because if you do, you are validating European colonialism and re-creating the conditions of war. A "clash of civilizations," as Samuel P. Huntington tried to frame the prospects of American diplomacy in a 1996 book, would have sounded merely bizarre from this standpoint. For again, civilization was a continuum: all human beings want and need both the development and the recognition of their natural talents, learned skills, and past efforts.

Fourth, power and standing in the world were not functions of military capacity or accomplishment; they were instead results of what Henry Luce called, with emphatic irony, "all the trivial ways"—"intellectual, scientific, and artistic"—all the ways in which the black aesthetic changed the United States, all the ways in which the United States changed the world, all the ways in which we citizens of the late twentieth century changed ourselves. Perhaps the most important achievement of the Open Door Notes was to announce to the world that from now on, power in the world is to be understood as a function of economic capacity, political pluralism, and cultural attainment, rather than the result of a huge military and a grimly determined officer corps.

The corollary of this announcement, an achievement in its own right, was the idea that multilateral institutions and cooperation would have to be the political infrastructure of peaceful economic development. The U.S. Congress rejected the League of Nations in 1919 on exactly these grounds—Article 10 of the League's covenant committed American military power, such as it was, to the preservation and protection of European spheres of influence. The United Nations was approved in 1945 on the same grounds—Article 51 of the UN charter outlaws unilateral use of armed force.

The original architects of an anticolonial imperialism were not naïve. They knew that the United States would have to build and eventually deploy significant military power to defend its growing overseas interests. "Nations with large interests abroad must necessarily encounter many difficulties," as *The Bankers' Magazine* explained in 1900, "which frequently can only be overcome by force of arms." But like the American people, these original architects had a deep suspicion of standing armies and an abiding aversion to the big government required to sustain them. Until the 1930s, their goal, often expressed in treaties, was to limit the spread of military technology (battleships in the 1920s, for example) in the hope of blunting the "balance-of-power" approach taken by the victors in the First World War.

Vietnam Syndrome

The Great Depression and the Second World War changed everything except the assumptions and imperatives at work in the original Open Door Notes. Yes, the military component of the federal budget did increase almost exponentially in the 1950s, in accordance with the Cold War agenda of "containing" Communism, and, yes, the United States did sink, slowly and surely, into the quagmire of Vietnam, a proxy war with China very much like the previous disaster in Korea. But the rationale for war in Southeast Asia was perfectly consistent with the principles of American foreign policy in the twentieth century as summarized above. The goal was to make sure that Japan did not revert to its traditional economic relationship with China, the recipient of most of its exports and surplus capital until 1949, when the Communists seized power. The goal was to make sure that Japan had another outlet for its enterprise and would, as a result, remain within the orbit of the "free world" now dominated by the United States. Here is how a study group sponsored by the Woodrow Wilson Foundation and the National Planning Association, which included two State Department alumni, a National City Bank economist, and the chair of Harvard's Department of Government—the mentor of both Samuel P. Huntington and Henry Kissinger—framed that goal in 1955: "The history of the 1930s should be a warning to the West, and especially to the United States, that failure to make sufficient economic opportunity for the expansion of Japan's exports and for Japanese economic growth can be disastrous for the security of the West and the peace of the world. The logical way to open this opportunity would be to make possible greater Japanese participation in the development of Southern Asia."

The social and intellectual results of the debacle in Vietnam did, however, make a big difference toward the end of the twentieth century: they did change everything in both interesting and dangerous ways. The social result was the All-Volunteer Army, which presupposed the end of the draft that had conscripted so many young men into a military still befuddled by the idea of civil rights (that is, the idea of racial equality). In the aftermath of Vietnam, the four major military branches rebuilt themselves from scratch, and they did it with the ideals of the 1960s in mind. The Marine Corps went farther than the others, but by the 1990s the American military was the most egalitarian social program in the United States. It fulfilled the goals of Lyndon Johnson's "Great Society" by becoming the most active, even strident, adherent of affirmative action, and in doing so it became the nation's least racist institution. It fulfilled, in this sense, the goals of the civil rights movement, but meanwhile it provided a portal to education for working-class kids of every kind, of every color.

The intellectual results were more ambiguous, of course. On the Left , the critique of American imperialism became much more forceful and apocalyptic. Jimmy Carter was elected president in 1976 in part because the Congress and the American people were so disgusted by the atrocities perpetrated in their name, from Saigon to Santiago. U.S. complicity in the 1973 overthrow of Salvador Allende, the democratically elected president of Chile, was especially galling and led directly to Senator Frank Church's indictment of the CIA in 1976. Carter's notion of "human rights" as the core principle of foreign policy has, by now, reshaped the very idea of diplomacy; in its absence, it is improbable that Augusto Pinochet—the general who led the coup against Allende—or Slobodan Milošević would have been arrested or tried in international courts of law. But in the late 1970s, it was an astonishing departure to make human rights the centerpiece of foreign policy. "Realism" had been the rule in the White House since 1968 because Henry Kissinger had been the presiding officer of American diplomacy.

On the Right, meanwhile, the critique of American foreign policy became much more pointed and persuasive. Ronald Reagan was elected president in 1980 in part because the Congress and the American people were so disgusted by the atrocities perpetrated by foreigners, from Luzon to Tehran—remember the hostages held for over a year by the Iranian Revolutionary Guard, starting in 1979? The simple fact that Carter had relinquished U.S. rights to the Panama Canal (Teddy Roosevelt's bully project) signified the twilight of American power, according to Reagan, but he promised to turn dusk to dawn.

The debate that ensued on U.S. foreign policy cannot be characterized, however, as a Left/Right divide that corresponds somehow to a liberal/conservative opposition. The Vietnam Syndrome took over the body politic in the late 1970s, when everybody acknowledged that we lost the war, and then asked why, and then wondered how the United States would regain what Henry Luce had called its "indefinable, unmistakable sign of leadership: prestige." This unfortunate syndrome had many symptoms, many manifestations, and many unintended consequences.

Then as now, the United States was the preeminent military power in the world. Why did it lose the Vietnam War to a guerilla movement that had one-tenth of the logistical capacity at the disposal of American forces—and no airplanes? There are four available explanations these days. First, the U.S. military was fighting the wrong war. It was using strategy and tactics suited to a war of maneuver, in which the object is to defeat another army on a field of battle, when it should have been fighting a war of position—engaging in counterinsurgency—and trying to win the "hearts and minds" of the local populations by (re)building the material foundations of their daily lives. Sound familiar? Second, the politicians in the Congress wouldn't permit the president to do what was necessary to win: they kept reining in the war powers of the executive branch, and in doing so they betrayed the American military and cancelled the American Century. By this account, mind you, a military resolution of the war was both possible and imminent. It would have happened, and soon, except that the Congress got in the way. Sound familiar?

Third, the New Left and the "liberal media" misled the civilian population on the benefits, the triumphs, and the accomplishments of the war—sound familiar?—so that by 1968 a majority of the American people opposed continued involvement. This third explanation feeds into and amplifies the second, and vice versa, since the Congress would presumably have been acting on the voters' wishes, and the media would presumably have been paying attention to public opinion. Fourth, the tattered morale and outright mutiny of American troops on the ground after 1968 finally made the elongation of the war impossible. The "Vietnamization" of the conflict under Richard Nixon and Henry Kissinger—their attempt to turn the war over to local populations—was the political admission of this sad cultural truth. Familiarity ends here.

Another Country in Another Century

Again, there is no firm Left/Right political valence in these extant explanations for the debacle in Vietnam. But the ending of the American Century was announced when two employees of President Gerald R. Ford—he was the jolly, slapstick politician who succeeded the impeached Nixon—seized on the second and third explanations and then, with the help of renegade intellectuals of the conservative kind, redefined the sources and meanings of international power in the 1990s. This story begins in the mid-1970s, when Dick Cheney and Donald Rumsfeld worked for Ford at the White

House, where they witnessed, with horror, the decline of the imperial presidency—the decline dictated by statutes such as the War Powers Act (1974) and the Foreign Intelligence Surveillance Act (1978), which forced the executive branch to acknowledge its responsibility to the Congress and the Constitution.

Rumsfeld and Cheney—and their numerous allies, among them Richard Armitage, Colin Powell, and Paul Wolfowitz—resurfaced in the Reagan years and moved into senior positions under George H. W. Bush in the late 1980s and early 1990s. Rumsfeld was then the elder Bush's emissary to Saddam Hussein, whom the United States supported in his long, bloody, brutal war against Iran. Cheney was secretary of defense during the first Gulf war of 1991, when he fiercely opposed a march up to Baghdad to overthrow Hussein after the international coalition assembled by the president had vanquished the Iraqi army in Kuwait—on the grounds that an invasion of Iraq meant long-term occupation, which would in turn endanger, not secure, U.S. interests in the Middle East by inflaming anti-American (and anti-Israeli) opinion there.

By that time, the Soviet Union had disintegrated, and so the urgent antagonisms of the Cold War had stopped making sense. What was America's mission in a world absent the "evil empire," as Reagan had called it? What was to be done? Cheney and Wolfowitz had good answers in 1992, and they would eventually change the way America's mission could be conceived and conducted. When they returned to power with the election of George W. Bush in 2000, they were already looking for a way to depart from the inherited tradition, from the principles of twentieth-century foreign policy. When the World Trade Center collapsed on September 11, 2001, they were intellectually equipped to incorporate the incident into conclusions they had already reached.

In the spring of 1992, Wolfowitz, Cheney's deputy at the Pentagon, had circulated a memorandum called "Defense Planning Guidance" (DPG), which would deeply inform the thinking and the attitudes of those consigned to outer-Beltway darkness after Bill Clinton's election in November. Every two years the Pentagon revises the DPG in preparation for congressional scrutiny of the Defense Department budget. This time around, the revision was supervised and completed by Zalmay Khalilzad, the Afghan exile authorized by Wolfowitz to rethink the document.

In doing so, that unelected delegate from a world elsewhere rewrote the principles of U.S. foreign policy by stating that its new purpose was to prevent the emergence of a Great Power rival, by military means if necessary. A lot of people noticed as he did it—the document was leaked to the *New York*

Times—but it didn't matter very much because there we were, already the indispensable nation, perhaps even the "hyperpower," bursting with armed force and poised to do nothing except congratulate ourselves. Wolfowitz himself disowned the document because the controversy it generated made him uncomfortable. Cheney praised it, however, saying to Khalilzad, "You've discovered a new rationale for our role in the world."

The 1992 DPG thereafter became the canonical text, the originary manifesto, of these "Vulcans," as James Mann calls them, when they were sent into exile by the Clinton presidency. By 1997 they had embraced and even enlarged Khalilzad's analysis by founding the Project for a New American Century (PNAC), along with William Kristol, Robert Kagan, Richard Perle, and other self-styled conservatives who wanted to "restore" America's standing in the world—that is, to recover from the malady of the Vietnam Syndrome and, accordingly, to stiffen the moral fiber of the nation as well as the world, as if the projection of American power abroad would reawaken the patriotic spirit of the American people at home.

PNAC was the social and intellectual origin of the second Gulf war, the current war in Iraq, in three related senses. First, its founders and members overpopulated the Bush administrations, even though some of its more outspoken residents, like Rumsfeld and Perle, disappeared in 2006. Second, PNAC's purposes were "Rebuilding America's Defenses" (the title of a 2000 publication) and defining world power as military might. Many critics of the war in Iraq have excoriated Donald Rumsfeld for treating the military with insufficient respect and for engaging the enemy with insufficient "boots on the ground," but they miss the point of invading on the cheap—the secretary of defense and his allies in the White House were trying to demonstrate how agile, mobile, and deadly American armed forces could be, all over the place, wherever necessary. In doing so, they hoped to redefine American "prestige" as a function of military power, as Robert Kagan had urged in his best-selling book of 1999, *Of Paradise and Power*. But in doing so they were also repudiating a founding principle of twentieth-century U.S. foreign policy—they were ending the American Century in the name of its revival.

Third, PNAC's 2000 publication titled "Rebuilding America's Defenses" proposed, in exact accordance with the 1992 DPG, that the premise and purpose of U.S. foreign policy should be "precluding the rise of a great power rival." This locution is quite novel in the annals of U.S. diplomacy—it is another abrupt break from the past—because the new (anticolonial) American imperialism invented and refined in the twentieth century was an attempted escape from the Great Power politics that had led so many times to so many wars after 1600.

The question for John Hay, Charles Conant, Frank Vanderlip, and their fellow architects of the international future was, How do we make the passage of the seat of empire peaceful? In the past, they knew, wars were the means by which one empire succeeded another. This succession was inevitable, they assumed—in fact, it was already happening in the passage of the seat of empire from the Thames to the Potomac, as Hay explained in his eulogy for McKinley in 1901. But was there a way to avoid these ugly intervals of warfare, especially now that they could become global? Hay and the others thought so, but their twofold assumption was that the passage of the seat of empire would continue—it would keep moving east to west, toward Asia—and that multilateral institutions would permit and enforce a peaceful passage.

PNAC's answers to these difficult questions were very different. A new American Century was, by definition, a way of precluding the passage of the seat of empire. By implication, it was going to be unilateral, and it was going to be the result of warfare, that is, of the superior military force residing in the United States. The war in Iraq cannot be attributed solely to PNAC—although, again, everywhere you look in the Bush administrations you will find a founder—but the National Security Strategy (NSS) document issued by the White House in September 2002, which became the official rationale for "preemptive" war, replicates key terms, categories, and arguments of PNAC alumni.

Go back to the DPG of 1992: "In the Middle East and Southwest Asia, our overall objective is to remain the predominant outside power in the region and preserve U.S. and Western access to the region's oil." Then fast forward to "Rebuilding America's Defenses," PNAC's manifesto of 2000, where "precluding the rise of a great power rival" is a major premise and a major purpose. And then read the NSS of 2002: "The U.S., has long maintained the option of preemptive actions to counter a sufficient threat to our national security."

Whose Ending?

These texts are cut from the same cloth because the same people are doing the stitching. The conclusion you must draw from this intellectual continuity is startling, and it makes you wonder how far these Vulcans were willing to go—it makes you ask, how determined were they to nullify the principles of twentieth-century American foreign policy? For the place you arrive after reading these documents is another country; at any rate it is neither the new world imagined by John Hay nor the new epoch charted by Henry Luce.

Now a century ago the founders of a new imperialism had to move beyond a colonial past they thought outmoded—so we should know that there is nothing wrong with the creative destruction of intellectual innovation. But we should also ask if the principles of American foreign policy in the twentieth century are just relics of the past, to be discarded in the name of a new global reality; we should ask if the Bush administration was too quick to dispense with the inherited tradition. The best way to answer is to ask what the Iraq war was about, without indulging fond dreams of executive competence and bureaucratic rectitude.

If we are to believe the utterances of the policymakers themselves, and there is no reason not to, this war had four broad purposes, all of them linked by a conception of government that is unnerving if not alarming—and all of them unrelated to the stated purposes of the invasion of Iraq (except in the fundamental sense that the removal of Saddam Hussein was the condition of every other purpose). To begin with, the world must be reminded of the fact that American military power is not only mightier than any other Great Power rival, but it is technologically and logistically equipped to fight on many fronts, with as few or as many forces as it takes to shock and awe the local population. Translation: We can destroy any enemy, anywhere, anytime, so do not pretend to be the heir to the empire that is the American Century.

Also, that military power will be deployed by a "unitary executive," an unapologetically extreme branch of government that has finally retrieved the commander in chief's rightful powers from the hapless, haphazard Congress and reasserted the prerogatives of the imperial presidency once claimed by Richard Nixon. Congress must be consulted by the president, according to this novel line of thinking, but in a time of war he acquires all the constitutional powers he needs to revoke the right of habeas corpus for "enemy combatants" and to prolong their detention and interrogation indefinitely. In a time of war, he also acquires all the constitutional powers he needs to violate the right to privacy enunciated by the Supreme Court in 1967. Translation: The Constitution legally and historically mandates the separation of powers, but in the entirely new circumstances determined by the end of the Cold War—determined, that is, by America's unique status as the last superpower standing—that separation is moot. We will keep the secrets.

In addition, the multilateral institutions that the United States has hitherto created and supported in shaping the world's future are no more useful—and no less objectionable—than the U.S. Congress when it comes to making foreign policy and deploying the military in the name of the new national interests and the new international threats which appeared in the aftermath of the Cold War. The United Nations is a fine idea, and the neighborhood is still desirable, but the multilateral commitments that once kept the peace have become excuses for inaction in the face of new threats to national security. Translation: Why should we keep listening to the nations we disarmed in the 1940s or entertaining the ideas of a less dangerous, more innocent age? If our deadly enemies are multiplying in the absence of the Soviet Union, why should we hesitate before attacking them with conventional forces?

And finally, perhaps most importantly, the impending movement, the probable passage, of the seat of empire is now unacceptable. The notion that America would ever relinquish its superiority is an anachronism produced by "Wilsonian idealism" back in the early twentieth century. Thus, China is not to be the new seat of empire in the mid-twenty-first century, even though it will be the largest, most productive economy in the world by 2030. It cannot be, because it is still a vaguely communist, strongly statist challenge to globalization as promoted and practiced by the United States. But how to stop this economic juggernaut in East Asia? How to slow or stop the passage in the seat of empire predicted and expected by the architects of an anticolonial imperialism in the early twentieth century? Translation: How do we slow China down, how do we make sure the American Century lasts for another hundred years? What if we turn the international spigot by controlling the third largest oil reserves in the Middle East—not by relying on the Saudis but by owning or developing those reserves in Iraq?

These are not the paranoid ravings of a vast, left-wing conspiracy chanting, "No Blood for Oil!" Here is how Alan Greenspan, the former chair of the Federal Reserve and a renowned conservative, characterized our situation a year before crude oil hit $100 per barrel in 2008: "The intense attention of the developed world to Middle Eastern political affairs has always been tied to oil security. . . . And whatever their publicized angst over Saddam Hussein's 'weapons of mass destruction' [please note the scare quotes, which in this context are expressions of sarcasm or contempt], American and British authorities were also concerned about violence in an area that harbors a resource indispensable for the functioning of the world economy. I am saddened that it is politically inconvenient to acknowledge what everyone knows: the Iraq war was largely about oil."

The Bush Doctrine, as enunciated in the NSS document of September 2002, was both the forecast of war in Iraq and the realization of the ideas residing in the program of the Project for a New American Century—and these ideas were, in turn, the distant echoes of the 1992 DPG. Its central claim, as we have already seen, is that "the option of preemptive actions" is an American tradition; it can be justified on historical grounds because the United States has been conquering territory and fighting "splendid little wars" since the eighteenth century. As Max Boot and Robert Kagan, two supporters of the Bush Doctrine, have explained, this nation has always been dangerous, prone to spasms of gun-toting military idiocy in the name of freedom. Andrew Bacevich, a brilliant historian of U.S. diplomacy, a fierce critic of the Bush Doctrine, and a former Army officer, agrees with them—he has suggested that the militarization of foreign policy in the late twentieth century was an inevitable result of the Cold War and then was somehow magnified in the aftermath of the Soviet Union's collapse. The difficulty of proving these arguments for continuity lies in the simple fact that the original architects of an Open Door World renounced territorial acquisition and colonial occupation as the proper objects of modern imperialism—they knew that the practices of the past were not sufficient to the requirements of the future, and they knew that a military rendition of world power would lead to world war.

Boot, a senior fellow at the Council on Foreign Relations, correctly cited three examples of "preemptive actions" before Iraq in trying to defend the NSS document of 2002: the Mexican War of 1846 to 1848, the Spanish-American War of 1898 to 1903, and the Vietnam War. The trouble here is that Americans are now generally agreed that the first two were imperialist wars of conquest and that the third was, at best, a disaster (even at the time, Congressman Abraham Lincoln insisted that the Mexican War was based on the "sheerest deception"). Preemptive military actions are everywhere you look in the record of human civilization, from Thermopylae to Baghdad. The question is not whether they happened; the question is whether our actions can be justified according to the moral criteria we have acquired since Nuremberg and Vietnam—and probably even earlier, in the aftermath of World War I.

As we have seen, the Open Door world as conceived by its original architects was a place in which military solutions to international disagreements were sometimes necessary but always a last resort; in which armed force did not exhaust the meanings of world power; in which unilateral "preemptive actions" had become obsolete, even destructive; in which multilateral institutions constrained such actions and enabled the sovereignty of all nations, in which economic growth and development were the necessary conditions of world peace; in which exclusive spheres of influence were the crucial constraint on such growth and development; and in which the colonial culture of racism—the "white man's burden"—could not thrive because it severed the continuum of civilization.

In addressing and shaping the second stage of globalization—when the whole world was first knit together by the new fiber of direct investment as well as trade, when the whole world could see the new horizon of modernity—these original architects of the Open Door believed they had found a way to reduce the role of militaries in the articulation of foreign policies and the conduct of international relations. They believed they had found a way to ease the inevitable passage of the seat of empire, perhaps even dispensing with war as its spastic, deadly accompaniment. So conceived, the American Century was a postimperialist design for a world accustomed to colonialism, racism, and war. Ending it will not be easy, then, because it contains real hope for a world free of fear and want and violence, a world in which freedom just is development. Still, we must ask in our own time, in this third stage of globalization, has the Open Door now been adjourned as an intellectual agenda? Is the ending of the American Century already accomplished?

"Virtual Sanctuaries": Globalization and the New Terrorist Movements

There is of course another way to read for that ending. This alternative reading would place the rise of terrorism at the center of the story we tell about the new global realities that changed the relation between America and the world—between the inside and the outside of what came to be called "the homeland." This reading would probably treat the formal declaration of a "war on terror" in 2001 as the inevitable result of the irrational (read: ethnic and religious) forces that gathered at the end of the twentieth century in furious opposition to modernity as exemplified and purveyed by the United States. American foreign policy was militarized, in other words, by the nature of the new threat to peaceful economic development on a global scale. It is a plausible reading because after the fall of the Soviet Union, terrorism did become the principal threat to orderly development as sponsored by the last remaining superpower (or the "hyperpower," according to French observers)—as early as 1994, soon after the first attack on the World Trade Center was carried out by Islamic militants, the State Department had defined terror as the central concern of U.S. foreign policy.

So let us revisit the late-twentieth-century scene of discussion on the rise of terrorism, particularly as this discussion was recast by later interpretations of 9/11. There was (and is) a rough consensus among analysts and policymakers on the salient features of the phenomenon. This background agreement remained even in view of serious disagreements on the origins, implications, and prevention of terrorism. To begin with, everyone agreed that the third stage of globalization was the medium and the method of new terrorist movements, in two related senses. First, their leaders often had cosmopolitan educations that made them citizens of a world without borders, while their rank-and-file members invariably understood how to use the most advanced communication technologies, including computers. The nine-year insurgency in Afghanistan against the Soviet invasion of 1979, for example, was the context in which Islamic militants from around the world first exchanged notes on how to divert or neutralize (not destroy) an overextended superpower. There they learned how to make the Internet their base—so that when the United States finally destroyed the al Qaeda training camps in Afghanistan (long before 9/11), jihadists found "virtual sanctuaries" in cyberspace, on hundreds of websites where they could teach each other how to use mobile phones as effective detonators, to fire rocket-propelled grenades, and to conduct a proper beheading.

Second, and more importantly, the typical terrorist movements of the late twentieth century were substate actors that refused to fight an old-fashioned war of maneuver in which the goal is to conquer a state and its territory; they chose instead to fight a newfangled war of position in which the goal is to discredit the enemy's legitimacy in the court of world opinion. This substate status and this strategic choice challenged the sovereignty of nation-states, a founding principle of modern law—at any rate they enacted a dispersal of power from states to society by ending the state's exclusive claim on the means of mass destruction and by merging the theater of combat with civil(ian) society. As John Yoo, the fierce critic of the Geneva Conventions who served in George Bush's Justice Department, explained, "Once, only nation-states had the resources to wage war. [Now] Al Qaeda is able to finance its jihad outside the traditional structure of the nation-state, and this may well extend to nuclear, biological, or chemical weapons." In enacting this dispersal of power, terrorist movements resembled the multinational corporations and nongovernmental organizations that were meanwhile challenging the regulatory reach and the moral standing of states. They also embodied the "decentering" of power from the core to the periphery of the modern world system which found its academic analog under the rubric of "postcolonial" studies.

Here is how Lawrence Freedman, an influential British authority on the subject, summarizes the linkages between the third stage of globalization and the rise of the new terrorism in the very late twentieth century: "Terrorism appeared as part of the underside of globalization. It was already becoming apparent that the consequence of the openness in the international system, economically as much as politically, was taking certain things out of control.

The result of globalization was the reduced power of states, the movement of capital and people around the world as governments opened up their borders. This created new opportunities for those who wished to inflict harm on the established [world] order."

Kurt Campbell and Michelle Flournoy more usefully emphasize that the terrorist groups brought together under al Qaeda's ideological umbrella were themselves components of the new world order convened by globalization: "By redirecting much of the energies of these groups from unsuccessful efforts to cause upheaval in their home countries into a broader assault on the West, bin Laden has created a genuine strategic threat. . . . By operating transnationally, [these] groups have found a way to get out of the box of facing off solely against national police in isolated theaters—conflicts they usually lose." Meanwhile Philip Bobbitt, the most important contemporary analyst of terrorism, reminds us that "when the boundaries between domestic and foreign threats were being erased" by globalization, maintaining the distinction between law (crime) and strategy (war) in addressing terrorism became difficult if not impossible.

The background agreement on the salient features of terrorism also included acknowledgment of its standing as a weapon of the weak, its willingness to target civilians with weapons of mass destruction, and its ideological cohesion around anti-Western, postliberal principles. Terrorism, whether practiced by Russian anarchists, Irish nationalists, diasporic Zionists, or Palestinian refugees, has always been the recourse of those who lack the mass support and the weaponry to wage conventional war against a modern nation-state. They have meant instead to sap the will of the enemy state by bringing the carnage of war to its civilian population—by making everyday life the theater of battle, thus erasing the distinction between combatant and noncombatant or, in a larger sense, between the public and the private, the outside and the inside. "The whole point is for the psychological impact to be greater than the actual physical act," Louis Richardson, the Harvard-based authority, explains. "Terrorism is indeed a weapon of the weak."

But the terrorists of the very late twentieth century were quite different from their predecessors among, say, the Irgun, the Zionist group led by Menachim Begin in the 1940s, or its mirror image, the Palestine Liberation Organization (PLO), led by Yasir Arafat from the 1960s until his death in 2004. Both of these groups targeted civilians in the hope of removing them and their armed representatives from territory they claimed as their ancestral homeland. Even so, neither would have considered, let alone undertaken, the annihilation of an entire city by means of chemical, biological, or nuclear weapons. The terrorist movements of the very late twentieth century did consider such a project. That is the big difference between, say, the Irish Republican Army (IRA) and al Qaeda: the latter, for example, killed almost as many innocent civilians in one day, September 11, 2001, as the IRA had in thirty years of trying.

Bobbitt illustrates the difference with a hypothetical scenario comparing the IRA, the PLO, and al Qaeda.

> Fearing popular revulsion, international disapproval, local repression, and threats to their own cohesion, and facing active dissuasion by those states that monopolized WMD even when they were willing to arm terrorists with other weapons, [the IRA and the PLO] turned away from such acquisitions. If someone had said to either Gerry Adams or Yasir Arafat, "I can get you a ten-kiloton nuclear weapon," one can imagine the reaction. A cautious gasp, a quick turning away—reflecting the apprehension that one has met an agent provocateur. But suppose such an offer were made to bin Laden? He would say, "What will it cost?"

The difference of scale between the old and the new terrorism is often explained by the ideological cohesion of the latter—the order-of-magnitude increase in the carnage caused by terrorist groups is an index of their religious intensity, many analysts say. They typically go on to say that this intensity magnifies an anti-Western, postliberal attitude toward the evidence of modernity. The special contribution of al Qaeda, in these terms, has been its graft of a renewed Islamic doctrine, on the one hand, and a variety of political grievances already forged by Muslims' resistance to Western imperialism—by Afghans, Iranians, Lebanese, and Palestinians—on the other.

Western observers often complain that Muslims never experienced a Reformation akin to the European upheaval that produced a separation of church and state and so allowed the emergence of political movements that required no religious support or justification. What these observers forget is that neither Martin Luther nor John Calvin, the Reformation's founding fathers, favored such a separation: the statutory distance between the sacred and the secular took three centuries to establish, and its measurement still changes as the result of political debate and judicial review. The intellectual renewal of Islam in the late twentieth century through the restatement and revision of original texts—particularly but not only the Koran—has, in fact, amounted to a reformation, but like the Christian precursor, it reinstates the refusal of a separation between holy writ and statutory law. Its inventors have insisted that the rules and prohibitions we can derive from the Koran (and, of course, from its acknowledged antecedents in the Old and New Testaments) are sufficient to the demands of modern governance.

Now, we may ridicule this position as an antimodern deviation from the secular example of the West. We may want, accordingly, to prescribe more economic development as the treatment needed to wake these backward fundamentalists from their benighted dream of a global Caliphate ruled from Mecca. But look more closely. There is nothing notably antimodern about either the religious fervor that would reintegrate the sacred and the secular—transcendent truth and mundane reality—or the political opposition to the liberal distinction between state and society. Indeed, all the successful revolutionary movements of the twentieth century, which occasionally used terrorism as an adjunct to their guerilla wars, tried to dismantle this liberal distinction on the grounds that it no longer made a difference. These movements, from fascism to communism, were uniformly anticapitalist and antiliberal, but they were also committed to the most strenuous versions of industrialized modernity. So we can say that the intellectual renewal of Islam carried out by the spiritual leaders of the Muslim Brotherhood in the 1950s (among them, Sayyid Qutb) and appropriated by al Qaeda in the 1990s does urge the erasure of the liberal distinction between state and society; but we should not conclude—as do Paul Berman from the Left and Norman Podhoretz from the Right—that this urge is the symptom of a nihilist sensibility which requires the obliteration of Western civilization.

If we do reach that conclusion, we will continue to mistake a postliberal doctrine for an antimodern ideology, and we will, as a result, continue to ignore the specific political grievances al Qaeda files on behalf of Muslims everywhere. We will continue, accordingly, to say that "they [the terrorists] hate us not because of what we do, but for the way we live" or that they are the moral equivalent of the Nazis. President Bush put it this way nine days after the towers fell: "They're the heirs of all the murderous ideologies of the 20th century. By sacrificing human life to serve their radical visions, by abandoning every value except the will to power, they follow in the path of fascism, Nazism, and totalitarianism." Thus, we will understand that there can be no political discussion or compromise with such brutes—we will realize that we must wage a borderless, endless war on terror, with all that implies for the militarization of U.S. foreign policy as such.

Bush and the liberal intellectuals who gathered under the banner of a war on terror were emphatic in claiming that the enemy has no political agenda except a "cult of death and irrationality," which somehow entails the end of the world as we know it. Here is Bush on October 6, 2005: "In fact, we're not facing a set of grievances that can be soothed [sic] and addressed. We're facing a radical ideology with unalterable objectives: to enslave whole nations and intimidate the world. No act of ours invited the rage of the killers—and no concession, bribe or act of appeasement would change or limit their plans for murder." Here is Berman at an even more delirious and incomprehensible pitch of prophetic dread in 2003: "The successes of the Islamist revolution were going to take place on the plane of the dead, or nowhere. Lived experience pronounced that sentence on the Islamist revolution—the lived experience of Europe, where each of the totalitarian movements [fascism and communism] proposed a total renovation of life, and each was driven to create the total renovation in death."

Sympathy for the Devil: The Rationality of Terrorism

But in fact, al Qaeda, like every other terrorist movement before it, has a legible political agenda that flows directly from its specific grievances against the West—especially against the United States, the exemplar of Western, liberal, imperialist capitalism. To be sure, this agenda is often animated by the religious vernacular that shapes public discourse in Muslim countries, but in essence it is a set of political goals with little room for the imagery of Armageddon. Osama bin Laden insisted in 2003, for example, that the American way of life was neither his personal concern nor the object of Islamic jihad: "Their leader, who is a fool whom all obey, was claiming that we were jealous of their way of life, while the truth—which the Pharaoh of our generation conceals—is that we strike at them because of the way they oppress us in the Muslim world, especially in Palestine and Iraq." Before and after the U.S. invasion of Iraq, moreover, he consistently listed three examples of such "oppression": the American military presence in the Arabian Peninsula; the U.S.-sponsored economic sanctions imposed by the United Nations on Iraq after the first Gulf war (which, according to a UNICEF report, killed five hundred thousand Iraqi children under the age of five between 1991 and 1998); and the unwavering American support for Israel during its ill-fated invasion of Lebanon and during its ongoing settlement of Palestinian territory.

Now, we may say that each of these three strategic positions was, or is, an important element in the national security of the United States, and with it the global order over which it presides. But in doing so, we must understand that none is a permanent or even a long-standing fixture of U.S. foreign policy—for all date from the very late twentieth century (the consummation and militarization of the U.S.-Israeli relation, for example, dates from Reagan's second term). We must also understand that each was, and is, a matter of choice by policymakers; alternatives to all three positions were, and are, presumably available, especially in view of the Soviet Union's defeat in

Afghanistan and its subsequent dissolution, both of which reduced Russian power in the Middle East. Finally, we must understand that the adoption of alternatives to these strategic positions does not entail any disruption in the American way of life.

So, regardless of what we think about, say, Israel's treatment of Palestinian claims—whether we think it is just or unjust—we can acknowledge that what we do (and support) in the Muslim precincts of the Middle East is far more significant than the way we live in North America. By the same token, we can acknowledge that what we do in that world elsewhere is subject to reconsideration and revision. Once we have made these acknowledgments, we can see that our approach to al Qaeda and related threats need not take the form of a borderless, endless "war on terror." We can see that this approach might well take the form of diplomacy, perhaps even changes in U.S. strategic positions. At least we can conclude that the militarization of American foreign policy is not the inevitable result of the terrorist threat to peaceful economic development on a global scale.

To boil this conclusion down to its essentials, let us ask an impertinent question: What if it had informed the U.S. response to the attacks on the World Trade Center and the Pentagon? We know, from our brief study of pragmatism and poststructuralism in chapter 3, that past events are effects of interpretation because real events just happen; they do not in their happening possess the formal qualities of narrative, which makes them significant—that is, actionable and thus consequential—by giving coherence to what is random, or at least meaningless, sequence. As William James once put it, "Day follows day, and its contents are simply added. The new contents themselves are not true, they simply come and are. Truth is what we say about them."

He might have added that the truth of what we say about the contents of any sequence, whether natural like the sunrise or artificial like the start of a war, is divisible or debatable; in other words, the truth we discover is always plural because our purposes in narrating, in speaking the truth about the sequence in question, are different. In the case at hand, for example, the narrative that determined a military rather than a diplomatic response to al Qaeda was the story told by George W. Bush soon after 9/11, then fleshed out by Paul Berman, Christopher Hitchens, David Frum, and Richard Perle, among many others—a story that portrayed bin Laden and his lieutenants as members of the same "cult of death and irrationality" that had turned Europe into a charnel house in the 1940s. Like the fascists before them, these were bizarre, evil, inexplicable men with whom there could be no bargaining. The consequence of this narrative was, and is, a borderless, endless "war on terror."

What if the story told soon after 9/11 had portrayed these men as rationally using the principal weapon of the weak in seeking to redress specific political grievances and to change recent American foreign policy? Clearly, war would not have been the only actionable answer, the only conceivable consequence. Changes in the relevant strategic positions would not necessarily have been the appropriate response either. But we would have known that the American way of life was not at stake in responding to the attacks of 9/11, that maintaining the distinction between law and strategy was necessary, and that bargaining with the enemy was therefore possible. The consequence of this narrative, this knowledge, would be a very different world than the one we now inhabit; at any rate, we can be sure that it would not be on a permanent war footing and that the Middle East would not still be the site of desperate armed struggle.

But it is notoriously difficult to prove a negative—which is why historians are not supposed to ask "what if" questions. Fortunately, there is another way to prove that, if our purpose is to explain, address, and contain the new terrorism, war is not the answer. It takes us to Iraq in the fourth year of the American invasion, when more than fifty U.S. soldiers and marines were dying every month at the hands of Shi'ite militias in Baghdad and Sunni insurgents in Anbar Province—both factions used recognizably terrorist tactics, including ethnic cleansing and suicide bombers—when "national reconciliation" by means of political compromise between the Muslim sects was still a joke, and when Iran was becoming the key player in the reconstruction of Iraq's battered infrastructure. This was the year of the so-called surge, which placed thirty thousand additional troops in Baghdad to pacify the center of armed resistance to the American occupation.

On the face of it, then, the "surge" of 2007 was a military solution to a military problem—the lack of security determined by terrorism, which made the day-to-day give-and-take of pluralist politics unthinkable. And on the face of it, the "surge" worked. Violence in Baghdad plummeted, and the peculiarly vicious Sunni insurgency in Anbar—where officers from Saddam Hussein's disbanded army had allied with a new offshoot of al Qaeda—quickly receded. By 2008, progress toward "national reconciliation" was enacted in a parliamentary compromise on sharing oil revenues among the Shi'ite majority and the Sunni and Kurdish minorities. In these terms, war was the answer to the rise of terrorist movements of resistance in Iraq: The logic of the larger, global war on terror was validated by the success of the "surge." Certainly the proponents of the war and the "surge" said as much.

But in fact, the so-called surge did not work as a military solution. It worked instead as a counterterrorist strategy that acknowledged the primacy of specific political grievances (most of which pertained to perceived inequities of proportionate power within postwar Iraq). Indeed the "surge" could not have worked as a military solution. According to the U.S. military's new *Field Manual*, prepared under the direction of the U.S. commander in Iraq during the "surge," an effective counterinsurgent force requires at least twenty combatants per one thousand members of the local population. By this calculation, 120,000 troops would have been required in Baghdad alone, a city of six million inhabitants. The difference was not, and could not have been, covered by Iraqi forces, which were still ethnically divided and still incapable of supplying their own logistical backing.

So the rapid fall of terrorist violence in Iraq between mid-2007 and late 2008 was not the result of a military victory. It was instead the result of Iran's orders to Shi'ite militias in Baghdad and the U.S. military's negotiations with the Sunni insurgents in Anbar. The most formidable militia in the capital was the Mahdi Army, led by the radical Shi'ite cleric Moktada al-Sadr, whose anti-American rhetoric had made him a national hero. This militia practically disappeared from the streets in 2007, when the force that trained it, Iran's Revolutionary Guard, ordered it to stand down. Meanwhile, in keeping with the new *Field Manual*'s political imperatives, the U.S. military bribed the Sunni tribal leaders and former Baathists of Anbar, who in turn armed their followers and disarmed their former allies from al Qaeda in Mesopotamia. In short, a war of position worked where a war of maneuver had failed. Or rather, war as such was not the answer in stabilizing Iraq.

The original architects of the Open Door believed that war as such was a problem, not a solution to perceived inequities in the distribution of global resources and opportunities, particularly since it spawned revolutionary movements—for example, both the communist and fascist movements of the 1920s were born in the throes of World War I—which in turn closed off huge swaths of the world market and created the conditions for trade war. Again, the Open Door world as conceived by these architects was a place in which military solutions to international disagreements were sometimes necessary but always a last resort; in which armed force did not exhaust the meanings of world power; in which unilateral "preemptive actions" had become obsolete, even destructive; in which multilateral institutions constrained such actions and thus enabled the sovereignty of all nations; in which economic growth and development were the necessary conditions of world peace; in which exclusive spheres of influence were the crucial obstacle to such growth and development; and in which the colonial culture of racism—the "white man's burden"—could not thrive because it severed the continuum of civilization.

In addressing and shaping the second stage of globalization, these original architects of the Open Door believed they had found a way to reduce the role of militaries in the articulation of foreign policies and the conduct of international relations. They believed they had found a way to ease the inevitable passage of the seat of empire, perhaps even dispensing with war as its spastic, deadly accompaniment. Perhaps we have accidentally rediscovered their way of thinking in fighting, and losing, a "war on terror" in Afghanistan, in Iraq, and at home. If that is the case, the American Century could have a happy ending after all.

~

Coda
Keep Arguing

Now that you've read this book, what do you know that you didn't before? That's the pragmatic test of any idea, category, or assertion. If there are no consequences, you can forget about it.

A better way to ask the same question is, what could you argue after reading this book? Here's a preliminary list.

You could argue that the Reagan Revolution was not a merely conservative movement and that, by their own account, the supply-side radicals who stormed the Keynesian citadel were repulsed by the Congress and the American people. You could argue that socialism was an active dimension of political and intellectual life in the late-twentieth-century United States—and your argument might well be confirmed by the new regulatory apparatus invented to address the economic crisis that began in 2008.

In short, you could argue that the country kept moving to the left after 1975, so that it was much more liberal at the end of the century than it was before Reagan took office. Not that conservatism was eclipsed—no, the point is that conservatives themselves kept worrying about the social and moral effects of free markets and consumer capitalism and that liberals were meanwhile evolving into what we used to call social democrats.

You could argue that higher education is better off these days precisely because the Left, broadly construed, took over the pilot disciplines of the liberal arts in the 1980s. You could correlate that takeover with the larger shift of American culture and politics to the left of center. You could even correlate that takeover with the increasing diversity of both the student body

133

and the faculty after the fourth great watershed in higher education. Look around, the university is a very different place than it used to be, and that's a good thing. Or, maybe not. But now you have an argument about it—and that's a very good thing.

You could argue that poststructuralism and postmodernism are not foreign imports but are, instead, homegrown theories that make good sense of the new world of the late twentieth century. You could even say that pragmatism, that venerable American philosophy, is the origin of it all, deconstruction included. Maybe you wouldn't want to go that far. You would, however, want to argue that modern individualism has been in question—a point of contention—since at least the 1890s, so that the notion of a "socially constructed self" was not exactly new in the 1990s. Or maybe it felt new because gender trouble was so clearly its origin.

You could argue that feminism changed everything, inside academia and out, but also that feminism, like liberalism or conservatism, is an extremely diverse set of attitudes toward history and thus contains a programmatic urge that is anything but uniform. You could also argue that the so-called culture wars of the 1990s were an intramural sport on the Left—or that the right-wing positions in these conflicts kept losing. Either way, you could say that Americans were trending left after Reagan, to the point where arguments over gay rights became a normal part of political discourse and the 1993 Pulitzer Prize went to an avowed Marxist whose play carried the subtitle of a "Gay Fantasia."

You could argue that the end of modernity was on view at the Cineplex in the late twentieth century, where horror became the movie mainstream and male masochism became commonplace. In other words, you could say that when the professors started talking about gender trouble in the big words of poststructuralism, they were translating the evidence available on screen, for example, from *I Spit on Your Grave*, a truly awful movie. Or not—think of *The Matrix*, which makes Jean Baudrillard and Cornel West, two professors, its patron saints. You could say, in conclusion, let's get over the either/or choice. By now we know this postmodern impulse goes both ways, up and down, as the line between lowbrow and highbrow culture dissolves in the late twentieth century.

You could argue that the antirealist tendency of late-twentieth-century TV—cartoons, angels, demons, vampires, everywhere!—signifies the stupidity of the audience. You could argue instead that this tendency has been deeply embedded in the American literary/artistic tradition since at least the 1820s. You could say, as a result, that all those supernatural creatures were gathering to remind us that freedom does not reside in the abolition of our earthly, particular circumstances but rather in our ability to reshape them in accordance with our purposes. You could say that real love requires bodies that matter—it requires passion rather than metaphysics or immortality. You might even say that angels in America have always been a reminder of this life, not the next.

You could argue that excrement is the raw material of our time—it is the way we recognize and handle the demonic forces and properties of globalization. Or just go ahead and call it a world of shit. It's where you live, no matter what your address, whether in Guatemala City or New York City. Everybody's insides are now outside, reminding us that the sacred "interiority" of modern individualism is at risk and that the universalization of exchange value is complete. You could go on to say that it is only in the cartoonish universe of late-twentieth-century TV that this excremental issue has been seriously, comically, and productively addressed, by drawing anal probes from outer space and singing in blackface about hell on earth.

You could argue that the music of the late twentieth century, in all its demented fury and unruly variations, was a way to address the gender trouble of that millennial time. You could say that the trademark genres of the moment—disco, punk, heavy metal, and hip-hop—were ways of reasoning in music that were just as profound as the professorial idiom on offer in the classroom. Maybe more so, because they performed the deconstruction and recombination of identities you heard about in lectures and read about in books.

You could argue that the "personal" computer is anything but. You could say that it removes you from the scene of modern individualism, where you brood in private, and that it delivers you unto a new world of public, social, anonymous discourse, where you try on new identities. Every day. And you get to Google yourself.

And you could argue that the American Century was both longer and shorter than you thought. It began earlier than even Henry Luce believed, and it ended only recently, with the militarization of American foreign policy. Or did it? You could argue that we still inhabit the world invented by the Open Door Notes. You could argue that this expansive place has been whirled away by the Bush Doctrine and the very idea of a "war on terror." Either way, you might be right.

So let's keep arguing.

~

Appendix
Their Great Depression and Ours

This essay was written and published at my blog in October 2008, then reprinted at History News Network (www.historynewsnetwork.org) and excerpted at TNR.com, American Prospect.com, Salon.com, Mother Jones .com, and a dozen other websites. It is reprinted here because it speaks directly to the questions raised in chapter 1 about supply-side economics.

I

Now that everybody is accustomed to citing the precedent of the Great Depression in diagnosing the recent economic turmoil—and now that a severe recession is unfolding—it may be useful to treat these episodes as historical events rather than theoretical puzzles. The key question that frames all others is simple: Are these comparable moments in the development of American capitalism? To answer this question is to explain their causes and consequences.

Contemporary economists seem to have reached an unlikely consensus in explaining the Great Depression—they blame government policy for complicating and exacerbating what was just another business cycle. This explanation is still gaining intellectual ground, and it deeply informed opposition to the bailout plan. The founding father here is Milton Friedman, the monetarist who argued that the Federal Reserve unknowingly raised real interest rates between 1930 and 1932 (nominal interest rates remained more or less stable, but as price deflation accelerated across the board, real rates went up), thus freezing the credit markets and destroying investor confidence.

But the argument that government was the problem, not the solution, has no predictable political valence. David Leonhardt's piece for the *New York Times* (10/1/08) is the liberal version of the same argument: if government does its minimal duty and restores liquidity to the credit markets, this crisis will not devolve into the debacle that was the Great Depression. Niall Ferguson's essay for *Time* magazine titled "The End of Prosperity" (10/6/08) takes a similar line: "Yet the underlying cause of the Great Depression—as Milton Friedman and Anna Jacobson Schwartz argued in their seminal book *A Monetary History of the United States, 1867–1960*, published in 1963—was not the stock market crash but a 'great contraction' of credit due to an epidemic of bank failures." Ben Bernanke's argument for the buyouts and the bailout derives, of course, from the same intellectual source. At Friedman's ninetieth birthday party in 2002, Bernanke, then a member of the Fed's board, said, "I would like to say to Milton and Anna: Regarding the Great Depression. You're right, we did it. We're very sorry. But thanks to you, we won't do it again."

The assumption that regulates the argument, whether conservative or liberal, is that these two crises are like any other and can be managed by a kind of financial triage, by treating the immediate symptoms and hoping the patient's otherwise healthy body will bring him back to a normal, steady state. Certain fragile or flamboyant or fraudulent institutions will be liquidated in the normal course of this standard-issue business cycle, and that is a good thing—otherwise the "moral hazard" of validating the "corrupt and incompetent practices of Wall Street and Washington," as John McCain puts it, will be incurred.

Crisis management, by this accounting, is an occasional activity that always addresses the same problems of liquidity and moral hazard. By the same accounting, the long-term causes of crisis must go unnoticed and untreated because they are temporary deviations from the norm of market-determined equilibrium and because the system appears to be the sum of its parts—if the central bank steps in with "ready lending" when investor confidence falters, these parts will realign themselves properly and equilibrium will be restored.

From this standpoint, the Great Depression and today's economic crisis are comparable not because they resulted from similar macroeconomic causes but because the severity of the credit freeze in both moments is equally great, and the scope of the financial solution must, then, be equally far-reaching. Then and now, as Anna Schwartz explained in an interview with the *Wall Street Journal* (10/18/08), a "credit tightening" accounts for the collapse of the boom.

There is another way to explain the Great Depression, of course. It requires looking at the changing structure, or "long waves," of economic growth and development, digging all the while for the "real," rather than the merely monetary, factors. This explanatory procedure focuses on "the fundamentals" and typically treats the financial system as a tertiary sector that merely registers the value of goods on offer—except when it becomes the repository of surplus capital generated elsewhere, that is, when personal savings and corporate profits cannot find productive outlets and flow instead into speculative channels.

The long-wave approach has fallen out of favor as more mainstream economists have adopted the assumptions enabled by the Friedman-Schwartz rendering of monetary history. This structural approach does, however, make room for crisis management at the moment of truth; here, too, the assumption is that financial triage will suffice during the economic emergency. When things settle down, when normal market conditions return, the question of long-term trends will remain.

The problem with the long-wave approach—the reason it has less traction than the tidy alternative offered by Friedman and Schwartz—is that it cannot specify any connection between macroeconomic realities and conditions in the financial markets. Michael Bernstein's brilliant book on the origins of the Great Depression, for example, treats the stock market crash of 1929 as a "random event" that complicated and amplified events happening elsewhere in the economy.

This theoretical standoff has crippled our ability to provide a comprehensive explanation for the Great Depression and thus to offer a convincing comparison between it and the current crisis. So let's start over—let's ask the kind of questions that are already foreclosed by the competing models. Was the Great Depression just another business cycle that the Fed screwed up because it didn't understand the money supply? Or was it a watershed event that registered and caused momentous structural changes in the sources of economic growth? Or would more astute crisis management have saved the day?

Does the current crisis bear any resemblance to the Great Depression? Or is it just another generic business cycle that requires an unprecedented level of government intervention because the staggering amount of bad debt has compromised the entire financial system?

The short answers, in order, are No, Yes, No, Yes, No.

Here are the long answers. The underlying cause of the Great Depression was not a short-term credit contraction engineered by central bankers who, unlike Ferguson and Bernanke, had not yet had the privilege of reading

Milton Friedman's big book. The underlying cause of that economic disaster was a fundamental shift of income shares away from wages/consumption to corporate profits that produced a tidal wave of surplus capital that could not be profitably invested in goods production—and, in fact, was not invested in good production. In terms of classical, neoclassical, and supply-side theory, this shift of income shares should have produced more investment and more jobs, but it didn't. Why not?

Look first at the new trends of the 1920s. This was the first decade in which the new consumer durables—autos, radios, refrigerators, and the like—became the driving force of economic growth as such. This was the first decade in which a measurable decline of net investment coincided with spectacular increases in nonfarm labor productivity and industrial output (roughly 60 percent for both). This was the first decade in which a relative decline of trade unions gave capital the leverage it needed to enlarge its share of revenue and national income at the expense of labor.

These three trends were the key ingredients in a recipe for disaster. At the very moment that higher private-sector wages and thus increased consumer expenditure, became the only available means to enforce the new pattern of economic growth, income shares shifted decisively away from wages toward profits. For example, 90 percent of taxpayers had less disposable income in 1929 than in 1922; meanwhile corporate profits rose 62 percent, dividends doubled, and the top 1 percent of taxpayers increased their disposable income by 63 percent. At the very moment that *net investment became unnecessary to enforce increased productivity and output*, income shares shifted decisively away from wages toward profits. For example, the value of fixed capital declined at the cutting edge of manufacturing—in steel and automobiles—even as productivity and output soared because capital-saving innovations reduced both capital/output ratios and the industrial labor force.

What could be done with the resulting surpluses piling up in corporate coffers? If you can increase labor productivity and industrial output without making net additions to the capital stock, what do you do with your rising profits? In other words, if you cannot invest those profits in goods production, where do you place them in the hope of a reasonable return?

The answer is simple—you place your growing surpluses in the most promising markets, in securities listed on the stock exchange, say, or in the Florida real estate boom, particularly in view of receding returns elsewhere. You also establish time deposits in commercial banks and start issuing paper in the call loan market that feeds speculative trading in securities.

At any rate that is what corporate CEOs *outside the financial sector* did between 1926 and 1929, to the tune of $6.6 billion. They had no place else to put their increased profits—they could not, and they did not, invest these profits in expanded productive capacity because merely maintaining and replacing the existing capital stock was enough to enlarge capacity, productivity, and output.

No wonder the stock market boomed, or rather no wonder a speculative bubble developed there. It was the single most important receptacle of the surplus capital generated by a decisive shift of income shares away from wages toward profits—and that surplus enforced rising demand for new issues of securities even after 1926. By 1929 about 70 percent of the proceeds from such IPOs were spent unproductively (that is, they were not used to invest in plant and equipment or to hire labor), according to Moody's Investors Service.

The stock market crashed in October 1929 because the nonfinancial firms abruptly pulled their $6.6 billion out of the call loan market. They had experienced the relative decline in demand for consumer durables, particularly autos, since 1926 and knew better than the banks that the outer limit of consumer demand had already been reached. Demand for stocks, whether new issues or old, disappeared accordingly, and the banks were left holding the proverbial bag—the bag full of "distressed assets" called securities listed on the stock exchange. That is why they failed so spectacularly in the early 1930s—again, not because of a "credit contraction" engineered by a clueless Fed but because the assets they were banking on and loaning against were suddenly worthless.

The financial shock of the Crash froze credit, including the novel instrument of installment credit for consumers, and thus amplified the income effects of the shift to profits that dominated the 1920s. Consumer durables, the new driving force of economic growth as such, suffered most in the first four years after the Crash. By 19341, demand for and output of automobiles was half of the levels of 1929; industrial output and national income were similarly halved, while unemployment reached almost 20 percent.

And yet recovery was on the way, even though increased capital investment was not—even though by 1934 nonfinancial corporations could borrow from Herbert Hoover's Reconstruction Finance Corporation at almost interest-free rates. By 1937, industrial output and national income had regained the levels of 1929, and the volume of new auto sales exceeded that of 1929. Meanwhile, however, net investment out of profits continued to decline so that by 1939 the capital stock per worker was lower than in 1929.

How did this unprecedented recovery happen? In terms of classical, neoclassical, and supply-side theory, it *couldn't have happened*—in these terms, investment out of profits must lead the way to growth by creating new jobs, thus increasing consumer expenditures and causing their feedback effects on profits and future investment. But as H. W. Arndt explained long ago in *The Economic Lessons of the Nineteen-Thirties* (1944), "Whereas in the past cyclical recoveries had generally been initiated by a rising demand for capital goods in response to renewed business confidence and new investment opportunities, and had only consequentially led to increased consumers' income and demand for consumption goods, the recovery of 1933–1937 seems to have been based and fed on rising demand for consumers' goods."

That rising demand was a result of net contributions to consumers' expenditures out of federal deficits and of new collective bargaining agreements, not the eradication of unemployment. In this sense, the shift of income shares away from profits toward wages, which permitted recovery was determined by government spending and enforced by labor movements.

So the underlying cause of the Great Depression was a distribution of income that, on the one hand, choked off growth in consumer durables—the industries that were the new sources of economic growth as such—and that, on the other hand, produced the tidal wave of surplus capital which produced the stock market bubble of the late 1920s. By the same token, recovery from this economic disaster registered—and caused—a momentous structural change by making demand for consumer durables the leading edge of growth.

II

So far I have asked five questions that would allow us to answer this one: Does the recent and recurring economic turmoil bear the comparisons to the Great Depression we hear every day, every hour? On my way to these questions, I noticed that mainstream economists' explanations of the Great Depression converge on the idea that a credit contraction engineered by the hapless Fed was the underlying cause of that debacle. They converge, that is, on the explanation offered by Milton Friedman and Anna Jacobson Schwartz in 1963 in *A Monetary History of the United States, 1867–1960*. In this sense, the presiding spirit of contemporary thinking about our current economic plight—from Niall Ferguson to Henry Paulson and Ben Bernanke—is Friedman's passionate faith in free markets.

I am not suggesting that there is some great irony or paradox lurking in the simple fact that a new regulatory regime resides in the programs proposed by Paulson and Bernanke. Saving the financial system is a complicated business that will produce innumerable unintended consequences. Instead, my point is that rigorous regulation, even government ownership of the commanding heights, is perfectly consistent with the development of capitalism.

Here, then, are the remainder of those five questions—the questions that are foreclosed by the theoretical consensus gathered around Friedman's assumptions about business cycles and crisis management.

Would more astute crisis management have prevented the economic disaster of the 1930s? Does the current crisis bear any resemblance to the Great Depression? Or is it just another generic business cycle that requires an unprecedented level of government intervention because the staggering amount of bad debt has compromised the entire financial system?

The short answers to these questions are No, Yes, and No. The long answers to the first two questions appeared in Part 1. Let's take up the last three here, always with the policy-relevant implications in view.

More astute crisis management could not have saved the day in the early 1930s, no matter how well-schooled the Fed's governors might have been. The economic crisis was caused by long-term structural trends that, in turn, devastated financial markets (particularly the stock market) and created a credit freeze—that is, a situation in which banks were refusing to lend and businesses were afraid to borrow. The financial meltdown was, to this extent, a function of a larger economic debacle caused by a significant shift of income shares toward profits, away from wages and consumption, at the very moment that increased consumer expenditures had become the fulcrum of economic growth as such (see Part 1).

So, even when the federal government offered all manner of unprecedented assistance to the banking system, including the Reconstruction Finance Corporation of 1932, nothing moved. It took a bank holiday and the Glass-Steagall Act—which barred commercial banks from loaning against collateral whose value was determined by the stock market—to resuscitate the banks, but by then they were mere spectators on the economic recovery created by net contributions to consumer expenditures out of federal deficits.

So the current crisis does bear a strong resemblance to the Great Depression, if only because its underlying cause is a recent redistribution of income toward profits, away from wages and consumption (of which more in a moment), and because all the unprecedented assistance offered to the banking system since the sale of Bear Stearns and the bankruptcy of Lehman Brothers in September—AIG, Washington Mutual, Fannie Mae, Freddie Mac, the bailout package, the equity stake initiative, and so on—has not thawed the credit freeze. The markets, here and elsewhere, have responded accordingly, with extraordinary volatility.

The liquidation of distressed assets after the Crash of 1929 was registered in the massive deflation that halved wholesale and retail prices by 1932. This outcome is precisely what Ben Bernanke and Henry Paulson have been trying desperately to prevent since August 2007—and before them, it is precisely what Alan Greenspan was trying to prevent by skirting the issue of the "housing bubble" and placing his faith in the new credit instruments fashioned out of securitized assets derived from home mortgages. Their great fear, at the outset of the crisis, was not another Great Depression but the deflationary spiral of Japan in the 1990s, after its central bank pricked a similar housing bubble by raising interest rates and disciplining the mortgage dealers.

On the one hand, these men feared deflation because they knew it would cramp the equity loan market, drive down housing prices, slow residential construction, erode consumer confidence, disrupt consumer borrowing, and reduce consumer demand across the board. Meanwhile, the market value of the assets undergirding the new credit instruments—securitized mortgages—would have to fall, and the larger edifice of the financial system would have to shrink as the banks recalculated the "normal" ratio between assets and liabilities. In sum, Greenspan, Bernanke, and Paulson understood that economic growth driven by increasing consumer expenditures—in this instance, increasing consumer debt "secured" by home mortgages—would grind to a halt if they didn't reinflate the bubble.

On the other hand, they feared deflation because they knew its effects on the world economy could prove disastrous. With deflation would come a dollar with greater purchasing power, to be sure, and thus lower trade and current account deficits, perhaps even a more manageable national debt. But so, too, would come lower U.S. demand for exports from China, India, and developing nations, and thus the real prospect of "decoupling"—that is, a world economy no longer held together by American demand for commodities, capital, and credit. The centrifugal forces unleashed by globalization would then have free rein; American economic leverage against the rising powers of the East would be accordingly diminished.

So Greenspan is not to be blamed for our current conditions, as every congressman and all the CNBC talking heads seem to think. Under the circumstances, which included the available intellectual—that is, theoretical—alternatives, he did pretty much what he had to, hoping all the while that the inevitable market correction would not be too severe. So have Bernanke and Paulson done their duty. There may well be corruption, fraud, stupidity, and chicanery at work in this mess, but they are much less important than the systemic forces that have brought us to the brink of another Great Depression.

The real difficulty in measuring the odds of another such disaster, and thus averting it, is that those available intellectual alternatives are now bunched on an extremely narrow spectrum of opinion—a spectrum that lights up a lot of trees but can't see the surrounding forest. Again, everyone, including Bernanke, now seems to think, along with Milton Friedman, that the underlying cause of the Great Depression was a credit contraction that froze the financial system between 1930 and 1932. Here is how Niall Ferguson put it in *Time* magazine for the week of October 13, 2008: "Yet the underlying cause of the Great Depression—as Milton Friedman and Anna Jacobson Schwartz argued in their seminal book *A Monetary History of the United States, 1867–1960*, published in 1963—was not the stock market crash but a 'great contraction' of credit due to an epidemic of bank failures."

M. Gregory Mankiw more recently joined this monetarist chorus in the *New York Times*, similarly suggesting that a credit contraction was the cause of that epic debacle: "The 1920s were a boom decade, and as it came to a close the Federal Reserve tried to rein in what might have been called the irrational exuberance of the era. In 1928, the Fed maneuvered to drive up interest rates. So interest-sensitive sectors like construction slowed." Then the crash came, and "banking panics" followed—the "money supply collapsed" and credit froze as fear gripped the "hearts of depositors." So the recovery after 1933 was a function of "monetary expansion" eased by the end of the gold standard; the "various market interventions" we know as the New Deal "weakened the recovery by impeding market forces" (*New York Times* 10/26/08).

By this accounting, pouring more money into the financial system ("monetary expansion") will fix it, and when it is fixed, the larger economy will find a new equilibrium at a reflated price level. The goal is to "recapitalize" the banks so that they can resume lending to businesses at a volume that sustains demand for labor and to consumers at a volume that sustains demand for finished goods. By the terms of the $700 billion bailout package and according to new (and unprecedented) initiatives by the Fed, this recapitalization will take three forms.

First, the Treasury will buy equity stakes in banks deemed crucial to reanimating the lifeless body of the financial system—to make this move is *not to nationalize these banks* by installing government as their owner but rather to provide "start-up" capital free and clear, as if Paulson were backing an IPO. Second, the Fed can buy short-term commercial paper from firms who need money to maintain inventory, pay vendors, and hire labor. This move opens the central bank's discount window to mutual funds as well as nonfinancial firms, presumably small businesses that have neither cash reserves nor credibility with local bankers.

Third, and most importantly, the Treasury will conduct an auction through which the mortgage-related distressed assets now held by lenders are liquidated—that is, are bought by the government for more than their market value but less than their nominal value. Once those assets are "off the books," banks will have sufficient unencumbered capital to resume loaning at volumes and rates conducive to renewed growth and equilibrium. Investor confidence will return as investment opportunities appear, so the logic runs, and new borrowing will soon follow. But because this auction can't take place until the Treasury sorts through the books of the firms holding distressed assets—a matter of months—the equity stake approach has become, at least for the time being, the government's most promising means of restoring investor confidence in the integrity of the financial system.

Let us suppose, then, that Ferguson, Paulson, and Bernanke are right to assume that monetary policy is both the necessary and the sufficient condition of crisis management under present circumstances. (Bernanke now says he's in favor of a "stimulus package," but this is like saying he's in favor of the sun rising tomorrow—the real question is what version of fiscal stimulus will take effect, not whether stimulus will be proposed by Congress and the president.) Let us suppose, in other words, that the recapitalization of the banks proceeds exactly according to plan and that interest rates keep falling because the Fed wants to encourage borrowing. Does the reflation and recovery of the larger economy naturally follow?

In theory, yes—that is, if Friedman was right to specify a credit contraction as the underlying cause of the Great Depression, then a credit expansion on the scale accomplished and proposed by Paulson and Bernanke should restore investor confidence and promote renewed economic growth; it should at least abort an economic disaster. But if a credit contraction was not the underlying cause of the Great Depression and its sequel in our own time, then no amount of credit expansion will restore investor confidence and promote renewed economic growth.

The historical record of the 1930s and the slow-motion crash of the stock market since 2007 would suggest that Friedman's theoretical answer to our question lacks explanatory adequacy—and that Paulson and Bernanke's practical program, *which follows the Friedman line*, has not restored, and cannot restore, investor confidence. The effective freeze of interbank lending that, contrary to recent news reports, was already an alarming index as early as September 2007 would suggest the same thing. ("The system has just completely frozen up—everyone is hoarding," said one bank treasurer back then. "The published LIBOR [London interbank overnight] rates are a fiction."

Moreover, a severe recession now waits on the other side of recapitalization, mainly because consumer confidence, spending, and borrowing have been compromised or diminished, if not destroyed, by the credit freeze and the stock market crash: "Discretionary spending is drying up as Americans grapple with higher food and energy prices, depressed home values and diminished retirement accounts" (*Wall Street Journal* 10/9/08). Every indicator, from unemployment claims to retail sales, now points toward an economic crisis on a scale that has no postwar parallel.

Monetary policy, no matter how imaginative and ambitious, can't address this crisis. For just as a credit contraction was not the underlying cause of the Great Depression, so the reflation and recovery of the larger economy were not, and are not, the natural consequences of a financial fix. Our questions must then become, what *was* the underlying cause of the Great Depression, and how does the current crisis recapitulate the historical sequence that produced the earlier economic disaster?

And finally, if monetary policy cannot solve the real economic problems that now face us, what more is to be done?

As I argue in Part 1, the Great Depression was the consequence of a massive shift of income shares to profits, away from wages and thus consumption, at the very moment—the Roaring Twenties—that expanded production of consumer durables became the crucial condition of economic growth as such. This shift produced a tidal wave of surplus capital that, *in the absence of any need for increased investment in productive capacity* (net investment declined steadily through the 1920s even as industrial productivity and output increased spectacularly), flowed inevitably into speculative channels, particularly the stock market bubble of the late 1920s; when the bubble burst—by my calculation, when nonfinancial firms abruptly pulled out of the call loan market—demand for securities listed on the stock exchange evaporated, and the banks were left holding billions of dollars in distressed assets. The credit freeze and the extraordinary deflation of the 1930s followed; not even the Reconstruction Finance Corporation could restore investor confidence and reflate the larger economy.

So recovery between 1933 and 1937 was *not* the result of renewed confidence and increased net investment determined by newly enlightened *monetary* policy (the percentage of replacement and maintenance expenditures in the total of private investment actually grew in the 1930s). It was instead the result of net contributions to consumer expenditures out of federal budget deficits. In other words, *fiscal policy under the New Deal reanimated the new growth pattern that had first appeared in the 1920s*—that is, it validated the consumer-led pattern that was eventually disrupted by the shift of income shares to profits, away from wages and consumption, between 1925 and 1929.

That consumer-led pattern of economic growth was the hallmark of the postwar boom—the heyday of "consumer culture." It lasted until 1973, when steady gains in median family income and nonfarm real wages slowed and even ended. Since then, this stagnation has persisted, although increases in labor productivity should have allowed commensurable gains in wages. Thus a measurable shift of income shares away from wages and consumption, toward profits, has characterized the pattern of economic growth and development over the last thirty-five years.

We don't need Paul Krugman or Robert Reich to verify the result—that is, the widening gap between rich and poor, or rather between capital and labor, profits and wages. Two archdefenders of free markets, Martin Wolf of the *Financial Times* and Alan Greenspan, have repeatedly emphasized the same trend. For example, last September Greenspan complained that "real compensation tends to parallel real productivity, and we have seen that for generations, but not now. It has veered off course for reasons I am not clear about" (*Financial Times* 9/17/07). A year earlier, Wolf similarly complained that "the normal link between productivity and real earnings is broken" and that the "distribution of U.S. earnings has, as a result, become significantly more unequal" (*Financial Times* 4/26/06).

The offset to this shift of income shares came in the form of increasing transfer payments—government spending on entitlements and social programs—since the 1960s; these payments were the fastest-growing component of labor income (10 percent per annum) from 1959 to 1999. The moment of truth reached in 1929 was accordingly postponed. But then George Bush's tax cuts produced a new tidal wave of surplus capital with no place to go except into real estate, where the boom in lending against assets that kept appreciating allowed the "securitization" of mortgages—that is, the conversion of consumer debt into promising investment vehicles.

No place to go except into real estate? Why not into the stock market or, better yet, directly into productive investment by purchasing new plant and equipment and creating new jobs? Here is how Wolf answered this question back in August 2007 when trying to explain why the global "savings glut"— this is how Ben Bernanke named his special concern before he became the chair of the Fed—was flowing to the United States: "If foreigners are net providers of funds, some groups in the U.S. must be net users: they must be spending more than their incomes and financing the difference by selling financial claims to others," Wolf began. "This required spending is in excess of potential gross domestic product by the size of the current account deficit [the difference between spending and income]. At its peak that difference was close to 7 percent of GDP. . . . Who did the offsetting spending since the stock market bubble burst in 2000? The short-term answer was 'the U.S. government.' The longer-term one was 'U.S. households.'"

Wolf argues that once the dot.com bubble burst, the Bush tax cuts and the resulting federal deficit became the "fiscal boost" that forestalled a "deep recession." Then he turns to the different, but similarly effective, "deficit" created by *consumer* debt: "Now look at U.S. households. They moved ever further into financial deficit (defined as household savings, less residential investment). Household spending grew considerably faster than incomes from the early 1990s to 2006 [as wages stagnated, credit cards became ubiquitous, and mortgage lenders became more aggressive]. By then they ran an aggregate financial deficit of close to 4 percent of GDP. *Nothing comparable has happened since the second world war, if ever.* Indeed, on average households have run small financial surpluses over the past six decades."

And while consumers were going deeper into debt to service the current account deficit and finance economic growth, corporations were abstaining from invest-ment: "The recent household deficit more than offset the persistent financial surplus in the business sector. For a period of six years—the longest since the second world war—U.S. business invested less than its retained earnings" (*Financial Times* 8/22/07).

Greenspan concurred: "Intended investment in the United States has been lagging in recent years, judging from the larger share of internal cash flow that has been returned to shareholders, presumably for lack of new in-vestment opportunities."

So the Bush tax cuts merely fueled the housing bubble—they did not, and could not, lead to increased productive investment. And that is the consis-tent lesson to be drawn from fiscal policy that corroborates the larger shift to profits away from wages and consumption. A fiscal policy that cuts taxes on the wealthy and lowers the capital gains levy will not, and cannot, work to restore growth because increased investment does not automatically flow from increased savings created by tax cuts—and, more importantly, *because the conversion of increased savings to increased private investment is simply un-necessary to fuel growth.*

The *Wall Street Journal* admitted as much in its lead editorial of October 23, 2008, titled "An Obamanomics Preview." It was an admission by omis-sion, to be sure, but it nonetheless makes my point. Here is how it works: "Af-ter the dot.com bust, President Bush compromised with Senate Democrats and delayed his marginal-rate income tax cuts in return for immediate tax rebates. The rebates goosed spending for a while, but provided no increase in incentives to invest. Only after 2003, when the marginal-rate cuts took effect immediately, combined with cuts in dividend and capital gains rates, did robust growth return. The expansion was healthy until it was overtaken by the housing bust and even resisted recession into this year."

By this account, robust growth after 2003 was a function of increased incentives to invest that were provided by reductions in tax rates on dividends and capital gains. But the *Journal's* editorial board cannot—and does not—claim that such growth was the consequence of increased investment because, as Wolf and Greenspan emphasize, rising profits did not flow into productive investment. Growth happened in the absence of increased investment. Again, savings created by tax cuts do not necessarily translate into investment, and, as the historical record cited by the *Journal* itself demonstrates, increased private investment is simply unnecessary to fuel growth.

This last simple fact is the sticking point. It has not been, and cannot be, acknowledged by existing economic theory, whether monetarist or not. That is why the following axiom, which is derived from study of the historical record rather than belief in the world disclosed by economic theory, will sound startling at the very least: *there is no correlation whatsoever between lower taxes on corporate or personal income, increased net investment, and economic growth.*

For example, the fifty corporations with the largest benefits from Ronald Reagan's tax cuts of 1981 reduced their investments over the next two years. Meanwhile, the share of national income from wages and salaries declined 5 percent between 1978 and 1986, while the share from investment (profits, dividends, rent) rose 27 percent as per the demands of supply-side theory—but net investment kept falling through the 1980s. In 1987, Peter G. Peterson, the Blackstone founder who was then chairman of the Council on Foreign Relations, called this performance "by far the weakest net investment effort in our postwar history." Yet economic growth resumed in the aftermath of recession, in 1982, and continued steadily until the sharp but brief downturn of 1992.

The responsible fiscal policy for the foreseeable future is, then, to raise taxes on the wealthy and to make net contributions to consumer expenditures out of federal deficits if necessary. When asked why he wants to make these moves, Barack Obama does not have to retreat to the "fairness" line of defense Joe Biden used when pressed by Sarah Palin in debate or, for that matter, by the leader of the liberal media, the *New York Times* itself, which has admonished the

Democratic candidate as follows: "Mr. Obama has said that he would raise taxes on the wealthy, starting next year, to help restore fairness to the tax code and to pay for his spending plans. With the economy tanking, however, it's hard to imagine how he could prudently do that" (10/7/08).

In fact, if our current crisis is comparable to the early stages of the Great Depression, it is hard to imagine a more prudent and more productive program.

~

Bibliographic Essay

What follows is part endnotes and part bibliographical essay. I have tried to indicate the sources from which I have drawn evidence and ideas and to cite readings that provide background for, verification of, or challenges to my arguments.

From Dusk to Dawn: Chapter 1: Origins and Effects of the Reagan Revolution

On the oil shock and stagflation in the 1970s, see John M. Blair, *The Control of Oil* (New York: Pantheon, 1976), Alan S. Blinder, *Economic Policy and the Great Stagflation* (New York: Academic Press, 1981), Mancur Olson, *The Rise and Decline of Nations* (New Haven, CT: Yale University Press, 1982), and Michael Bruno and Jeffrey D. Sachs, *Economics of Worldwide Stagflation* (Cambridge, MA: Harvard University Press, 1985). James Q. Wilson's "cultural" diagnosis of the urban crisis, *Thinking About Crime* (New York: Basic, 1975), was revised and reissued three times by 1985. Martin Scorsese's filmic depictions of the related dangers are *Mean Streets* (1973) and *Taxi Driver* (1978).

On the Keynesian consensus and the supply-side challenge, see Theodore Rosenof, *Economics in the Long Run: New Deal Theorists and Their Legacies, 1933–1993* (Chapel Hill: University of North Carolina Press, 1997), and Herbert Stein, *Presidential Economics: The Making of Economic Policy from Roosevelt to Reagan and Beyond* (New York: Simon & Schuster, 1984). David

Stockman quotations are taken from *The Triumph of Politics: How the Reagan Revolution Failed* (New York: Harper & Row, 1986); compare this account against Paul Craig Roberts, *The Supply-Side Revolution* (Cambridge, MA: Harvard University Press, 1984). Martin Feldstein's work can be sampled in Martin Feldstein, ed., *Taxes and Capital Formation* (Chicago: University of Chicago Press for the National Bureau of Economic Research, 1987).

Paraphrases and quotations of George Gilder are taken from *Sexual Suicide* (New York: Quadrangle, 1973) and *Wealth and Poverty* (New York: Basic, 1981). The left-wing version of the very same concerns is Barbara Ehrenreich, *The Hearts of Men: American Dreams and the Flight from Commitment* (Garden City, NY: Doubleday, 1983). Charles Murray's *Losing Ground: American Social Policy, 1950–1980* (New York: Basic, 1984) was a sensation that still lives on as an underground cult classic among conservative activists, as does a later, even more controversial book, *The Bell Curve: Intelligence and Class Structure in American Life* (New York: Free Press, 1994), coauthored with Richard C. Herrnstein.

Henry Kaufman, Felix Rohatyn, and Lloyd Cutler, among others, are quoted and discussed in James Livingston, "The Presidency and the People," *Democracy* 3 (1983). See also Lester Thurow, *The Zero-Sum Society* (New York: Penguin, 1981), Ira Magaziner and Robert B. Reich, *Minding America's Business* (New York: Vintage, 1982), and Michel Crozier, Samuel P. Huntington, Joji Watanuki, *The Crisis of Democracy: Report on the Governability of Democracies to the Trilateral Commission* (New York: New York University Press, 1975), for evidence of bipartisan worries about the economic effects of the dysfunctional political culture inherited from the centrifugal 1960s.

The economic theories of Milton Friedman and Friedrich von Hayek take the form of political manifestoes in, respectively, *Capitalism and Freedom* (Chicago: University of Chicago Press, 1962) and *The Road to Serfdom* (Chicago: University of Chicago Press, 1950); see the appendix above titled "Their Great Depression and Ours," on how Friedman's ideas became the mainstream in thinking about business cycles like the 2008–2009 economic crisis. Related ideas are explored in Ludwig von Mises, *Human Action* (New Haven, CT: Yale University Press, 1949). Irving Kristol's doubts about such ideas are registered in *Two Cheers for Capitalism* (New York: Basic, 1978); quotations are taken from here. Herbert Croly's seminal books are *The Promise of American Life* (1912) and *Progressive Democracy* (New York: Scribner's, 1914); like his friend Theodore Roosevelt, Croly was a big-government liberal who believed that state capitalism was the obvious alternative to socialism as it was developing on the American scene. When conservatives like

Kristol and John McCain cloak themselves in the mantle of TR and Croly, we should not, then, debunk their supposed hypocrisy; we should instead ask whether their fear of actually existing socialism is warranted by the available evidence.

Michael Novak's ambitious gloss on Max Weber is *The Spirit of Democratic Capitalism* (New York: Simon & Schuster, 1982); all quotations are taken from here. His competition was Daniel Bell, *The Coming of Post-Industrial Society* (New York: Basic, 1973) and Charles Lindblom, *Politics and Markets* (New York: Harper, 1977). The journal founded by Bell and Irving Kristol, *The Public Interest* (now *The National Interest*), contains the poignant record of the neoconservative movement away from consensus on the moral ambiguities of capitalism. The long-term effort of American intellectuals to map a twentieth-century world not governed by the heartless logic of anonymous market forces is brilliantly evoked by Howard Brick, *Transcending Capitalism* (Ithaca, NY: Cornell University Press 2004).

Liberation Theology did threaten to become the mainstream of Catholic doctrine in the 1970s and 1980s, at least in the Western Hemisphere: see Phillip Berryman's primer, *Liberation Theology* (New York: Random House, 1987), and David Tombs, *Latin American Liberation Theology* (Boston: Brill, 2002). Quotations and paraphrases in the text are from *Gaudium at Spes* (1965) and "Justice in the World" (1971). See also Gustavo Gutierrez, *A Theology of Liberation*, trans. Sister Caridad Inda and John Eagleson (Maryknoll, NY: Orbis, 1973), which is probably the single most important document of the movement.

Barrington Moore's *Social Origins of Dictatorship and Democracy* (Boston: Beacon, 1966) should be compared with Maurice Dobb, *Studies in the Development of Capitalism*, rev. ed. (New York: International, 1963), T. S. Ashton, ed., *The Brenner Debate* (New York: Cambridge University Press, 1987), and the primary source itself, Karl Marx, *Capital*, trans. Samuel Moore and Edward Aveling, 3 vols. (Chicago: Kerr, 1906–1909), especially the treatment of "primitive accumulation" in volume 1.

Figures on taxes, incomes, and the like are from Robert S. McIntyre and Dean C. Tipps, "How the Reagan Tax Policies Are Affecting the American Taxpayer and the Economy," which is a revision of an earlier piece by McIntyre, "The Failure of Tax Incentives," both distributed by Citizens for Tax Justice (1983). Peter G. Peterson said the same thing about the atrophy of net investment in a long list of publications, beginning with "The Morning After," *The Atlantic* 260, no. 4 (October 1987). On long-term trends in capital formation and investment, see Simon Kuznets, *Capital in the American*

Economy (Princeton, NJ: Princeton University Press for the National Bureau of Economic Research, 1961), and James Livingston, *Pragmatism and the Political Economy of Cultural Revolution, 1850–1940* (Chapel Hill: University of North Carolina Press, 1994), part 1.

In the 1950s and 1960s, it was not unusual for theorists to belittle the role of capital formation and net private investment in determining the pace and the pattern of economic growth and meanwhile to define "technical change," whether exogenous or endogenous (that is, whether a function of profit-maximizing activity or not), as the real source of growth. Among the economists who did so were Robert Solow, Moses Abramovitz, Solomon Fabricant, Kenneth Kurihara, Wassily Leontief, Harold Vatter, Edward Denison, and Edmund Phelps. By my reading, their contributions were part of a larger theoretical controversy started by Joan Robinson and Piero Sraffa (the latter in *The Production of Commodities by Means of Commodities* [Cambridge: Cambridge University Press, 1960]), which questioned the explanatory adequacy of production functions in measuring and evaluating the marginal product of capital. Since the 1970s and 1980s, their voices have been drowned out by supply-side economics and its policy-relevant urge to cut taxes and provide incentives to private investment; but in the twenty-first century's second decade, as we struggle to deal with an economic crisis with no postwar parallel, we can perhaps begin to hear them again.

On transfer payments as a growing component of income as such, circa 1959 to 1999, see Edward L. Whalen, *A Guided Tour of the United States Economy* (Westport, CT: Quorum Press, 2002). Robert Bork's pathetic lament about the 1960s is *Slouching Towards Gomorrah*, 2nd ed. (New York: HarperCollins, 2002).

Chapter 2: "Tenured Radicals" in the Ivory Tower

Full disclosure: I am a beneficiary of what Clark Kerr called the great transformation of higher education and a participant observer as well. I lived through the upheavals that remade the university in the image of a transnational America. I was granted a PhD by Northern Illinois University (NIU), a small land-grant teacher's college until 1962, when certain liberal arts departments established doctoral programs and the physical plant expanded to accommodate swelling numbers of high school graduates who fully expected to go to college. By the time I received my degree in 1980, undergraduate enrollment at NIU was approximately twenty-five thousand. Since then, I have taught in a suburban community college, a small liberal arts college, two maximum-security prisons, and four large state universities in the Midwest, the Upper South, and the Northeast. In my view, the great transformation of higher education is a magnificent achievement because it enriched the argument about what it means to be an American and gave working-class kids like Nancy Hewitt, Bonnie Smith, and Christopher Fisher, my colleagues at Rutgers, and Marvin Rosen, my mentor at NIU, a chance at the of a professor.

The history of higher education before and after the land-grant colleges is traced in Bill Readings, *The University in Ruins* (Cambridge, MA: Harvard University Press, 1996), Richard Hofstadter and C. DeWitt Hardy, *The Development and Scope of Higher Education in the U.S.* (New York: Columbia University Press, 1952), Bernard Bailyn, *Education in the Forming of American Society* (New York: Vintage, 1960), Christopher Newfield, *Ivy and Industry: Business and the Making of the American University, 1880–1980* (Durham, NC: Duke University Press, 2003), Seymour Martin Lipset and Everett Ladd, *The Divided Academy* (New York: McGraw-Hill, 1975), and Clark Kerr, *The Great Transformation of Higher Education, 1960–1980* (Albany: State University of New York, 1991). Figures and quotations are taken from the last two texts. See also Seymour Martin Lipset, *Rebellion in the University*, rev. ed. (New Brunswick, NJ: Transaction, 1993), and Howard Dickman, ed., *The Imperiled University* (New Brunswick, NJ: Transaction, 1993).

On the common curricular concerns of liberals and conservatives, see Arthur Schlesinger Jr., *The Disuniting of America: Reflections on a Multicultural Society*, rev. ed. (New York: Norton, 1998), Lynne Cheney, *Telling the Truth* (New York: Simon & Schuster, 1995), Roger Kimball, *Tenured Radicals: How Politics Has Corrupted Our Higher Education*, rev. ed. (Chicago: Elephant Paperbacks, 1998), and Robert Bork, *Slouching Towards Gomorrah*, as cited in chapter 1. Quoted remarks are taken from these texts and again from Irving Kristol, *Two Cheers for Capitalism*, as cited in chapter 1.

On the eclipse of "pioneer individualism" and the rise of "social selfhood" at the turn of the twentieth century, see James Livingston, *Pragmatism, Feminism, and Democracy: Rethinking the Politics of American History* (New York: Routledge, 2001). A. Lawrence Lowell's *Public Opinion and Popular Government* (New York: Longmans, 1913) is part of a larger debate on the relation of the new "social self" to the future of democracy, a debate that pitted John Dewey against Walter Lippmann in the 1920s; its distant echoes can be heard in contemporary arguments over the utility of identity politics and the rationality of the American electorate.

Chapter 3: The Creators and Constituents of the "Postmodern Condition"

The postmodern condition is a many-splendored thing. As I suggest in this chapter, agreement on its meanings is tenuous at best; only the chronology seems secure, but even here you can roam freely throughout the twentieth century. Among the most influential accounts are Ihab Hassan, *The Dismemberment of Orpheus: Toward a Postmodern Literature* (New York: Oxford, 1971), Jean-François Lyotard, *The Post-Modern Condition*, trans. Geoff Bennington and Brian Massumi (1979; rpt. Minneapolis: University of Minnesota Press, 1984), David Harvey, *The Condition of Post-Modernity* (Cambridge, MA: Blackwell, 1989), and Fredric Jameson, *Postmodernism, or The Cultural Logic of Late Capitalism* (Durham, NC: Duke University Press, 1991). To my mind, the most useful accounts are Margaret Rose, *The Post-Modern and the Post-Industrial: A Critical Analysis* (Cambridge, MA: MIT Press, 1991); Donald M. Lowe, *History of Bourgeois Perception* (Chicago: University of Chicago Press, 1982), and *The Body in Late-Capitalist USA* (Durham, NC: Duke University Press, 1999); and Gianni Vattimo, *The End of Modernity*, trans. Jon Snyder (Baltimore: Johns Hopkins University Press, 1988).

Quoted remarks of Lynne Cheney and Alan Bloom are taken, respectively, from *Telling the Truth*, as cited in chapter 2, and *The Closing of the American Mind* (New York: Simon & Schuster, 1987). The argument that the idea of a postmodern condition has American antecedents is drawn from James Livingston, *Pragmatism and the Political Economy of Cultural Revolution*, as cited in chapter 1; Livingston, *Pragmatism, Feminism, and Democracy*, as cited in chapter 2; and Livingston, "Pragmatism, Nihilism, and Democracy: What Is Called Thinking at the End of Modernity?" forthcoming in John Stuhr, ed., *One Hundred Years of Pragmatism* (Bloomington: Indiana University Press). My procedure in these works is to trace the relevant intellectual genealogies—for example, the connective citations and the philosophical idioms that link William James, Josiah Royce, Jean Wahl, and Alexandre Kojeve, or William James, Edmund Husserl, Carl Schmitt, and Martin Heidegger—rather than merely to note the strong resemblance between the early scandal of pragmatism and the latter sensation of postmodernism (or, as Judith Butler would have it, poststructuralism). Both words, "scandal" and "sensation," also apply to the reception of Thomas Kuhn, *The Structure of Scientific Revolutions* (Chicago: University of Chicago Press, 1962).

On poststructuralism, semiotics, deconstruction, and the Heideggerian backstory, see Kaja Silverman, *The Subject of Semiotics* (New York: Oxford University Press, 1982), Jonathan Culler, *The Pursuit of Signs* (Ithaca, NY:

Cornell University Press, 1981), Judith Butler, *Subjects of Desire: Hegelian Reflections in 20th-Century France* (New York: Columbia University Press, 1987), Harold Bloom et al., *Deconstruction and Criticism* (New York: Continuum, 1979), Jacques Derrida, *Writing and Difference*, trans. Alan Bass (Chicago: University of Chicago Press, 1978), Tom Cohen, ed., *Jacques Derrida and the Humanities* (New York: Cambridge University Press, 2001), Hubert L. Dreyfus, *Being-in-the-World: A Commentary on Being and Time, Division I* (Cambridge, MA: MIT Press, 1991), and the big event itself, Martin Heidegger, *Being and Time*, trans. John Macquarrie and Edward Robinson (New York: Harper & Row, 1962).

For feminist appropriations and inflections of poststructuralism, as well as Karl Marx, Sigmund Freud, Friedrich Nietzsche, Claude Lévi-Strauss, and many other "classical" social theorists, see, for example, Joan Kelly, *Women, History, and Theory* (Chicago: University of Chicago Press, 1984), Jane Gallop, *The Daughter's Seduction: Feminism and Psychoanalysis* (Ithaca, NY: Cornell University Press, 1982), Susan Suleiman, *Subversive Intent: Gender, Politics, and the Avant-Garde* (Cambridge, MA: Harvard University Press, 1990), Alice Jardine, *Gynesis: Configurations of Woman and Modernity* (Ithaca, NY: Cornell University Press, 1986), and Jane Flax, *Thinking Fragments: Psychoanalysis, Feminism, and Postmodernism in the Contemporary West* (Berkeley: University of California Press, 1990). As Joan Kelly observed in "The Doubled Vision of Feminist Theory," reprinted in the collection of essays cited above, historians of women were drawn to cross-disciplinary ways of addressing their subjects because the "split vision of social reality" determined by the received tradition was inadequate to the apprehension of a world in which the distinctions between public and private, the personal and the political, had stopped making a difference: "Our analyses, regardless of the tradition they originate in, increasingly treat the family in relation to society; treat sexual and reproductive experience in terms of political economy; and treat productive relations of class in connection with sex hierarchy. In establishing these connections, feminist thought is moving beyond the split vision of social reality it inherited from the recent past. . . . That is, we are moving beyond a nineteenth-century conception of society because our actual vantage point has shifted."

The seminal works discussed in the text are Gayle Rubin, "Notes on the Traffic in Women: Toward a Political Economy of Sex," in Rayna Reiter, ed., *Toward an Anthropology of Women* (New York: Monthly Review Press, 1975), Joan W. Scott, "Gender: A Useful Category of Historical Analysis," *The American Historical Review* 91 (1986), and Judith Butler, *Gender Trouble: Feminism and the Subversion of Identity* (New York: Routledge, 1990).

The historiographical background of such theoretical forays—that is, the empirical, anomalous evidence that demanded a paradigm shift of the kind attempted by Rubin, Scott, and Butler—can be sampled in Gerda Lerner, *The Majority Finds Its Past: Placing Women in History* (New York: Oxford University Press, 1979), Mary Jo Buhle, *Women and American Socialism, 1870–1920* (Urbana: University of Illinois Press, 1981), Suzanne Lebsock, *The Free Women of Petersburg* (New York: Norton, 1984), Bonnie Smith, *Ladies of the Leisure Class: The Bourgeoisies of Northern France in the 19th Century* (Princeton, NJ: Princeton University Press, 1981), Alice Kessler-Harris, *Out to Work: A History of Wage-Earning Women in the U.S.* (New York: Oxford University Press, 1982), Nancy Cott, *The Bonds of Womanhood* (New Haven, CT: Yale University Press, 1977), and Linda Gordon, *Woman's Body, Woman' Right: Birth Control in America*, rev. ed. (New York: Penguin, 1990).

On the culture wars as an intramural sport on the left or, at any rate, as a debate conducted within a narrow ideological spectrum that remained more or less liberal, see Jonathan Rieder, ed., *The Fractious Nation?* (Berkeley: University of California Press, 2003), and Alan Wolfe, *One Nation, After All* (New York: Penguin, 1998). See also the works cited in the text: Richard Rorty, *Achieving Our Country* (Cambridge, MA: Harvard University Press, 1998), volume 45 of *Social Text* (1995), Linda Nicholson, ed., *Feminist Contentions* (New York: Routledge, 1995), and Martha Nussbaum in the September 21, 1999, issue of *The New Republic*.

Frank Lentricchia's complaint against Michel Foucault is found in *Ariel and the Police* (Madison: University of Wisconsin Press, 1988). See otherwise works by Harvey and Jameson as cited above in the notes for this chapter. Quoted remarks of Robert Bork and William Bennett are taken, respectively, from *Slouching Towards Gomorrah*, as cited in chapter 1, and *The De-Valuing of America: The Fight for Our Children and Our Culture* (New York: Summit Books, 1992).

Chapter 4: "Signs of Signs:" Watching the End of Modernity at the Cineplex

Pat Robertson's quoted remarks are taken from Frederick Detwiler, *Standing in the Premises of God: The Christian Right's Fight to Redefine America's Public Schools* (New York: New York University Press, 1999).

The possibilities of periodization according to Samuel P. Huntington and Daniel Bell are on display, respectively, in *The Clash of Civilizations* (New York: Simon & Schuster, 1996), a book that grew out of an article in *Foreign*

Affairs, and *The Cultural Contradictions of Capitalism* rev. ed. (New York: Basic, 1996), a book that reads as the autobiography of an entire generation of left-wing intellectuals. See Raymond Williams, *Problems in Materialism and Culture: Selected Essays* (London: Verso, 1980), for insight into how modern social formations sponsor divergent cultures, but always with his admonition from *Culture and Society, 1780–1950* (London: Chatto & Windus, 1958) in mind: "The area of a culture, it would seem, is usually proportionate to the area of a language rather than the area of a class."

I chose the movies discussed in this chapter for three reasons: they were immensely popular when released or have powerfully shaped subsequent filmmaking, they remain many-layered texts worthy of close reading, and I still love watching them, even at their most irritating or frightful extremes. The readings offered here are my own, but they are informed throughout by the work of film theorists and historians such as Paul Smith, Bill Nichols, Virginia Wexman, Laura Mulvey, Robert Ray, Mary Ann Doane, Teresa de Lauretis, and Barbara Creed. I am particularly indebted, however, to Carol Clover, *Men, Women and Chain Saws: Gender in the Modern Horror Film* (Princeton, NJ: Princeton University Press, 1992); Kaja Silverman, *The Acoustic Mirror* (Bloomington: Indiana University Press, 1988), and *Male Subjectivity at the Margins* (New York: Routledge, 1992); David Savran, *Taking It Like a Man: White Masculinity, Masochism, and Contemporary American Culture* (Princeton, NJ: Princeton University Press, 1998); Robin Wood, *Hollywood from Vietnam to Reagan* (New York: Columbia University Press, 1986); and Noel Carroll, *The Philosophy of Horror, or Paradoxes of the Heart* (New York: Routledge, 1990).

A representative sample of Jean Baudrillard's ideas can be found in *The Mirror of Production*, trans. Mark Poster (St. Louis, MO: Telos, 1975). On the end of modernity as an instance of the world Baudrillard maps, see also the works cited in chapter 3.

Sigmund Freud's ideas about masochism are found in "A Child Is Being Beaten" (1924) and "The Economic Problem of Masochism" (1924), in *The Standard Edition of the Complete Psychological Works*, trans. James Strachey (London: Hogarth, 1959), vols. 17 and 19. Clover, Silverman, and Savran have interesting disagreements on the uses of these ideas in diagnosing male masochism at the movies, all of which turn on inflections of Judith Butler's performative theory of gender. My own test of Freud's ideas on male masochism can be found in a five-part essay on *300*, the film adaptation of Frank Miller's graphic novel, which I wrote in 2007 for my blog, www.politcsandletters.com.

On crime, gunslingers, and gangsters as both symptoms and attempted cures of massive social change, see Kenneth Burke, *Attitudes Toward History*, rev. ed. (Boston: Beacon, 1962), Michael Denning, *Mechanic Accents: Dime Novels and Working Class Culture* (New York: Verso, 1987), Robert Warshow, *The Immediate Experience* (Garden City, NY: Doubleday, 1962), Robert Sklar, *City Boys: Cagney, Bogart, Garfield* (Princeton, NJ: Princeton University Press, 1992), and Francis Fukuyama, *The Great Disruption* (New York: Free Press, 1999). D. H. Lawrence read what is now canonical American literature as evidence of the crimes or tragedies that founded American culture in *Studies in Classic American Literature* (n.p., 1923). Three other seminal readings of the same moment are Lewis Mumford, *The Golden Day* (New York: Boni & Liverwright, 1926), F. O. Matthiessen, *American Renaissance* (New York: Oxford University Press, 1941), and R. W. B. Lewis, *The American Adam* (Chicago: University of Chicago Press, 1955). A brilliant rewriting of these readings is Jonathan Arac, *Critical Genealogies* (New York, Columbia University Press, 1987).

My first take on *The Little Mermaid* was published by *Cineaste* in 1990 and later revised and enlarged to include *Toy Story* in "Cartoon Politics: The Case of the Purloined Parents," an essay in Van Gosse and Richard Moser, eds., *The World the Sixties Made* (Philadelphia: Temple University Press, 2002). The political transparency or putative uniformity of Disney texts—the notion that these are "self-evidently reactionary parables of the American Right"—is rigorously challenged by Eleanor Bryce and Martin McQuillan, *Deconstructing Disney* (London: Pluto, 1999); I disagree with most of their readings, mainly because they often reduce cartoon figures to representations of neoliberal (Thatcherite) politics, but this is a brilliant, jarring, indispensable book. Susan Faludi takes the "downsizing of Dad" very seriously in *Stiffed: The Betrayal of the American Man* (New York: HarperCollins, 1999).

Chapter 5: "Angels in America:" Technologies of Desire and Recognition

On animation in film, see Paul Wells, *Understanding Animation* (New York: Routledge, 1998), and two useful collections, Elizabeth Bell, Lynda Haas, and Laura Sells, eds., *From Mouse to Mermaid: The Politics of Film, Gender, and Culture* (Bloomington: Indiana University Press, 1995), and Kevin Sandler, ed., *Reading the Rabbit* (New Brunswick, NJ: Rutgers University Press); Norman Klein quotes are from here. My debt to Scott McCloud,

Understanding Comics: The Invisible Art (New York: Harper, 1994), is bound-less, but I disagree with his periodization of the relation between words and images in the modern Western world. Even so, if I am right, his argument about the cultural force of comics in the twentieth century becomes all the more important. See also the Old Testament, as it were, by the graphic novel's founding father, Will Eisner, *Comics and Sequential Art* (Tamarac, FL: Poorhouse Press, 1985), and Kirk Varnedoe and Adam Gopnick, *High and Low: Modern Art [and] Popular Culture* (New York: Museum of Modern Art/Abrams, 1990).

On performance art, the key text is Moira Roth, *The Amazing Decade: Women and Performance Art in America, 1970–1980* (Los Angeles: Astro Artz, 1983). See also Rozika Parker and Griselda Pollock, eds., *Framing Feminism: Art and the Women's Movement, 1970–1985* (New York: Pandora, 1987).

My questions about Bugs Bunny owe a great deal to Shannen Dee Williams, a graduate student in history at Rutgers University, who forced me to rethink Lawrence Levine's treatment of the Trickster in *Black Culture and Black Consciousness* (New York: Oxford University Press, 1977), and, more immediately, to reread Constance Rourke, *American Humor* (Garden City, NY: Doubleday, 1931). The Trickster is of course a transhistorical figure, from Hermes the Thief to Br'er Rabbit, but his resonance in modern American culture is colored by his central position within the African American folk tradition. That Bugs and his carrot were inspired by Clark Gable's fast-talking character in *It's a Wonderful Life*, Frank Capra's Oscar-winning movie of 1934, emphasizes the Trickster's liminal function, for this movie is an allegory of class struggle (and reconciliation) that authorizes the hard-boiled cynicism of Gable's subaltern standpoint.

On anal erotism and anality more generally, the basic texts are Sigmund Freud, "Character and Anal Erotism" (1908), "The Predisposition to Obsessional Neurosis" (1913), and "On the Transformation of Instincts with Special Reference to Anal Erotism" (1916), in the *Collected Papers*, 8th ed. (London: Hogarth, 1952), each of which is a kind of commentary on the *Three Essays on Sexuality* (1905), the book that Freud repeatedly revised between 1910 and 1925. See also Sandor Ferenczi, "The Ontogenesis of the Interest in Money," in *First Contributions to Psycho-Analysis* (London: Hogarth, 1952). My appropriation of these texts is mediated and informed by Norman O. Brown, *Life against Death: The Psychoanalytical Meaning of History* (Middletown, CT: Wesleyan University Press, 1959), Michael T. Taussig, *The Devil and Commodity Fetishism in Latin America* (Chapel Hill: University of North Carolina Press, 1980), Dan Sabbath and Mandel Hall, *End Product: The First Taboo* (New York: Urizen, 1977), Julia Kristeva, *Powers of Horror: An Essay on Abjection*, trans. Leon Roudiez (New York: Columbia University Press, 1982), and Jacqueline Rose, *Sexuality in the Field of Vision* (London: Verso, 1986).

Norman O. Brown is the most forceful advocate of treating Freud as a theorist of culture—or a philosopher of history—but along these same lines, see also Jonathan Lear, *Love and Its Place in Nature* (Chicago: University of Chicago Press, 1990), Geza Roheim, *The Origin and Function of Culture* (1943; rpt. Garden City, NY: Anchor Books, 1971), Jean Laplanche, *Life and Death in Psychoanalysis*, trans. Jeffrey Mehlman (Baltimore: Johns Hopkins University Press, 1976), Herbert Marcuse, *Eros and Civilization* (Boston: Beacon, 1955), Giles Deleuze and Felix Guattari, *Anti-Oedipus: Capitalism and Schizophrenia*, trans. Robert Hurley, Mark Seem, and Helen R. Lane (Minneapolis: University of Minnesota Press, 1983), and Theresa Brennan, *History after Lacan* (New York: Routledge, 1993).

Richard Chase argued long ago that romance has been the mainstream of American literature: see *The American Novel and Its Tradition* (Garden City, NY: Doubleday, 1957). Compare this argument against Jane Tompkins, *Sensational Designs: The Cultural Work of American Fiction, 1790–1860* (New York: Oxford University Press, 1984), Fredric Jameson, *The Political Unconscious: Narrative as a Socially Symbolic Act* (Ithaca, NY: Cornell University Press, 1981), M. H. Abrams, *Natural Supernaturalism: Tradition and Revolution in Romantic Literature* (New York: Norton, 1971), and my "Hegelian" reading of *Sister Carrie* in Miriam Gogol, ed., *Theodore Dreiser: Beyond Naturalism* (New York: New York University Press, 1995).

The "posthuman future" on display in biotechnology is mapped in Francis Fukuyama, *Our Posthuman Future* (New York: Farrar, Straus and Giroux, 2002). A very different angle on the same future—one in which angels, demons, cyborgs, vampires, and other out-of-body experiences become normal—is taken in N. Katherine Hayles, *How We Became Posthuman* (Chicago: University of Chicago Press, 1999), a disturbing and brilliant book that addresses the effects of computer technology on "liberal subjectivity." See also Rob Latham, *Consuming Youth: Vampires, Cyborgs, and the Culture of Consumption* (Chicago: University of Chicago Press, 2002), for a fascinating study of how the imaginary intersections between vampires and cyborgs, bodies and machines are animated by postindustrial regimes of production.

On America's music as an Atlantic phenomenon, see Ned Sublette, *Cuba and Its Music* (Chicago: Chicago Review Press, 2004), Nick Tosches, *Country: The Biggest American Music* (New York: Dell, 1977), Gilbert Chase,

America's Music, 3rd rev. ed. (Urbana: University of Illinois Press, 1992), and Christopher Small, *Music of the Common Tongue* (Hanover, NH: Wesleyan University Press, 1987).

On the blues as such, the basic, indispensable texts are Albert Murray, *Stomping the Blues* (New York: McGraw-Hill, 1976), and *The Hero and the Blues* (Columbia: University of Missouri Press, 1982); Charles Keil, *Urban Blues* (Chicago: University of Chicago Press, 1966); Leroi Jones [Amiri Baraka], *Blues People: Negro Music in White America* (New York: Morrow, 1963); Francis Davis, *The History of the Blues* (New York: Hyperion, 1995); William Ferris, *Blues from the Delta* (New York: DaCapo, 1978); Robert Palmer, *Deep Blues* (New York: Penguin, 1981); and Abbe Niles, "The Story of the Blues," in W. C. Handy, ed., *Blues: An Anthology*, 4th ed. (1926; rpt. New York: DaCapo Press, 1990). The Wynton Marsalis quotation is taken from Herman Gray, *Cultural Moves: African Americans and the Politics of Representation* (Berkeley: University of California Press, 2005).

On the black aesthetic, see Harold Cruse, *The Crisis of the Negro Intellectual* (New York: Morrow, 1967). With respect to its purchase on the mainstream of American culture—a purchase typically mediated by the commodity forms, the mechanical means, and the commercial imperatives of mass markets—see Michael Eric Dyson, *Reflecting Black: African-American Cultural Criticism* (Minneapolis: University of Minnesota Press, 1993); Leon Wynter, *American Skin: Pop Culture, Big Business, and the End of White America* (New York: Crown, 2002); Greg Tate, ed., *Everything but the Burden: What White People Are Taking from Black Culture* (New York: Broadway Books, 2003); Nelson George, *Blackface: Reflections on African-Americans and the Movies* (New York: Harper, 1994), and *Elevating the Game: Black Men and Basketball* (New York: HarperCollins, 1992); Todd Boyd, *Young, Black, Rich and Famous: The Rise of the NBA, the Hip-Hop Invasion, and the Transformation of American Culture* (New York: Doubleday, 2003). Notice that these are "primary sources" written in an anthropological mode by participant-observers.

On punk, Madonna, heavy metal, and the broader arc of the music scene at the end of the twentieth century, see Clinton Hevlin, *From the Velvets to the Voidoids* (London: Penguin, 1993), Susan McClary, *Feminine Endings: Music, Gender, and Sexuality* (Minneapolis: University of Minnesota Press, 1991), Robert Micklitsch, *From Hegel to Madonna* (Albany: State University of New York, 1998), Cathy Schwichtenberg, ed., *The Madonna Connection* (Boulder, CO: Westview, 1993), Robert Walser, *Running with the Devil: Power, Gender, and Madness in Heavy Metal Music* (Hanover, NH: Wesleyan University Press, 1993), Barry Shank, *Dissonant Identities: The Rock 'n' Roll Scene in Austin, Texas* (Hanover, NH: Wesleyan University Press, 1994),

Aaron Fox, *Real Country: Music and Language in Working-Class Culture* (Durham, NC: Duke University Press, 2004), Ian Christie, *Sound of the Beast: The Complete Headbanging History of Heavy Metal* (New York: HarperCollins, 2003), and George Lipsitz, *Dangerous Crossroads* (New York: Verso, 1994). The anthropological attitude of the participant-observer regulates these sources, too, as I suppose it must in view of the simple fact that music is typically embodied as performance.

On hip-hop, quotations and paraphrases are taken from Tricia Rose, *Black Noise: Rap Music and Black Culture in Contemporary America* (Hanover, NH: Wesleyan University Press, 1994), S. H. Fernandez Jr., *The New Beats: Exploring the Music, Culture, and Attitudes of Hip-hop* (New York: Doubleday, 1994), and Andrew Ross, *No Respect: Intellectuals and Popular Culture* (New York: Routledge, 1989). See, more generally, Michael Eric Dyson, *Between God and Gangsta Rap* (New York: Oxford University Press, 1996), Nelson George, *Hip-hop America* (New York: Viking, 1998), Janice Rahn, *Painting without Permission: Hip-hop Graffiti Subculture* (Westport, CT: Bergin & Garvey, 2002), and Tricia Rose, *The Hip-hop Wars* (New York: Basic, 2008). In many recent books informed by the methods and sensibilities of cultural studies, the text (music/dance) in question recedes, and the context (society/scene) becomes both the means and end of the analysis: see, for example, M. T. Kato, *From Kung Fu to Hip-Hop: Globalization, Revolution, and Popular Culture* (Albany: State University of New York, 2007). On the other hand, there are at least two invaluable ethnographies: Jeff Chang, *Can't Stop Won't Stop: A History of the Hip-Hop Generation* (New York: Picador, 2005), and Joseph G. Schloss, *Making Beats: The Art of Sample-Based Hip-Hop* (Middletown, CT: Wesleyan University Press, 2004).

On technology and cultural meaning, change, and literacy, the essential books are Donna Haraway, *Simians, Cyborgs, and Women: The Reinvention of Nature* (London: Routledge, 1991), Richard Lanham, *The Economics of Attention* (Chicago: University of Chicago Press, 2004), Mark Poster, *The Mode of Information: Poststructuralism and Social Context* (Chicago: University of Chicago Press, 1990), Howard Rheingold, *Virtual Reality* (New York: Summit, 1991), James R. Beninger, *The Control Revolution: Technological and Economic Origins of the Information Society* (Cambridge, MA: Harvard University Press, 1986), Allucquiere Rosenne Stone, *The War of Technology and Desire at the Close of the Mechanical Age* (Cambridge, MA: MIT Press, 1995), Dan Schiller, *Digital Capitalism: Networking the Global Market System* (Cambridge, MA: MIT Press, 1999), Ted Friedman, *Electric Dreams: The Computer in American Culture* (New York: New York University Press, 2005), and Katherine Hayles as cited above in the notes for this chapter. The presiding spirit of these studies remains Walter J. Ong, *The Presence of the Word* (New Haven, CT: Yale University Press, 1967).

My use of the phrase "artificial intelligence" is not meant as a contribution to the debates on the topic, all of which circle the metaphysical and practical meanings of "mind," "consciousness," and "human nature." Good introductions to the issues at stake are Margaret A. Boden, ed., *The Philosophy of Artificial Intelligence* (New York: Oxford University Press, 1990), and Brian P. Bloomfield, ed., *The Question of Artificial Intelligence* (New York: Methuen, 1987). See also Hubert Dreyfus, *Being-in-the-World*, as cited in chapter 3.

Chapter 6: The Ending of the "American Century"

In this chapter, I write as an heir to the intellectual legacy of the "revisionist" diplomatic history perfected at the University of Wisconsin in the 1950s and 1960s. The exemplar of this tradition is William Appleman Williams, whose pathbreaking book of 1959, *The Tragedy of American Diplomacy*, 3rd ed. (New York: Dell, 1972), was consciously indebted to Charles A. Beard, *The Idea of National Interest* (New York: Macmillan, 1934). Both texts are deftly situated and appropriated by Andrew Bacevich in *American Empire* (Cambridge, MA: Harvard University Press, 1999), a book that brilliantly renews the "revisionist" tradition. In my view, however, the best treatment of the Open Door policy and the meanings of the American Century is Martin J. Sklar, "The American Century: A Twice-Told Tale," a still unpublished paper originally intended for inclusion in Michael J. Hogan's indispensable collection of essays titled *The Ambiguous Legacy: U.S. Foreign Relations in the "American Century"* (New York: Cambridge University Press, 1999); the Henry Luce piece is reprinted here. The abridged, published version of Sklar's paper is in David G. Becker and Richard L. Sklar, eds., *Imperialism and World Politics* (Westport, CT: Praeger, 1999). A comparable long view of empires and imperialisms which also accords with my argument about the American Century in this chapter is Strobe Talbott, *The Great Experiment: The Story of Ancient Empires, Modern States, and the Quest for a Global Nation* (New York: Simon & Schuster, 2008).

The "revisionist" position on American diplomacy inspired and informed by Williams and his mentor at the University of Wisconsin, Fred Harvey Harrington, is often characterized by historians and political scientists as an instance of economic determinism because the revisionists, among them Walter LaFeber, Thomas McCormick, Lloyd Gardner, Marilyn Young, Emily Rosenberg, Carl Parrini, Joan Hoff, Michael Hunt, and Bruce Cumings, emphasize the relation between the development of American capitalism and the evolution of U.S. foreign policy. In fact, the revisionists have indeed paid attention to the economic dimension of the Open Door, but they have never equated foreign relations and dollar diplomacy. Their goal has always been to dismantle the stale opposition of "realism versus idealism," which still regulates conventional thinking about the making of U.S. foreign policy; the means to this end is the revisionists' recognition that (1) until the very late twentieth century, policymakers saw no contradiction between their commitment to the globalization of capitalism and the realization of the highest possible morality, and (2) that capitalism is more than an economic phenomenon to be comprehended in terms of economic history.

On globalization, there are already too many prize-winning books that should never have been published. Most of them go by the name of "American Empire." The brilliant exception to this rule is Michael Hardt and Antonio Negri, *Empire* (Cambridge, MA: Harvard University Press, 1999), an ambitious attempt to periodize modern imperialism that inevitably cites the American example as the template of the future. On the first stage of globalization, that is, on the creation of a world market in the sixteenth, seventeenth, and eighteenth centuries by European exploration and conquest, see Immanuel Wallerstein, *The Modern World-System* (New York: Academic Press, 1976); Perry Anderson, *Lineages of the Absolutist State* (London: Verso, 1974); E. E. Rich and C. H. Wilson, eds., *The Cambridge Economic History of Europe* (Cambridge: Cambridge University Press, 1967), vol. 4; Sidney W. Mintz, *Sweetness and Power: The Place of Sugar in Modern History* (New York: Penguin, 1985); Philip D. Curtin, *The Rise and Fall of the Plantation System* (New York: Cambridge University Press, 1998); and Giovanni Arrighi, *The Long Twentieth Century* (New York: Verso, 1994). In *Croissance et regression en Europe XIVe–XVIIIe siècles: receuil d'articles* (Paris: Librairie Armand Colin, 1972), M. Malowist mistakenly claims that Poland and Russia developed "very differently" under the pressures of a world market in agricultural raw materials—Wallerstein and Anderson follow his lead—but this study of the "second serfdom" east of the Elbe remains the best book on the crucial issue of early modern *underdevelopment in Europe* as a function of globalization; it is contextualized and corrected in James Livingston, "Russia and Western Trade, 1550–1790: Studies in the Origins of Economic Backwardness" (master's thesis, Northern Illinois University, 1975).

On the second stage of globalization, circa 1870 to 1960, the basic texts are J. A. Hobson, *Imperialism* (1902; rpt. London: Allen & Unwin, 1938), V. I. Lenin, *Imperialism: The Highest Stage of Capitalism* (1914; rpt. New York: International, 1939), and Charles A. Conant, *The United States in the Orient* (1901; rpt. Port Washington, NY: Kennikat, 1971); quotations are from here. As Carl Parrini and Martin J. Sklar have shown, the pro-capitalist theory of imperialism developed by Conant, which stresses the problem of surplus capital, is quite similar to, and indeed feeds directly into, the anticapitalist theories of Hobson and Lenin. See Parrini's fugitive pieces on Conant in Lloyd Gardner, ed., *Redefining the Past* (Corvallis: Oregon State University Press, 1984), and in Walter LaFeber and Thomas McCormick, eds., *Behind the Throne: Servants of Power to Imperial Presidents, 1898–1968* (Madison: University of Wisconsin Press, 1993); and Martin J. Sklar, *The Corporate Reconstruction of American Capitalism, 1890–1916: The Market, the Law, and Politics* (New York: Cambridge University Press, 1988). See also Giovanni Arrighi, *The Geometry of Imperialism* (New York: Verso, 1983), Rosa Luxemburg, *The Accumulation of Capital* (New York: Monthly Review, 1968), Eric Wolf, *Peasant Wars of the 20th Century* (New York: Harper & Row, 1969), Bill Warren, *Imperialism, Pioneer of Capitalism* (London: New Left Books, 1980), and Herbert Feis, *Europe: The World's Banker, 1870–1914* (New York: Norton, 1965). On the threat from Germany of a renewed Napoleonic empire encompassing the Eurasian land mass, see H. C. Meyer, *Mitteleuropa in German Thought and Action, 1815–1945* (The Hague, 1955), R. J. S. Hoffman, *Great Britain and the German Trade Rivalry, 1875–1914* (New York: Russell & Russell, 1964), and Fritz Fischer, *Germany's Aims in the First World War* (New York: Norton, 1967).

On the third stage of globalization, see David Harvey, *The New Imperialism* (New York: Oxford University Press, 2003), Joseph Stiglitz, *Globalization and Its Discontents* (New York: Norton, 2003), Zbigniew Brzezinski, *The Choice: Global Domination or Global Leadership* (New York: Basic, 2004), Jagdish Bhagwati, *In Defense of Globalization* (New York: Oxford, 2004), Niall Ferguson, *Colossus: The Price of America's Empire* (New York: Penguin, 2004), Leo Panitch and Martijn Konigs, eds., *American Empire and the Political Economy of Global Finance* (New York: Palgrave, 2008), and Marc Chandler, *Making Sense of the Dollar* (New York: Bloomberg, 2009).

The rationale for anticommunist war in Southeast Asia is adumbrated in William Y. Elliott et al. (the Woodrow Wilson Study Group and the National Planning Association), *The Political Economy of American Foreign Policy* (New York: Holt, 1955), and explained fully in William Borden, *The Pacific Alliance: U.S. Foreign Economic Policy and Japanese Trade Recovery, 1947–1955* (Madison: University of Wisconsin Press, 1984).

For the extant explanations of the military disaster in Vietnam, see Robert Buzzanco, *Masters of War: Military Dissent and Politics in the Vietnam Era* (New York: Cambridge University Press, 1996), and David L. Anderson and John Ernst, eds., *The War That Never Ends: New Perspectives on the Vietnam*

War (Lexington: University of Kentucky Press, 2007). On the reconstruction of the armed services in the aftermath of the Vietnam debacle, the place to start is Thomas Ricks, *Making the Corps* (New York: Scribners, 1997). See also work forthcoming from Jennifer Mittelstadt of Penn State, which treats the all-volunteer army as an instance of the welfare state; she presented her preliminary findings at the annual meeting of the American Historical Association in January 2008 and in a lecture at Rutgers University on February 6, 2009.

The architects of the war on Iraq have received lavish attention. See, for example, Bob Woodward, *Plan of Attack* (New York: Simon & Schuster, 2004), and Frank Rich, *The Greatest Story Ever Sold* (New York: Penguin, 2006). I have relied on James Mann, *Rise of the Vulcans* (New York: Penguin, 2004); Cheney is quoted from here. Meanwhile, dozens of books on the invasion of, and insurgency in, Iraq have appeared since 2003. Among the most useful and provocative are John B. Judis, *The Folly of Empire* (New York: Scribner's, 2004), Rashid Khalidi, *Resurrecting Empire* (Boston: Beacon, 2004), Thomas Ricks, *Fiasco: The American Military Adventure in Iraq* (New York: Penguin, 2006), Francis Fukuyama, *America at the Crossroads* (New Haven, CT: Yale University Press, 2006), and George Packer, *The Assassin's Gate: America in Iraq* (New York: Farrar, Straus and Giroux, 2005). See also the new *Counterinsurgency Field Manual of the U.S. Army and the U.S. Marine Corps* (Chicago: University of Chicago Press, 2007), with a foreword by Gen. David H. Petraeus. On the price of oil as measured by the aims of the Iraq war, see Alan Greenspan, *The Age of Turbulence* (New York: Penguin, 2007).

The National Security Strategy document of September 2002 is accessible online; its intellectual genealogy can also be traced online through the Project for a New American Century.

On the new terrorism of the late twentieth century and the American efforts to address, contain, and defeat it in view—or not—of the constraints imposed by domestic and international law, see Paul Berman, *Terror and Liberalism* (New York: Norton, 2003), Richard Posner, *Not a Suicide Pact: The Constitution in a Time of National Emergency* (New York: Oxford University Press, 2006), Mark Danner, *Torture and Truth: America, Abu Ghraib, and the War on Terror* (New York: New York Review of Books, 2004), John Yoo, *War by Other Means: An Insider's Account of the War on Terror* (New York: Atlantic Monthly, 2006), David Frum and Richard Perle, *An End to Evil: How to Win the War on Terror* (New York: Random House, 2003), Richard C. Clarke, *Against All Enemies: Inside America's War on Terror* (New York: Free Press, 2004), Louise Richardson, *What Terrorists Want* (New York:

Random House, 2006), Michael Scheuer, *Imperial Hubris: Why the West Is Losing the War on Terror* (Washington, DC: Potomac Books, 2004), Walter Laqueur, *The New Terrorism: Fanaticism and the Arms of Mass Destruction* (New York: Oxford University Press, 1999), Kurt M. Campbell and Michelle A. Flournoy, *To Prevail: An American Strategy for the Campaign against Terrorism* (Washington, DC: Center for Strategic and International Studies Press, 2006), and Lawrence Freedman, ed., *Superterrorism: Policy Responses* (Oxford: Blackwell, 2002). To my mind, the two most important contributions to the discussion are Philip Bobbitt, *Terror and Consent: The Wars for the 21st Century* (New York: Knopf, 2008), and Audrey Kurth Cronin, "Behind the Curve: Globalization and International Terrorism," *International Security* 27 (2002–2003); I do not agree with their conclusions, but their analysis of the phenomenon and their assessment of plausible countermeasures are indispensable to serious thinking about the new terrorist movements.

Index

~

About the Author

James Livingston has taught history at Rutgers, the State University of New Jersey, since 1988. Before then he taught in a junior college, three state universities, a small liberal arts college, and a maximum security prison. He has written on Shakespeare, Poe, Dreiser, and Disney as well as the origins of the Federal Reserve System and the connection between pragmatism and feminism. This is his fourth book. He is currently a fellow at the Cullman Center for Scholars and Writers of the New York Public Library, where he is writing two books, one a biography of Horace Kallen, the founding father of cultural pluralism, the other on the long-wave origins of the economic crisis that began in 2007.